ALSO BY MARK HUBAND

The Kingdom: Saudi Arabia and the Challenge of the 21st Century (joint editor)

Brutal Truths, Fragile Myths: Power Politics and Western Adventurism in the Arab World

The Skull Beneath the Skin: Africa After the Cold War

Egypt, Regional Leader and Global Player: A Market for the 21st Century

Egypt Leading the Way: Institution Building and Stability in the Financial System

Warriors of the Prophet: The Struggle for Islam

The Liberian Civil War

For my brother Paul

TRADING

Spies and Intelligence in an Age of Terror

SECRETS

Mark Huband

I.B. TAURIS

LONDON · NEW YORK

Published in 2013 by I.B.Tauris & Co. Ltd
6 Salem Road, London W2 4BU
175 Fifth Avenue, New York NY 10010
www.ibtauris.com

Distributed in the United States and Canada Exclusively by Palgrave
Macmillan, 175 Fifth Avenue, New York NY 10010

ISBN 978 1 84885 843 5

A full CIP record for this book is available from the British Library
A full CIP record for this book is available from the Library of Congress
Library of Congress catalog card: available

Typeset in Calisto by Dexter Haven Associates Ltd, London
Printed and bound in Great Britain by TJ International, Padstow, Cornwall

CONTENTS

LIST OF ABBREVIATIONS

ANC: African National Congress, the main South African anti-apartheid movement, today the country's largest political party

ASU: Active Service Unit, the terrorist cells deployed by the IRA during both the 1919–21 War of Independence and the Troubles of the 1970s and 1980s

Chief: Chief of the Secret Intelligence Service, SIS, the UK's foreign intelligence service

CIA: Central Intelligence Agency, the US foreign intelligence service

CIA CTC: Counter-Terrorism Center, the unit within the CIA focused on terrorism

CPSU: Communist Party of the Soviet Union

CSRT: Combatant Status Review Tribunal, a legal process held for detainees at Guantanamo Bay

CTC: Counter-Terrorism Command, the UK police unit leading the domestic counter-terrorism effort, created in 2002

DG: Director General, the head of MI5, the UK's domestic security service

DGSE: General Directorate of External Security (French: Direction Générale de la Sécurité Extérieure), France's foreign intelligence service

DIA: Defense Intelligence Agency, the intelligence-gathering unit of the US Department of Defense

DIS: Defence Intelligence Staff, the intelligence unit of the UK Ministry of Defence

DMP: Dublin Metropolitan Police, the police force of the Irish capital under British rule

EMPTA: O-Ethyl methylphosphonothioic acid, a dual-use chemical used for pesticides and as a precursor in the synthesis of nerve agents

ESB: External Security Bureau, Sudan's foreign intelligence service

FAA: Forças Armadas Angolanas, the Angolan army, created in 1991

FNLA: National Front for the Liberation of Angola (Portuguese: Frente Nacional de Libertação de Angola), the Angolan political movement

FBI: Federal Bureau of Investigation, the US domestic intelligence-gathering agency

FRU: Force Research Unit, an intelligence unit created by the British Army operating in Northern Ireland

Garda: Garda Síochána na hÉireann, the police force of the Republic of Ireland

GCHQ: Government Communications Headquarters, the UK Government's gatherer of signals intelligence, located in Cheltenham, UK; equivalent of the NSA in the United States

GHQ: General Headquarters, the headquarters of the British Army in Dublin until 1922

GIA: Armed Islamic Group (French: Groupe Islamique Armée), an Algerian Islamist organisation

GRU: Main Intelligence Directorate (Russian: Glavnoye Razvedyvatel'noye Upravleniye) the foreign-military-intelligence service of the Russian Army, created in 1918 and still operational

GWOT: 'Global War on Terror', the abbreviated term given to President George W. Bush's post-9/11 strategy for countering al-Qaeda

ISI: Inter-Services Intelligence agency, Pakistan's intelligence service

IRBM: Intermediate-range ballistic missile

ISG: Iraq Survey Group, the 1200-strong team of weapons experts, intelligence officers and military personnel sent to Iraq to search for WMD

JIC: Joint Intelligence Committee, the UK Government committee wherein intelligence gathered by the intelligence agencies is pooled

JTAC: Joint Terrorism Analysis Centre, the UK multi-agency 'clearing house' for terrorism-related intelligence

LIST OF ABBREVIATIONS

KGB: The Committee for State Security (Russian: Komitet gosudarstvennoy bezopasnosti), foreign-intelligence service of the Soviet Union, created in 1954, disbanded in 1991

LIFG: Libyan Islamic Fighting Group (Arabic: al-Harakat al-Islamiya al-Libiya), a Libya-focused affiliate of al-Qaeda

MI5: The UK's domestic security service, also referred to as the Security Service

MoD: Ministry of Defence, the UK's Defence Ministry

MPLA: Popular Movement for the Liberation of Angola (Portuguese: Movimento Popular de Libertação de Angola), the Angolan political movement

MBTI: Myers Briggs Type Indicator, a management tool used by GCHQ to place staff in appropriate roles according to personality type

NSA: National Security Agency, the US agency for gathering electronic and 'signals' intelligence; equivalent of the UK's GCHQ

OSCT: Office for Security and Counter-Terrorism, the UK Home Office department coordinating all UK counter-terrorist activity

PIRA: The Provisional Irish Republican Army, the Northern Ireland republican terrorist group, also referred to as 'the IRA'

PoWs: prisoners of war

RAF: Royal Air Force, the UK's airforce

RIC: Royal Irish Constabulary, the national police force of Ireland under British rule

RUC: Royal Ulster Constabulary, the police force in Northern Ireland between 1922 and 2001, when it was renamed the Police Service of Northern Ireland (PSNI)

SAS: Special Air Service, the special-forces regiment of the British Army

SEALs: Sea Air and Land teams, elite troops of the US Navy, a unit of which was responsible for the capturing and killing of the al-Qaeda leader Osama bin Laden on 2 May 2011

SIS: Secret Intelligence Service, the UK's foreign intelligence service, known also as MI6

SISM: Military Intelligence and Security Service (Italian: Servizio per le Informazioni e la Sicurezza Militare, Italy's military-intelligence service between 1977 and 2007; on 1 August 2007 SISMI was replaced by the Intelligence and External Security Agency (Italian: Agenzia Informazioni e la Sicurezza Esterna), the AISE

SST: Sensitive Site Team, specialist teams sent to Iraq to search for WMD

TASS: Telegraph Agency of the Soviet Union (Russian: Telegrafnoye agentstvo Sovetskovo Soyuza), the news agency of the Soviet Union

TOW: US anti-tank missile

UNITA: National Union for the Total Independence of Angola (Portuguese: União Nacional para a Independência Total de Angola), the Angolan political movement

UNSCOM: United Nations Special Commission, the UN body charged with assessing Iraq's weapons capability

USSR: Union of Soviet Socialist Republics, the Soviet Union, disbanded in 1991

WMD: Weapons of Mass Destruction

ACKNOWLEDGEMENTS

It is a revealing irony that even though parts of this book refer to the greater visibility which today characterises the approach of intelligence and security services in different parts of the world, those who are not mentioned by name in the pages that follow and who have assisted me with the research that forms the heart of what I have learned, must remain anonymous. But as there is no secret about the openness on the part of the agencies towards those of us who are keen to understand better how they operate and what they contribute to a better understanding of global issues, I hope it is not a breach of confidence to thank those from within the intelligence and security services of the countries mentioned here for their great help, patience and consideration. While this book is in no way 'official' – and has not been officially 'approved' for publication – it could not have been written without their assistance over the past twenty years; I am deeply grateful for all that they have been prepared to explain and share.

PROLOGUE

Where Rome's Quirinal Hill dips down to the cool shadows of the Piazza Barberini, and the sound of water trickles from the Fontana di Tritone, the streets rise narrowly between tall, silent residences, which by mid-morning are tightly shuttered against the summer heat.

My arrival there, on 17 June 2004, was part of a journey that had begun more than a year earlier, when President George W. Bush had delivered his January 2003 'State of the Union' address, in which he had told the world that 'the British Government has learned that Saddam Hussein recently sought significant quantities of uranium from Africa'.

It was 3 p.m. Water from the fountain was the only sound breaking into the afternoon heat which gripped the slumbering city. A call to my mobile phone earlier in the day had included instructions as to when I should reach that spot beside the newsagent's stall on the edge of the Piazza. I had killed time all morning, wondering what I was going to learn from the Italian with the very precise English who had called me while I was stumbling through the process of ordering breakfast in the dining room of a nearby hotel. I was to make my way to Piazza Barberini, where I should wait beside the newspaper stall until I received another call, the voice had told me.

I waited for what seemed like hours.

Twice, the newspaper seller asked me if I wanted to buy the titles I was nonchalantly leafing through. Business was slow. I bought a copy of the *Financial Times*, the newspaper for which I was writing at that time, and thought of the London office, where the 'opinion leaders' and 'old hands' would be busying themselves. Of spies few of them knew much, one very senior editor on one occasion having had to ask an officer from the Secret Intelligence Service (SIS, Britain's foreign-intelligence service, better known as MI6) who had been sent to accompany him to a lunch with the SIS Chief, 'What exactly is the difference between MI5 and MI6?'[1]

It was awkward for many in the media that there were people and organisations – spies and intelligence agencies – whose knowledge might be built on greater detail, harsher 'truths' and the ubiquitous reality of uncertainty than was acceptable to the grandees of journalism. As the *FT*'s Security Correspondent – charged with reporting on these issues – I trod a very fine line when tasked to report not only on the issues of terrorism and weapons proliferation – as I did between 2001 and 2005 – but also on secret intelligence itself; for when the Bush Administration and the Blair Government decided to use intelligence in a public manner to justify their invasion of Iraq, the story came to be not just about the intelligence on these issues, but about the credibility of the agencies themselves. Never before had the CIA, SIS, MI5 and other intelligence services, been under such scrutiny. They became *the story* – and it thus became necessary to know them and the people within them, in order that as a reporter it would be possible to write with balance and authority. The challenge was to achieve this without on the one hand being viewed as 'too close' to the spies and on the other doing so without sending the people who were the story – the spies themselves – back into the shadows from which they had been forced to emerge.

It was during a speech to newspaper editors on 28 October 2010 – the first such by a serving Chief of SIS – that Sir John Sawers reminded his audience of Machiavelli's maxim on how to win a war: 'Surprise is the essential factor in victory.'[2]

For centuries, the art of surprise has been practised by political leaders, military officers and intelligence operatives. In his work *The Art of War* Machiavelli writes, 'Nothing makes a leader greater than to guess the designs of the enemy.'[3] Despite the ever-widening range of tools in their various arsenals, it is the *surprise* use of the unmanned 'drone' from which Hellfire missiles are launched on unsuspecting terrorists hiding in the rugged desert of Yemen or the mountains of Pakistan's Tribal Areas, or of undetectable data-mining to demonstrate vastly superior computer power when tracking bomb plots, or of the crucial tip-off which enables identification of a ship carrying a lethal cargo through the Suez Canal, which is what turns knowledge into power and intelligence into action.

In the years that have passed since the terrorist attacks on New York and Washington on 11 September 2001, part of the trauma caused to Americans and the wider world has lain in the realisation that the ability to *surprise* had been lost to the other side. For centuries, the value of secret intelligence has lain as much in what you know as in what 'the enemy' does not know that you know. It is not always the case that intelligence need be acted upon: knowing the enemy's intentions, determining how one's interests will be served by perhaps steering the enemy to take this step rather than that one, seeking to infiltrate the enemy camp in order to seek to manipulate decision-making and actions – these various approaches are all part of the intelligence arsenal. Surprise is the most potent weapon of all, a well-kept secret not only helping maximise the physical impact of whatever action may follow from intelligence gathering, but also having a potentially even more significant psychological impact. For it was not only the devastation and death caused by the 9/11 attacks which were the blow to the United States; as devastating to the American psyche was the fact that the attacks had been planned and executed beneath a veil of secrecy which revealed how successfully the 'bad guys' had learned the intelligence rulebook. The shock which changed the world – after which it was widely predicted nothing would be the same again, and since which nothing has – emerged out of the realisation that the West was the sitting duck and that the terrorists had surprise on their side.

But it was a strange sort of surprise.

The threats had been made public for so long – in statements, *fatwas* and previous terrorist acts. It was an event that was 'bound to happen', according to those mavericks within the CIA who – while in retrospect arguing that they had all but predicted the 9/11 attacks – have been ignored or sidelined throughout history, *because* they are mavericks. Imagining the unimaginable, anticipating the worst, expecting the catastrophe, is not what civilised societies want to spend their time doing; they want to spend their time being civilised. That is why the mavericks are dismissed: people don't want to hear from people who are ahead of their time; they want to hear about the here and now.

Although it would be inaccurate to suggest that the world's intelligence agencies are staffed by people who spend much time considering their roles in this way, their role in fact meets a core wish of most people not to have to think too much about the danger, the threat and the mishap that may be lurking around the next corner. What this actually involves leads – quite naturally – back to what Machiavelli said in his most famous work, *The Prince*, in which he elaborated on how the leader must act if he is to provide the fullest possible defence for his people. The prince – in today's parlance, the state – must

> follow incessantly the chase, by which he accustoms his body to hardships, and learns something of the nature of localities... Which knowledge is useful in two ways. Firstly, he learns to know his country, and is better able to undertake its defence; afterwards, by means of the knowledge and observation of the locality, he understands with ease any other which it may be necessary for him to study thereafter... And the prince that lacks this skill lacks the essential which it is desirable that a captain should possess, for it teaches him to surprise his enemy, to select quarters, to lead armies, to array the battle, to besiege town to advantage.[4]

Only with knowledge of the terrain over which he rules can the leader expect to 'surprise his enemy'; and only if he can possess knowledge that he hopes his enemy doesn't have and which he hopes his enemy doesn't know he has, can he use what then becomes intelligence to help him further his aims. In the context of the twenty-first century – as this book seeks to illustrate, in the conversations with senior intelligence officers and others which follow – a particular shock to security and intelligence services was the realisation that the terrorist threat had emerged near-invisibly, within their own societies; not only had they failed to grasp the reality – in terms of both the terrorists' most deep-seated motivation and ultimate intentions – of the changing global terrain; they had also failed to grasp how motivations and intentions had manifested even in their own countries.

Such conditions go some way to explaining why Machiavelli's name still trips so regularly off the tongues of the powerful, the aspirational and – occasionally – the pretentious. Not only is what he writes of relevance today, but the fact that he is still taken into consideration suggests that the current state of the world is not unprecedented. Lessons from the past are not easily forgotten; what changes is the way in which they are taught and the means by which they are implemented. President Bush's implementation of the measures he saw as necessary and right in response to the 11 September terrorist attacks were and are – for those incarcerated and tortured in the dungeons and *oubliettes* of Guantanamo Bay – medieval. The vengeful violence resembles medieval statecraft, while the thinking behind it demonstrates how little of the Renaissance which had produced Machiavelli was inherited by Bush's America.

But at the core of the hurt that Americans felt in the wake of 9/11 was the shock – the 'surprise' – which is what the gathering, analysis and assessment of secret intelligence is supposed to prevent.

SIS – like the CIA, and the wider global intelligence community – was ill-prepared for the issues into which it was publicly plunged, as the debate about intelligence was played out in public. But it responded energetically, by seeking ways of supplementing intelligence which was already public with informal efforts to explain to a curious population what intelligence is and what it is not, how far it can be considered the 'truth', and what the limitations on its value are when decisions have to be made.

The only way to improve public knowledge – and, in the process, to neutralise some of the criticism that was being levelled at the intelligence service – was to talk to the public through the media. During the Cold War, intelligence services on all sides sought out friendly journalists, who would hungrily scavenge for stories about spies, honey-traps and double agents; their newsroom colleagues would sometimes wonder whether these reporters were in fact agents of the agencies, which some indeed were, and are. But unprecedented public scrutiny and media comment are not the most significant factors to have transformed the lives of spies in the age of terror into which the world was plunged on 9/11. More significant has been the changed relationship between spies and their targets, as recruiting spies on the inside of the enemy camp has become more difficult. This book is intended to explain the 'before and after' – that is, the long period during which modern spy-craft was developed before 9/11, and what has happened since.

The period 'before' started in the year 1798, its genesis lying in the efforts of the nation which would become the most ubiquitous global power since the Romans, to stifle rebellion in a troublesome part of its empire. The imperial power was Britain; the focus of its ire was Ireland.

As much as – and perhaps more than – any other relationship, that between Britain and Ireland is responsible for creating modern spy-craft. Britain's fast-expanding imperial presence during the nineteenth century meant that in one form or another its intelligence-gathering methods spread around the world. But even while it enjoyed overwhelming military power for much of that century, its capacity to identify, understand and act against plots aimed at undermining that power depended on far more subtle means than maintaining ranks of red-coated riflemen at forts dotted around the world. It depended on intelligence gathering, which in turn depended on understanding the social and political trends prevailing within subject populations, then on identifying – or 'making' – spies from within those populations, and – crucially – finding the means to ensure that these spies would be both reliable and discreet.

Out of this need grew the 'trade' in secrets, with spies becoming sellers of secrets and intelligence agencies the market to which they would sell.

It was through its ability and readiness to conduct this trade that the British came to lead the world in intelligence gathering; Britain was a willing buyer, its spies willing sellers. Whether for money, influence, respectability or the desire to 'do good', the ability of Britain's spymasters to identify likely informers or respond adeptly when informers turned up on their doorsteps, became key elements in the practice of wielding imperial power.

Ireland – under both British rule until 1921 and in Northern Ireland following the outbreak of the Troubles in 1969 – was where most of what has been learned about spying was first attempted. Moreover, Britain's global role and influence mean that the lessons learned there have not been confined to the spy-craft developed by spymasters in London; British practice has helped design what is called the 'intelligence machinery' around the world, among Britain's former colonies, among its allies, and even within countries with which it has no shared history.

Rooted as it is in the raw and cynical view that 'everybody has their price', the spy-craft developed by the British in Ireland was dependent on there being a market in which the sellers remained ready to sell secrets. But the two centuries during which the world's first global intelligence service developed its craft, came to an end when the sellers of secrets could not be found within the ranks of the enemy. It is the most dramatic change in the history of modern spying that al-Qaeda and its associated organisations drew people to their ranks who – most evidence suggests – were not open to trading secrets. As a consequence, the spies were left in crisis.

The Cold War which had replaced the intelligence agencies' focus on colonial-era intelligence gathering had demanded the creation of a new range of weapons; misinformation was central to the cat-and-mouse game played between 1945 and 1990, while ideological opposition within the ranks of the KGB led to vital intelligence being passed to the West. While this was a different kind of 'trade', it was a 'trade' nevertheless: Russians opposed to Soviet influence generally did not require payment, the prospect of bringing down the 'empire' being adequate incentive to betray the regime they served and despised. So, when the Soviet empire fell – its conflict with the West having wrought havoc mostly in the Cold War 'theatres' of Africa – Western spies found themselves ill-prepared for a threat posed not by dealmakers but by religious zealots. For two centuries it had usually been possible to find a trader – either a seller or a giver – through whom secrets could be obtained. With the arrival of al-Qaeda, the market dried up. This book tells the story of how dependent the world's spies came to be on the market which had been carefully nurtured since 1798, how the Cold War permitted them to fine-tune the practice, and how they then struggled with the threat from an organisation which could not be bought.

The drying up of the trade in secrets after 9/11 then brought a second revolution in spy-craft: if nobody within the enemy camp was prepared to trade, then the rules of the market would have to be changed. Instead of being offered inducements, those who might once have been informers would become prisoners; instead of permitting targets to 'run' and thus be observed from a distance, they would be captured, interrogated, isolated and tortured. Thus what had once been a craft characterised often by subtle persuasion in safe houses became a global rampage in which the most wanted were transported blindfold to the new citadel of intelligence gathering: Guantanamo Bay.

Stepping into this new and highly unpredictable world, as a reporter in need of information that could be believed or dismissed, weighed and assessed, was a risk. I wanted to learn more than it was possible to learn from open-source material, think-tanks, experts and commentators. What was happening in the world of terrorism, intelligence and weapons proliferation was unprecedented, so I sought out the widest possible range of sources – from the few well-informed Muslim dissidents who had not gone to ground in the wake of 9/11, to intelligence officers in countries which ranged from the Philippines to Saudi Arabia, from Italy to the United States. I was aware that doing so was bound to tickle the appetite of journalism's chattering classes. It was no surprise to me to find – on leaving the *Financial Times* in 2005 – that one of the more repugnant grandees on the staff had penned the following in my leaving card: 'Hope life's easier with just the one employer, "Old Boy".' The inference – that by developing intelligence sources in order to fulfil the task given me by the newspaper, I had also been working for the intelligence services – hurt, as had been intended. It was also shocking for the ignorance it revealed as to how journalistic reporting on these issues now had to be done. With the last superpower in a state of extreme shock, with the world deeply divided over how to respond to 9/11, and with the realisation that people once seen as ranting hot-heads were in fact capable of perpetrating devastating acts, it was not only the framework of international relations which had been overturned, but also the knowledge which underpinned that framework; intelligence was central to this knowledge – the United States and its allies needed to demonstrate that they grasped the reality of global political trends, in order both to prevent the shock of further 'surprise' and to regain global credibility and influence. American influence was challenged by the revelation of its vulnerability, and regaining it required rapidly regaining the intelligence advantage over al-Qaeda and its affiliates. Achieving this necessitated an understanding of just how redundant the established practices of intelligence gathering had become, in the face of this new, seemingly impenetrable and evidently global threat.

To grasp just how significant has been the revolution in the role of secret intelligence which it has been necessary to implement since 9/11, requires an understanding of how the major global intelligence services had evolved prior to the events of that day. What intelligence officers and agencies believed they could learn, assess and act upon was rooted in long-tested practices based on an understanding of what motivates people to act as they do: the influence of circumstance on the recruitment of spies, the thrill of secrecy, perhaps a belief in doing good. The elements have been common over centuries while also being highly personalised, and in modern times date back to British efforts to quash the first signs of Irish nationalism in 1798. Since that time, the practice had been based on the 'trade' in secrets – secrets passed on in return for money or prestige, perhaps out of revenge, or to clear a conscience. Spies are made in different ways, often purely as a result of how their handler within an intelligence service recruits, manages and rewards them. And it was the need to understand just how 9/11 had or – in this case – had not overturned what had been long-established that was the reason I found myself in Rome on that hot afternoon in June 2004, standing beside a newspaper stall on a near-deserted square waiting for my mobile to ring.

When it did, I jumped.

1

'THE CRAFT OF CHEAT AND IMPOSTER'

Peter Clarke and I were sitting on the polished leather armchairs which nestle in strategically placed clusters and thus allow visitors to the coffee room of the Rubens Hotel to remain out of earshot of whoever may be sitting nearby. Convenient for Whitehall and the various counter-terrorist agencies today dotted around Victoria and along the banks of the Thames, the Rubens' rather over-decorous rooms and hallways, replete with private corners, soft lighting and a busy street outside from which it is easy to step in or out, make it the perfect spot for a quiet chat about secret intelligence.

Ever the police officer, whose professional life had begun in 1977 as a 'bobby on the beat' and culminated in his appointment in 2002 as head of the UK's counter-terrorist police, Clarke chose his words with care. On the one hand he was keen to explain, on the other studious to avoid divulging operational secrets. We had met many times. As we sipped our cappuccinos he was at the early stage of a new, post-Met career in the private sector. Denied access to secret intelligence, his observations may have gone the way of many who have left government service and sought greater financial rewards as 'advisors' and 'experts' with the burgeoning number of security companies and private intelligence outfits which today operate with varying degrees of success behind the grand front doors of Mayfair. But he was not one of those former state servants who these days seek to enhance their value by combining guesswork with obfuscation while hinting at remaining privy to intelligence long after their official passes have been handed back. Instead, his observations remained as frank and well-considered as they had been between 2002 and 2008 when he had led what became known as the Counter-Terrorism Command (CTC), whose operations had thwarted major terrorist attacks across Britain.

The threats are no secret. It is the operational details that are. But dominating the intelligence-gathering strategy is a challenge of a kind that some say dates back to the efforts of Queen Elizabeth I's spymaster Thomas Walsingham to unearth 'Catholic' conspiracies to unseat the Virgin Queen. The challenge remains the same: how to find people who know what is about to happen, and to stop it before it does.

Just as Walsingham's efforts had depended on spies, so do the successes and failures of modern intelligence gathering. The complex individuals whose readiness to betray trust, take risks and often earn little or nothing for their efforts, are today as central to the world of espionage as they were five hundred years ago. Even though telephone intercepts and electronic data mining now lead the way in intelligence gathering, people – and their intentions – are still at the centre of spying, whether it be in seeking to unearth terrorist plots, understanding the intentions of 'rogue' regimes, or discerning social trends which may lead to revolutions.

But after five hundred years or more of learning each other's ways, the spies are still being thwarted by the spied-upon – the latter remain adept at preventing their organisations from being infiltrated, their plans from being thwarted and their networks being uncovered.

For the intelligence officers whose stock-in-trade is to recruit those who can step inside the plots, learn the plotters' secrets and take steps to halt plots before they happen, the role they now play is, increasingly, to explain to the linguists and others who are listening-in to bugged telephone calls what it is they are really hearing. While the brilliant minds of the headset-wearing staff of the UK Government's listening station GCHQ are taking notes as they eavesdrop conversations, it is the SIS or MI5 officer standing nearby – who has been following the evolution of a terrorist cell or a clandestine weapons-trafficking operation – who is often best placed to put the pieces together. The combination of operational bravado, strategic cunning and collective memory brought together in the intelligence agencies can perhaps then turn a mystery into a target, by – as one long-serving officer once told me – providing that 'crucial five per cent' of the overall picture that is often all to which the secret-intelligence content of an investigation may amount.

In the wake of 9/11, much that it was thought had been learned over many years appeared redundant. But in the weeks and months which followed that day, as both MI5 and SIS found they were grappling with the implications for themselves and their American counterparts of President Bush's global rampage, I heard Britain's spies often voice the view: we understand terrorism because of our experience of Northern Ireland. I wondered how much real substance there was to this claim, and wondered whether the uniqueness of historical events meant that there were no such things as 'lessons' – only 'techniques'. Having spent the decade prior to 9/11 living in and writing about the Muslim world, I found it challenging immediately to make the comparison between the specific political goals of the Provisional IRA and the global intentions of al-Qaeda. Was the claim by those within the UK intelligence services a rather spurious one, intended as much to get the Americans off their backs as to make them listen? Moreover, what experience of Ireland was really being referred to?

I had never worked as a reporter in Ireland, neither in Northern Ireland nor in the Republic. How the experience of operating in one place could inform action in another was a major question facing MI5 as it sought to tailor its experience of Northern Ireland to the new threat from home-grown Islamist extremism. And at least one of the answers seemed implied in what Peter Clarke said on that bright February morning in 2009. Reflecting on the challenge from radical Islamic groups which faced the colleagues he had left behind at the Met, he told me,

> What has been missing is anything coming up from the communities, in terms of intelligence. I can't think of any major case that has resulted from intelligence coming up from the ground. In the Irish days [of the 1970s and 1980s] it was fairly easy to say to people: look out for suspicious activity. But this has changed. These days what you're asking people to do is to look out for changes in behaviour – like people becoming more observant in their religious life.[1]

The implication of his comment was significant: the old methods of intelligence gathering *had* become redundant.

But just as identifying the motives of the enemy is crucial to understanding how to contend with the threat, so understanding the community from which the enemy comes is crucial to gauging how to recruit people from within it who are prepared to spy on it. Until 2004, MI5 had been unable to infiltrate effectively any of the two hundred or so Islamic groups – most of them small, numbering fewer than ten people – who were surveillance targets as part of Britain's domestic counter-terrorist effort. It was only with the 'airlines plot' revealed in August 2006 – which involved plans simultaneously to blow up aircraft as they flew across the Atlantic – that really significant intelligence was derived from MI5 infiltration of the group of plotters.

Meanwhile, a common feature of the UK agencies' assessment of how well – or badly – they were coping with the long-gestating challenge which culminated in the attacks on 9/11, was comparison with the past.

Like all such institutions, the agencies of which the intelligence machinery is comprised house generations of staff who share a single experience. Just as in the armed forces there are the Falklands and 'Gulf War One' generations, in SIS there are those who will forever be associated with life behind the Iron Curtain, while others rather like being referred to as the 'Camel Corps' of Arabic and Persian speakers. Within MI5 there is an entire generation of intelligence officers who lived and breathed Northern Ireland for two decades or more, but who are today working with a new intake of recruits who may never set foot in the province.

In light of the generational changes, and the obvious need the agencies have to 'move on' in response to events, and to seek to grapple with what is happening *today*, it is not surprising that history is sometimes consigned to the bottom drawer. Despite the references to the experience of MI5 in Northern Ireland throughout much of the Troubles as having informed the counter-terrorism effort post-9/11, the real ability to learn from past experience remains tentative, as Britain's leading academic scholar of intelligence, Christopher Andrew, writes in *The Defence of the Realm: The Authorized History of MI5*:

Had the intelligence community and the security forces been aware at the beginning of the Troubles of the problems caused half a century earlier [during the Irish War of Independence, 1919–21] by the lack of co-ordination between the military, the police and the metropolitan intelligence agencies, similar kinds of confusion would have been less likely to recur.[2]

Within the generation of intelligence officers who cut their teeth in Belfast and South Armagh during the 1970s and 1980s, there is a keenness to place today's experience of terrorism within the wider context of intelligence gathering as a profession that has been crafted and fine-tuned over many years, and which has evolved its practices in response to events – a profession which has an established and tested tradecraft. But as he eyed the traffic that passed beneath the open window of his office in the heart of Victoria, a senior security official with long experience of counter-terrorism in the UK seemed to express – with a frankness that is always disarming when coming from an old hand in a profession renowned for its skills in the art of deception – how challenging it was to apply old lessons to new realities. Referring to radical Muslim groups in Britain, he told me,

There has been a change in the dynamic of all this. Our understanding has been increasing throughout. There was a lack of that with 9/11. Up until 2005 it felt like a period of great turmoil. It felt as though we were throwing every desk officer we had into it. It was very difficult to get a strategic grip. Late 2005 was our worst period. It was getting alarming. It really did feel like a desperate scramble during that period.[3]

And what was it that he was able to look back on pre-9/11 that placed his current post-9/11 role in context? His response was clear:

The early days in Northern Ireland were a desperate scramble. It takes a little bit of time to catch your breath. It's quite a different feel. But it's fairly normal. We are in a better position now. The PIRA (that is, the Provisional IRA) were a hierarchical terrorist outfit with clear command and control and a good leadership. But the overall terrorist problem in the UK [in the twenty-first century] is much wider and more networked, so you don't see the group. Terrorist groups have an environment that they adapt to. The Islamist groups are much more varied than the IRA. Nationality does have an impact on some of this.

15

As the hum of Central London filtered up from the street below, the room fell quiet for a moment. A phrase – 'alert not alarm' – which had been a governmental mantra in the aftermath of 9/11, and which was intended to stir the population out of any complacency while simultaneously discouraging panic, passed through my mind; I wondered whether the man sitting before me in white shirt and dark, plain tie, leaning slightly forward in his chair as he made his points, was in fact the last line of defence. If he could understand how false the apparent calm outside his office window was, and if he had the insight, accumulated knowledge and capacity to hand which would ultimately thwart the bombers, then the calm might become believable after all. Understanding is the key – along with the capacity to place isolated events into broader contexts, and take steps that will then neutralise the threat; only then can it be known whether the knowledge base – the intelligence – is sound. He broke the silence:

> The experience of being in Northern Ireland gave us a realisation of the signals that you get by being on the ground. We recognised that we needed people up front (that is, based in localities across the province) to make communication shorter. It could not be done by sending messages from London.

I asked him which period he was specifically referring to. 'All of it,' he replied. 'Throughout the conflict – from the 1970s, until today.'

But the experience had actually started many years earlier.

Understanding the security and intelligence implications of the radicalism that has evolved into twenty-first-century terrorism and the 'home-grown' threat rooted within Islam's 'jihadist-salafist' trend, is little different from the task the British faced when they first encountered the challenge to the comfortable lives of the English landowners who had ruled Ireland since 1556. That challenge burst onto the Irish political landscape with the emergence of the secretive Society of United Irishmen, and the adoption of its revolutionary constitution on 10 May 1795.[4] The ensuing rebellion, which challenged the British domination of Irish political life, erupted in 1798 under the military command of the fifth son of the Duke of Leinster, Lord Edward Fitzgerald.

Central to the success of the British in thwarting the challenge to its administrators in Dublin Castle were the informers put in place within the ranks of the United Irishmen by Edward Cooke, Under-Secretary for Civil Affairs in the British administration, who was the 'man on the ground' sent by the British Prime Minister, William Pitt the Younger.

In his classic study of Irish nationalism, the historian Richard English argues that the rebellion of 1798 failed because 'from the start, the United Irishmen had been riddled with government informers (a theme which was to recur in later Irish republican conspiracies).'[5] But while secret intelligence determined the outcome of the rebellion – Britain's spies providing the key intelligence which led to the arrest and execution of the rebel leadership – the task of deciding how best to use their intelligence advantage was often the larger challenge for the British. Knowing the enemy better than he knows you, while seeking to ensure that he doesn't know how much you know about him, lies at the heart of spy-craft. But what real advantage does that offer if the intelligence target has emerged from within a domestic movement whose aims have a deep social root, and whose support base may be deepened and broadened if it can portray itself as 'victimised' and spied upon? Within the United Kingdom, today's major focus on gathering intelligence in order to thwart terrorist plots – which, it must be said, is far from being the only focus – is entangled within this conundrum; by using the overwhelming power of the state – including its intelligence-gathering capacity – to confront the threat from violent extremism, does the state run the risk that its success will drive more people to violence, as anger rises among those sympathetic to the cause?

Pitt's use of secret intelligence throughout his two terms as premier (1783–1801 and 1804–6) was – despite having some precedents – groundbreaking in terms of its scale, sophistication and the financial resources devoted to it. Just as would be the case during the Troubles of the 1970s and 1980s, traitors, opportunists and occasionally men and women sincerely seeking non-violent means to address the political crises, were ready and willing to engage in the trade in secrets that is the lifeblood of the intelligence machinery.

One of the first of these 'touts' – as informers are known in Ireland – was Thomas Reynolds, a Dublin silk mercer in dire straits, who was paid a lump sum of £5000 and given an annual pension of £1000 for life in return for his betrayal of the independence cause to Cooke and the British authorities, as the 1798 rebellion took hold. Reynolds would later became British consul, first in Iceland then in Copenhagen, before settling in Paris, where he died in 1836, having earned a total of £54,740 from the British Government in return for the information he had provided nearly thirty years earlier.[6]

But Reynolds's role as a tout is relatively minor when considered beside that of the spy who came next – a philandering, lying, vain chancer and newspaper proprietor called Francis Higgins. It was Higgins's intelligence gathering on behalf of Cooke which ultimately led to the failure of the Irish rebellion, his character having gone down in the history of spying as illustrative of the 'perfect spy' upon whom intelligence agencies have forever been dependent.

In an account of Higgins's activities published in London and Dublin in 1866, based on contemporary records, the writer William Fitzpatrick – a fierce critic of Higgins – cites newspaper accounts from the time when he writes, 'Notwithstanding the repeated assurances of the said Higgins, and the said several pretences to his being a person of fortune or business, he now appears to be a person of low and indigent circumstances, of infamous life and character, and that he supported himself by the craft of cheat and imposter.'[7]

His role as a spy on behalf of Dublin Castle is best revealed by Higgins himself.

Rarely in the history of espionage has the evidence of a spy's attitudes, purpose and character been so abundantly revealed as in the 158 letters he sent to Cooke and his predecessor Sackville Hamilton between 1795 and 1801, and which appear to have been his primary means of communicating with the Castle. From the moment of the United Irishmen's decision to go 'underground', Higgins wrote detailed accounts of where meetings of the clandestine organisation were taking place, who was present and what was discussed. Seemingly as regular as the information flow, however, were his requests for payment; a letter to Hamilton dated 10 April 1795 providing details of the activities of the 'Roman Catholick Committee of Correspondence', and stating,

However, Dear Sir, I should stop here not knowing on what terms I am to go on, how the paper [that is Higgins's newspaper, the *Freeman's Journal*] is circumstanced…I am besides unpaid…You know, Sir, I entirely relied on your kind attention and committed myself to your direction. I am fearful your hurry of business prevents my not being recollected. When, Dear Sir, shall I attend you?[8]

A few days later he provided an account of various financial challenges facing the Irish rebels, and again took the opportunity to explain to Hamilton that 'whatever intelligence I receive I am compelled to defray the expense out of my own pocket and that without receiving any emolument…I hope, Dear Sir…that you will have the kindness to put the Treasury Bill due in train of payment for yours faithfully to command.'[9]

But it was not until two years after Higgins had launched his role as informer that the network of agents he was operating on behalf of the British netted its most valuable spy. In a letter to Thomas Pelham – Chief Secretary to Ireland (1795–98), and Cooke's superior – Higgins writes, 'One of the persons from whom I have received information is a young barrister and of whom I had no more suspicion of his being a United Irishman (alias a Defender) than of myself.' The barrister in question was Francis Magan, a rebel insider who, as Higgins writes, took some convincing before agreeing to become a spy. In one letter Higgins explains Magan's demands:

The terms are! inviolable secrecy of name, and reward. At the same time he appeals to the *Almighty God* and calls him to be witness that no earthly consideration should influence him to make any discovery if it was not in the fullness of hope it may be used to save thousands and the blood and lives of innocent people in the metropolis.[10]

Convinced of the honourable nature of his motives, Magan by March 1798 also knew his value, as Higgins wrote to Cooke ten days before the arrest of most of the rebel leadership at a Dublin house: 'M[agan] requested I should call on you this day for cash, which he got and some borrowed is expended in subscriptions, donations, lottery and dinners etc.'[11]

As the rebellion of May 1798 drew closer, Higgins's letters to Cooke focused on the whereabouts, plans and movements of Lord Edward Fitzgerald, the military leader of the United Irishmen. On 18 May

Higgins related how details of the uprising then underway in several parts of the country had been discussed at Magan's own house, including plans to launch attacks in Dublin itself a few days later – information he followed with a robust complaint that money due to Magan 'should have been given at once'.[12]

Due to Magan's intelligence, the army was waiting for Fitzgerald, who, during a series of skirmishes, was shot, captured, beaten with rifle butts and taken to Newgate prison, where he died of his untended wounds on 4 June.

Stemming from an incident that bears an uncanny resemblance to modern tales of senior civil servants accidentally leaving their briefcases full of top-secret documents on commuter trains, much of the detail of 'Secret Service' activity in Ireland at that time emerged by mistake. In his account of *The United Irishmen: their lives and times*, published in 1867, a Dublin doctor, Richard Madden, provides two entire lists of payments made by the British colonial administration to its informers in Ireland.[13] Over a quarter-century earlier, in 1841, while he was preparing the first volume of his history, Madden had been browsing in a second-hand bookshop on Henry Street, Dublin when two volumes caught his eye. One was the *Catalogue of the Plants of County Dublin*, the other *Catalogue of the Pinelli Library*. Both were stamped 'Library, Dublin Castle', and had been thrown out as rubbish but then bought by the shop owner in one lot, along with reports, manuscripts and papers deemed no longer worth keeping. It was among the loose papers included in the lot that Dr Madden espied one entitled 'Account of Secret Service Money Applied in Detecting Treasonable Conspiracies, Pursuant to the Provisions of the Civil List Act of 1793'. On it, neatly dated, and detailing who was paid, when, how much and at whose behest, was the entire network of 'setters' (that is, agent handlers) and touts who together saved the British colonial administration. As the account shows, for a cost of £53,547.13s.1d, which did not include the subsequent pensions paid to spies, Dublin Castle was able to buy its way out of a political crisis; and as the entry for 20 June 1798 reveals, £1000 was paid for 'FH discovery of LEF' – a payment to Higgins in return for the intelligence that led to the arrest and death of Lord Edward Fitzgerald.

As befits a man who had thus far 'supported himself by the craft of cheat and imposter', Higgins – according to his biographer William Fitzpatrick's account – pocketed the money himself and never paid it to Magan, despite the latter's importance.

The role of Magan and other spies run by Higgins on the Government's behalf, was vital to Pitt's success in steering through Parliament the Acts of Union which cemented Ireland's place within the 'United Kingdom of Great Britain and Ireland'. Moreover, the same network proved invaluable as the rebellion under the leadership of the next nationalist hero, Robert Emmet, began to take shape in 1802.

In 1798 the authorities in Dublin Castle had ended the uprising led by Fitzgerald, but it had been a close-run thing. Intelligence, as the official quoted earlier told me – two hundred years after the deaths of the first modern Irish nationalists – can 'provide that crucial five per cent' of the overall picture. That five per cent – when it is an address, the time of a meeting, or an account of an individual's movements – may have more value than the remaining ninety-five per cent if what it contains can alone turn disparate strands into a coherent whole. It should not be overlooked, however, that political solutions are not intended to emerge from intelligence operations, just as intelligence operations alone are not intended to provide politicians with justification for their actions. Nor do intelligence officers consider their role as being to do more than react to events today in order to prevent or manipulate the events of tomorrow, as one senior officer with long experience of Northern Ireland in the 1970s once made clear to me: 'The fundamental job of the intelligence community is not analytical. It's about understanding what people are up to.'[14]

The 'what' rather than the 'why' is what drives the intelligence gathering, and it is this particular focus on the 'what' that became embedded in the spy-craft long before it became evident that such a thing as spy-craft actually existed. The approach today is remarkably similar to that of the 1790s, as one of the architects of Britain's post-9/11 counter-terrorism strategy told me: 'We are not investigating communities, and we don't claim to try and understand the dynamics within communities.' Recruiting people – agents – from within those communities who are prepared to spy for the state remains as singularly crucial for the intelligence agencies today as it was for their predecessors in 1798. Reflecting on this core practice in the post-9/11 world, the official went on to say,

> We have made progress, but it's asking a lot, to get people to help. Some of the agents do feel that what is happening – supposedly in their name – they do not like. Some have fallen out with the terrorist groups and feel that this [working as agents] is a way of getting their own back. Some want to make money. There are many reasons why there are people willing to help, though one of the consistent factors is a desire to do good.[15]

But the importance of establishing and understanding *why* those who become the targets of intelligence operations behave as they do, is neglected at the intelligence agencies' peril. The experience in the Ireland of the 1790s taught the British, and subsequently the administrations of their other imperial possessions, much about how it was that spies could be recruited and networks successfully maintained. But it was ultimately the British failure to understand that the Irish nationalist enemy had learned from its past mistakes which turned the tide in Ireland. Aware that the British Army could not be defeated on the battlefield, the Irish Republican Army which led the fight against British rule in 1919–21 knew it would have to fight an asymmetric war if it were to end colonial rule – and intelligence was the cornerstone of this campaign. Its success was dependent upon the IRA's ability to infiltrate the British administration in Ireland – infiltration dependent upon the British only understanding once it was too late just how widespread was Irish antipathy towards them. Eighty years later, the global capabilities of al-Qaeda depended upon precisely the same strategy, as Western countries found themselves targeted by extremism emerging from within their own societies; they were to pay a heavy price for focusing largely on what might be about to happen, having failed to discern in advance the reasons why radical sentiments had laid such deep roots.

2

THE FIRST INTELLIGENCE WAR

It was out of Britain's experience in Ireland that something akin to a spies' 'blueprint' can be seen to have emerged – a blueprint which still, today, counts as a foundation upon which much of what is typical of modern spying has been built. Although the product of many years' accumulated experience, multiple, crucial relationships were first tested within the Irish intelligence arena. The recruitment of touts, the evolution of counter-espionage techniques, the eruption of a war based largely on the practice of outwitting the other side's intelligence capacity – and later the crucial role played by spies in establishing and operating secret 'back channels' between enemies – were all developed to unprecedented lengths in the two hundred years of intelligence activities in Ireland which followed the uprising of 1798.

But as the leaders of the United Irishmen were marched to the gallows, the readiness of spies to trade their secrets – either for money or revenge or perhaps something as simple as personal satisfaction – had ultimately served only to give the Anglo-Irish landowners and the political power in Dublin Castle a little more time to await the end of their primacy. Intelligence gathering had not turned the tide of history: it had merely brought short-term advantage, having been decisive in steering events in a direction that would inevitably be forced into reverse by the power of underlying anti-British social currents.

When the scion of a leading nationalist Protestant family, Robert Emmet, led in 1803 a revolt on the streets of Dublin whose participants proclaimed 'we are not against property, – we war against no religious sect...we war against English dominion',[1] the sentiments were not unfamiliar to the British. But when Emmet's followers took to the streets of Dublin on 23 July, the Castle authorities were taken completely by surprise. Without their network of spies – Francis Higgins having by then moved on – the authorities were largely in the dark when seeking to assess how the nationalist trend had evolved since the rebellion of five years earlier. The scale of their ignorance is reflected in the brutality of their response to the uprising. Emmet's call to arms in 1803 unleashed violence that flew rapidly out of control, and culminated in Emmet himself being captured, tried, hanged and beheaded. There was no spying this time – just raw brutality, as the British sought blatantly to reassert their authority. Smaller uprisings followed in the 1840s and 1860s, but were quite easily quashed.

It was illustrative of how piecemeal intelligence operations could be – rather than being an ongoing part of broader security operations – that when the Easter Rising of 24–30 April 1916 brought an array of nationalist groups onto the streets of Dublin, the British were again taken by surprise. It was then that intelligence which 'was effective in crushing Irish separatist movements throughout the nineteenth century',[2] as the academic Peter McMahon writes, was the crucial missing ingredient. But forewarning of the Easter Rising had been flowing through the corridors of Whitehall for two years prior to the bloodshed, dating back to 29 October 1914, when Adler Christenson – the 'translator, messenger, travelling companion and sexual partner'[3] of the Irish diplomat-turned-revolutionary Sir Roger Casement – appeared at the door of the British embassy in Norway to betray his friend.

Casement had been a highly regarded diplomat in the British Foreign Service before becoming a virulent critic of colonialism following experiences in the Belgian Congo and Peru, where the ill-treatment of indigenous peoples stirred his anger at injustices committed by external powers. On resigning from the Foreign Service in 1913, he focused his attention on the aspiration of Irish independence from Britain. On his arrival at the embassy, Christensen handed the British minister,

Mansfeld de Carbonnel Findlay, a copy of a letter of introduction from the German ambassador in Washington to the German Chancellor, and provided details of Casement's travels from New York to Berlin, where he had sought German support for a rebellion in Ireland that would be mounted using Irish prisoners captured by Germany in France and Belgium. The newly created MI5 – formed in 1909 – then began gathering intelligence on Casement, most of it coming from Irish soldiers who had been approached by him to join the 'Irish Brigade' while in German captivity.

MI5's focus on the activities of Irish people in the United States was also intensified when it was realised that encrypted telegraph traffic between rebels based in Ireland and potential supporters in Germany was being channelled through the German embassy in Washington – fortuitously, via a telegraph route that passed through British territory. Decryption of the messages in 'Room 40' of the Admiralty provided a detailed understanding of Irish hopes and German responses.

But then – in a move which illustrated both how to use and how not to use intelligence – nothing was done in response to what had been learned; none of the intelligence gathered by Whitehall was shared with the Administration in Dublin, for reasons which in his history of MI5, published in 2009, the historian Christopher Andrew points out may have been deliberate. Andrew cites a note contained in UK Home Office files quoting Casement as relating how Captain Reginald 'Blinker' Hall – the Director of Naval Intelligence – had said of the impending Easter Rising, 'It's a festering sore, it's much better it should come to a head.'[4]

The importance of all that the 'intelligence machinery' had learned in Ireland – specifically, the importance of informers and the need to maintain networks of spies – had nevertheless become clear in 1916, though as much through success as through failure, as Andrew writes: 'It was the experience of Irish republican revolutionaries that led to the creation of the first domestic political surveillance agency (the Special Branch).'[5] But the intelligence machinery – MI5, and its sister foreign intelligence service, SIS – had also begun to learn as much about how to use intelligence as how to not use it: the Easter Rising could perhaps have been stopped in its tracks had Christenson's intelligence been passed on: it was not – because knowledge was, it was felt, better not acted upon.

Sitting in the quiet corner of a restaurant that had been carved out of the cavernous cellar of a refurbished warehouse in a city in the English Midlands, the two men I had arranged to meet who are part of today's intelligence machinery were as challenged by such anomalies as their predecessors had been.

After Britain 'lost' Ireland in 1921, the targets of the intelligence agencies became Europe's anarchists, communists and fascists. The only real change at the end of the Second World War was the location: London and Dublin were at peace, London and Moscow were at war. The war might be 'cold', but it was war nevertheless. Then terrorism came along, punching an asymmetric hole into the symmetry of the Cold War, putting Ireland once again back on the agenda, as 'the Troubles' that erupted in 1969 added blood to the sweat and tears of Britain's gloomy post-colonial era. But the Irish anomaly was not really an anomaly at all; the intelligence success of 1798 was really the exception: only in 1798 had intelligence been used effectively to prevent the event from happening at all.

This was not lost on the two men I had arranged to meet in the Midlands, as they mused on the successes and failures of the craft they had inherited from their predecessors.

As the attentive waitress fussed a little too much over our requirements, there were times when she seemed to want to overhear what it was we were discussing. Ever since the town of Tipton had become notorious as the home town of three men who would become inmates of the US naval base at Guantanamo Bay, and later as the epicentre of an extremist plot to televise the beheading of a British Muslim soldier, parts of the Midlands had become a focus for the intelligence agencies.

While phone taps and other signals intelligence – so-called 'sigint' – as well as tip-offs from allied intelligence services overseas, can help furnish the intelligence picture, rarely has the value of intelligence provided by agents on the ground been surpassed, which is why in 2005 – in the wake of the 7 July suicide bombings in London, which had left 52 people dead – MI5 accelerated its plans to open regional offices in several large UK cities. The waitress finally left us alone, and an old lesson seemed in the process of being relearned, as one of my interlocutors told me how it is that the communities in the suburbs that surrounded us where we sat had become central to intelligence gathering:

> The process of contextualising the situation is now borne out of real evidence. We are now better able to identify the trends we need to follow, more clearly. In terms of prioritising, greater local knowledge is giving us a much better context. It seems now that we have a much clearer understanding of where the threat is and where it might come from.[6]

Shortage of funds has been as much a feature in the refocusing process as has been the shift from suspects such as the firebrands who emerged in the wake of 9/11 to a much wider net of unknown, unnoticed people – so-called 'clean skins'. But long before 9/11 and the catastrophe of Iraq emerged as intelligence failures caused in part by a misreading of the *context*, ground-level intelligence had been proven to have the power to change the course of history entirely. This was not a reality later confined to the streets of Baghdad or Kabul; it was far closer to home – on the streets of Dublin, where the intelligence advantage was on the other side, and Britain lost a colony.

Odious and one-sided as he appears to have been, the agent-runner of 1798, Francis Higgins, had succeeded in explaining to the colonial power a great deal about street-level opinion. In the immediate aftermath of the 1916 Easter Rising it became clear that 'what the British government needed...was not tactical intelligence on the activities of the Irish Volunteers, but political intelligence on the momentous shifts in Irish opinion'.[7] In this the authorities in Dublin Castle were dangerously lacking, and the world's first 'intelligence war' came to be fought when Michael Collins – the intelligence chief of the Irish Republican Army and leader of a group of assassins within the IRA known as 'the Squad' – declared his aim as being to 'put out the eyes of the British',[8] that is, to prevent them from ever becoming fully cognisant of the reality they were facing. It was an approach rooted in his very accurate assessment of why previous republican uprisings had failed: while the Irish had held the moral high ground, the British had retained the intelligence advantage. But successive rebel leaders, from Lord Edward Fitzgerald onwards, had learned that in the confusion and chaos of wartime, the rightness of the cause does not win battles; in the asymmetric battle between Irish nationalism and the British Empire, intelligence – and the occasional, carefully targeted assassinations which it led to – was the only weapon available. To beat the British, the IRA needed spies of its own.

The success or failure of Collins's strategy depended substantially on the success his network of spies had in countering the efforts of those despatched or recruited by Britain. He said it himself: 'Without her spies England was helpless. It was only by means of their accumulated and accumulating knowledge that the British machine could operate ... Without their police throughout the country, how could they find the men they "wanted"?'[9]

So deep and broad was the anti-British sentiment in Ireland in the period 1916–21 that infiltration of the key security and communications services of the state was not only sought but possible. Thus it was that mail sorters and telephone operators who handled the Dublin Castle post and telecommunications were recruited to the nationalist cause, the former routinely copying mail destined for Whitehall and elsewhere, the latter taking note of who was speaking with whom. From a special crimes sergeant in Tralee, Collins obtained the cipher code for Royal Irish Constabulary (RIC) communications, which 'laid the foundation of the elaborate scheme of intelligence in the post offices'[10] and sometimes allowed the IRA to decode messages from provincial police stations even before they had been decoded by RIC headquarters staff. This process was made even easier for Collins when his own cousin, Nancy O'Brien, was appointed by the Dublin Castle authorities as a cipher clerk; she was given the job, the British authorities said, 'because she was someone they could trust'.[11]

On 19 December 1919 the Squad formally became the precursor of the 'Active Service Units' – the ASUs – that would spearhead the IRA terrorist campaign in the 1970s and 1980s. Intelligence – both using it and confronting its use by the enemy – was at its core. As Collins told the first meeting of the Squad,

> any of us who had read Irish history would know that no organisation in the past had an intelligence system through which spies and informers could be dealt with, but that now the position was going to be rectified by the formation of an intelligence branch, an Active Service Unit or whatever else it is called.[12]

Their efforts quickly bore fruit: by 11 December 1919 they and other IRA-linked groups had killed 169 police officers and 52 soldiers, most of whose identities, routines and locations had been gathered prior to the attacks by spies informing the Squad. The tally led Lord French – who in May 1918 had been appointed Viceroy, Lord Lieutenant of Ireland and Supreme Commander of the British Army in Ireland – to focus very specifically on the paucity of British intelligence that would have enabled the Castle authorities to counter the insurgency: 'Our secret service is completely non-existent. What masquerades for such a service is nothing but a delusion and a snare. The [Dublin Metropolitan Police, the DMP] are absolutely demoralised and the RIC will be in the same case very soon if we do not quickly set our house in order.'[13]

His concerns were well-founded: on 19 December a unit of the Squad ambushed French himself while his convoy was on its way to the vice-regal lodge at Phoenix Park, his life only being saved by an intelligence failure: the attackers thought French was in the second car of the convoy when in fact he had been in the first and was able to crash through the barrage of gunfire.

Desperate to take the intelligence fight to the IRA, senior officials in Dublin Castle waited for a knock at the door from somebody with insights into the nationalist movement who could help them understand the threat before it struck again.

It was then that they found somebody with whom to trade secrets.

Just as Edward Cooke – Under-Secretary at the Castle in the 1790s – had been approached by Francis Higgins, it was the good fortune of one of Cooke's successors in the post, the last-ever Under-Secretary, James MacMahon, to find a letter on his desk on or around 11 November 1919. The sender was Henry Quinlisk, and his story had started in a German prisoner-of-war camp at Limburg in 1916, in which he had been incarcerated since shortly after his arrival and capture in France when a corporal in the Royal Irish Regiment.[14] At Limburg he had been approached by the diplomat-turned-rebel Sir Roger Casement as he sought to recruit Irish PoWs to the Irish Brigade that he intended would – with German support – launch an uprising against the British.

Quinlisk was among those who had been supportive of Casement, though he was not released from German detention until the end of

World War I – too late to participate in the Easter Rising. In April 1919 he arrived in England, and was arrested for his involvement in the 'Casement Brigade' – as it was called in newspaper reports – but then released after two months, and returned to Ireland, where he was approached by the IRA.

Quinlisk – who 'cut a dashing figure, and was quite a man for the ladies'[15] – appears to have tried hard to ingratiate himself with Michael Collins, though his efforts to become a part of the IRA inner circle seem to have failed. Due to his support for Casement, Quinlisk – who introduced himself as 'Quinn' – had automatically had his army pay terminated even while he was a PoW at Limburg; but even this deprivation didn't discourage him from penning a note to Under-Secretary MacMahon at Dublin Castle, which read,

> I was the man who assisted Casement in Germany and since coming home have been connected with Sinn Féin. I have decided to tell all I know of that organisation and my information would be of use to the authorities. The scoundrel Michael Collins has treated me scurily [sic] and I now am going to wash my hands of the whole business.[16]

Quinlisk's motives for turning against his erstwhile companions strongly resemble those of the touts who would play a vital role in the Troubles which erupted in Northern Ireland in 1969. When Quinlisk was invited to introduce himself at the Castle headquarters of 'G Division', the police department focused on subversion, it was one of Collins's spies – Ned Broy – who typed the subsequent report for the G Division head Forbes Redmond, and who passed a carbon copy to Collins. But the canny Quinlisk had taken the precaution of telling Collins in advance that he planned to approach the Castle – the implication being that he intended to spy on the authority's behalf but pass on all he knew to Collins. The double game was on, and Quinlisk's first task for the Castle was to inform the British of Collins's whereabouts.

Simultaneously, the newly renamed Secret Intelligence Service (SIS) – which had been born out of the Secret Service Bureau created in 1909, where it had earned its more familiar name of MI6 – was making in-roads into the IRA, this time via contacts in London.

Collins had sent a former RIC officer, Thomas McElligott, to London in December 1919, with the task of establishing contacts within the

Metropolitan Police, twelve thousand of whose members had gone on strike on 30 August 1918. Seeking to capitalise on the anti-government ferment in England, McElligott – who had been dismissed from the RIC when he sought to create a trade union within the force – visited the headquarters of the striking police officers, and was there approached by 'John Jameson', a supposed Marxist with sympathies for the strikers, whose arms and hands were tattooed with Japanese women, snakes, flowers and a bird, and who had 'rings' tattooed on three of his fingers.

Jameson, an Irishman, introduced himself to the striking police officers as 'chief delegate of the Soldiers, Sailors and Airmen's Union'. About to answer to his questions, McElligott noticed the General Secretary of the National Union of Police and Prison Officers, which was leading the police strike, put a finger to his lips as if to say he should refrain from telling Jameson too much. In his memoir, *The Spy in the Castle*, Collins's most important spy – David Neligan – tells of how McElligott later had it explained to him: 'The London strikers had been warned by those in a position to know that Jameson was a secret service man come as a spy [for the British].'[17]

Despite this warning, however, McElligott brought Jameson to Dublin and introduced him to Michael Collins. Discussions focused on plans to arm the IRA – discussions which Jameson (whose real name was John Charles Byrne) quickly relayed to Redmond at G Division. However, this part of the game was quickly up, when Redmond blustered to his staff, 'You are a bright lot. [But] not one of you has been able to get on to Collins' track for a month, and there is a man only two days in Dublin and has already seen him.'[18] When Ned Broy heard this he – along with Collins – quickly realised that Redmond was speaking of the tattooed 'Marxist' John Byrne, alias Jameson. They decided to let Byrne/Jameson 'run' for a time, while the Squad focused on Redmond himself. Spoilt by the plethora of intelligence concerning his every move, the G Division head was gunned down on 21 January 1920, with Byrne/Jameson obliged to act as a lookout as two others shot Redmond in the back and head on Harcourt Street – a killing that sent the so-called 'G Men' scurrying into Dublin Castle, from where they would hardly re-emerge until the War for Independence ended eighteen months later.

Then it was Byrne/Jameson's turn.

Despite having sought to prove his loyalty to the cause by arranging the supply of small arms to the IRA, the tattooed spy failed to convince Collins he was genuine. His fate was sealed when a consignment of Webley revolvers he had brought from England was hidden in a basement on Bachelor's Walk, Dublin on 2 March 1920. Hours after they had been hidden, Collins learned from his contacts in the Castle that the basement was to be raided by G Division. Thirty years later Joe Dolan, a former member of the Squad, would recount the events of that day: 'Paddy [O']Daly, Tom Kilcoyne and Ben Barrett were to carry out the execution. Tom Kilcoyne, Ben Barrett and myself met outside Gardiner Street Church and proceeded on bicycles to the place of execution as pre-arranged.'[19] Byrne was then taken to an isolated spot, asked if he wanted to pray, responded to his executioners' claim that they were 'only doing our duty' by telling them 'and I have done mine', and was shot in the heart and the head.[20]

Byrne was later described at a British Government Cabinet meeting as 'the best Secret Service man we had'.[21] Now, British intelligence was in crisis, and in April 1920 Lloyd George's Government decided to up its game, Viceroy Lord French having written to Andrew Bonar Law – at that time Lord Privy Seal and Leader of the Commons in Lloyd George's coalition – that 'Administration in Ireland is, I believe, as bad as it is possible for it to be.'[22] So it was that in an effort to address the worsening situation Winston Churchill – at that time Secretary of State for War and Air – followed the recommendation of his newly appointed Army chief in Ireland, General Hugh Tudor, by handing the new role of 'Chief of Intelligence' in Ireland to 'a wicked little white snake' called Ormonde de l'Épée Winter.

This seemingly unflattering description of colonial Ireland's first and last Chief of Intelligence was that of Mark Sturgis, appointed Assistant Under-Secretary as part of the same overhaul of the beleaguered Administration at Dublin Castle. As if to soften his depiction of the monocle-wearing Winter, Sturgis then seemed to crystallise the necessary contradictions of the intelligence professional by adding of the man, 'He is a marvel ... and can do everything.'[23]

But Sturgis was wrong.

The opinion – or perhaps assumption – that intelligence officers 'can do everything', that their anonymity and resourcefulness make them as all-powerful as they are infallible, is a myth which has been perpetuated down the decades, often in fiction, but often by the fact of intelligence agencies having – until the post-9/11 era, when it became necessary to highlight the limits on intelligence capability – allowed the myths to perpetuate by never denying them.

Sturgis – just like followers of Ian Fleming's James Bond, or Prime Minister Tony Blair when he sought to justify the invasion of Iraq purely on the basis of intelligence – thought that he had the ultimate weapon when Winter turned up at Dublin Castle in April 1920. But as would be made clear to me eighty years later, many months after the threat from al-Qaeda had fully emerged, intelligence gathering could sometimes – perhaps often – succeed only in convincing the professionals within the broader decision-making machinery of government that 'the situation is complicated ... and very difficult to predict'. Sturgis, perhaps like the Chief Secretary for Ireland, Hamar Greenwood – who, even before taking up his post in April 1920, was noted for having 'talked the most awful tosh about shooting Sinn Féiners on sight, and without evidence, and frightfulness generally'[24] – must have *hoped* that intelligence would indeed be *the* secret weapon that could 'do everything'. Unfortunately for the British, they had no way of knowing that it was too late, as in their ignorance of what was taking place all around them in Dublin and in the countryside beyond, they admitted into the Castle's inner intelligence sanctum the man regarded by one member of Michael Collins's Squad as 'the best intelligence officer I ever met in my life'.[25]

In April 1918 David Neligan had set off from Templeglantine, County Limerick on his police career, because 'father was ageing and near pension-time; there was no future in the place for me. I decided to clear out.'[26] Three months later he was organising confidential G Division files in the office of the DMP secretary, and gaining his first taste of the conflict in which the Castle authorities were engaged.

It was a mark of how desperate the British had become that with similar ease Neligan was in the autumn of 1919 appointed to the plain-clothes branch of G Division itself, as he wrote in his breezily written memoir:

Being heartily tired of uniform and beat duty, I applied and was accepted. This was due to no merit on my part as the shootings had made this service unpopular with the general run of the force. The Castle was faced with a tough situation. Never before had such a determined and lethal attack been made on the British intelligence forces nor one directed with such ruthless efficiency.[27]

It was Neligan himself who on occasion exemplified this 'efficiency', as it was he who – on being addressed with others by the G Division head Forbes Redmond in November 1919 – realised that the man referred to by Redmond as having seen Michael Collins after 'only two days in Dublin' was the tattooed spy Byrne. Having been instrumental in Byrne's assassination, Neligan – who would later become spymaster of the Irish Free State following the Treaty with Britain that ended the war in July 1921 – reflects both philosophically and almost admiringly on this Irishman who served the British crown, writing, 'How true that nations suffer most from their sons who go over to the enemy! It must be said that this man was really smart.'[28]

Neligan's admiration perhaps drew on his own experience, as he was by that time fulfilling a similar function for the IRA as that which Byrne was providing for the British, leading him to reflect later on the value of agents:

> The British were very often lucky enough to have their man in the right place. They are, of course, most careful not to expose him. This was a lesson [Michael] Collins was slow to learn…Espionage is one of the toughest games played. An agent in the right place is hard to find, but when he is found he should be regarded as a pearl beyond price, like a good wife. Everything should be let go by the board rather than that he should be exposed. There are basic laws in that game and that is the first one.[29]

But a core dilemma facing intelligence agencies is how to respond to what they learn.

For Michael Collins, intelligence gathering had the basic aim of allowing the Squad to identify targets and kill them; there had to be a connection between spying and action. It was Collins's success in gathering intelligence while largely keeping his agents free of suspicion which turned the war in his favour, bringing as it did:

considerable success in thwarting British rule during 1919–21: through paramilitary action, intelligence work, political gesture, and the provocation of state clumsiness. By early 1921 significant sections of the Irish nationalist population were sympathetic enough to the IRA rebels to make British government of nationalist Ireland impossible in normal ways.[30]

Central to the impossibility of governing 'in normal ways' was the disarray within the intelligence apparatus. The Castle authorities – even after the arrival of Greenwood, Winter, the new Commander-in-Chief of British forces, General Sir Nevil Macready, and, at Winston Churchill's insistence, nearly a thousand extra 'Auxiliary' troops drawn from English and Irish forces – were becoming 'blind' not only to *where* the threat they faced was coming from but also to *what* it was they were really confronting. Moreover, when intelligence gathered by the DMP or others cast an accurate light on what was taking place, it was often

> trumped by prejudice and miscalculation. The influential belief – shared by many in Dublin Castle and the Cabinet – that the real source of rebellion (as opposed to the armed struggle) was a tiny 'murder gang' ignored police reports of the spread and depth of the republican movement and nationalist anger…[While the] abandonment of the army's counter-insurgency effort in April 1920 effectively threw away a growing intelligence advantage (at least in the south).[31]

The sense was manifest of mistakes made and opportunities lost, 1920 seeing the Castle authorities lurching towards defeat. Evidence of how acute was the ongoing sense of failure emerged immediately after that defeat, in a remarkably candid, confidential assessment by an anonymous team of officials within the intelligence branch of Army General Headquarters in Dublin. The *Record of the Rebellion in Ireland in 1920–21, and the Part Played by the Army in Dealing with It (Intelligence)*[32] pulls no punches in its methodical and factual account of how and why Ireland was 'lost' to the British. Its resonance today is striking, with the same themes emerging from its pages as are apparent daily in the issues facing Western and other intelligence services as they have sought to grapple with the challenge from al-Qaeda and its associated organisations. Just as will be described later, the GHQ staff who wrote the *Record* early on pointed to the intelligence value of captured IRA prisoners; the difficulty of infiltrating the organisation and 'running' agents within it had proved – as the experiences of Byrne and others had shown – extremely difficult, the *Record* detailing how

> Secret Service was on the whole a failure in Ireland. For many reasons it was practically impossible to place a man in any inner circle. For Irishmen, the risks of discovery and of its consequent results were too great; the Sinn Féin movement was so general, the proportion of Irishmen outside it so small, and any stranger in a country district so suspected that consistent, regular and unsuspected informers, such as had been employed on other occasions, were almost unobtainable at any price.[33]

The alternative was to arrest IRA suspects and interrogate them over periods of time, as events unfolded and leads could be followed up. Today, the same process has been – and is – underway in the prison camp at Guantanamo Bay. But in 1920, pressure for the humane treatment of prisoners seems – somewhat surprisingly – to have been considerable; much to the chagrin of the GHQ staff, a number of IRA prisoners were released on 14 April after going on hunger strike, the *Record* stating that their release 'was a severe blow to Intelligence in Ireland…Informers who had begun to come forward in the preceding months, now became afraid to do so and military intelligence grew both more necessary and harder to obtain.'[34]

But the *Record* of 1920–21 then provides another lesson for today's spies, regarding those of the 'enemy' that have been captured. In a section entitled 'Sources of Information' the Castle staff wrote,

> Interrogation is usually confused with cross-examination which is a very different matter requiring a different kind of skill. There are a few golden rules for interrogation, viz: – (a) *Brutal Methods are a Mistake.* – Many innocent men were imprisoned because brutal interrogators, who believed that every Irishman was a Sinn Féiner, so treated them that, in the hope of escaping further ill-treatment, they confessed that they were soldiers of the I.R.A. (b) *Detailed Local Knowledge is Essential*, and usually the most successful interrogator was the local intelligence officer who knew about the neighbourhood or village of the man he was examining, the names of his friends and of the local I.R.A. officers. For senior intelligence officers to conduct interrogation was, with few exceptions, generally a waste of time to all concerned.[35]

Despite the slowly dawning realisation within Dublin Castle that its own ranks were riddled with spies, they continued to have no choice but to appoint local people to sensitive positions. But the more they drew Dubliners and others into their embrace the more weakened they were; 'the people' were against them, and the tide could not be turned. As the *Record* states on recognising the Irish 'abhorrence' of informers (a feeling perhaps rooted in their having been such a demeaning though constant feature of Anglo–Irish history),

> This feeling made it very difficult to obtain information during 1920–21, apart from the fact that the bulk of the people were our enemies and were therefore far more incorruptible than has been the case in former Irish movements. The offer of large rewards (a £10,000 reward was offered for the capture of Michael Collins) produced no results, partly for the above reason and partly because the people were terrorised more thoroughly than has ever been the case before.[36]

But it then goes on to highlight the hopelessness of the British position by stating, '[Had] agents been planted five years ago throughout the country they would, assuming the policy as actually carried out not to have been altered, in all probability have become ardent Sinn Féiners by 1920.'[37]

In such circumstances, all that the IRA needed to do was to continue identifying the individuals upon which the Castle authorities relied, and send the Squad to assassinate them. To do so Collins could rely on the need the British had for local people as bureaucrats. British ignorance of how infested with IRA spies the Castle was – and of how high the price is when the motives driving a population are not understood – reached its peak when David Neligan resigned from the DMP on 11 May 1920. Under pressure from Collins to get back into the heart of the intelligence structure, however, Neligan then reapplied for a position, and was quickly reappointed, this time within the upper ranks of G Division. By then the Division and the DMP in general 'had practically ceased to function'[38] owing to the fear of the Squad which pervaded its ranks. As the *Record* explains, agents working for the army had provided useful intelligence regarding the locations of IRA arms dumps: 'These sources, however, were almost entirely dried up in February [1920] when the I.R.A … began a series of murders of persons who they believed might have given information... [The] terror created was such that all who had been given information previously were silenced.'[39]

Ormonde de l'Épée Winter's response to the climate of fear that pervaded Dublin's intelligence machinery was to place greater responsibility for it into the hands of a reformed Crimes Special Branch, with input from a newly formed 'London Bureau', which provided additional intelligence officers – some on secondment from the Indian Civil Service – as well as a greater role for the Army. By November 1920 his strategy was having some success in apprehending IRA activists, though as the *Record* says, 'That intelligence as a whole obtained such good results in Dublin was due mainly to personal effort rather than good organisation;'[40] it later returns to this theme with regard to areas outside the capital, stating, 'In the south military intelligence depended very largely on the goodwill and enthusiasm of [Army] units.'[41]

In response Collins decided to act, drawing upon the address book of British spies, uniformed military intelligence officers and Crimes Special Branch personnel living around Dublin, which had been provided mostly by an army typist and IRA informer at the Castle, Lily Mernin. Prime targets were the 'Cairo Gang', a group of informers named after the Grafton Street café they frequented, along with the uniformed British military intelligence officers who lived mostly in hotels and guesthouses in various parts of the city. The Squad, with support from the Dublin IRA, struck on Sunday 21 November 1920. By the end of the morning, of the thirty-five people on the hit-list they had killed eleven at nine different addresses – most of them as they were waking up. Neligan's perspective from inside Dublin Castle is one of the most vivid:

> Terror gripped the invincible spy system of England. An agent in the castle whose pals had been victims shot himself. He was buried with the others, in England. The attack was so well organised, so unexpected, and so ruthlessly executed that the effect was paralysing. This was bringing it home to them in earnest. It can be said that the enemy never recovered from the blow.[42]

The intelligence war which brought the British to their knees in Ireland and culminated in the creation of the Irish Free State on 6 December 1922 illustrated what can happen when one side in a conflict is able not only to seize the advantage in intelligence gathering, but also to harness it effectively to the deeper political sentiments present within the population from which its spies are drawn. In 1919 Britain had very few friends in Ireland; by 1921 it was an administration on the run. Personal animosity towards Michael Collins had encouraged figures such as Quinlisk to approach the British with offers of a trade in secrets, but the limits on what the British could do to seize back the intelligence advantage were as evident to Winter as they were invisible to Mark Sturgis – the man who believed that Winter was the spy who could 'do anything'.

Eighty years later, as the battle with al-Qaeda lurched from one shock to another, deliberation over what secret intelligence could and could not do was ongoing.

Seen from across St James's Park, Whitehall in 2002 looked largely unchanged from the days when Winston Churchill and Lloyd George sat locked in debate about the means by which Britain should best address the 'Irish Question'. Only the concrete flowerbeds and reinforced bollards complete with portcullis insignia picked out in gold paint which began to spring up along the perimeters of government buildings in the aftermath of 9/11, marked a change in the appearance of Britain's centre of political power. But the issues to which the intelligence machinery had to gear itself up were the same, as newspaper pages were being turned by elderly men enveloped by the leather armchairs of the grand room in which I learned of how the shape of new threats was being discerned: 'Some of them have been caught – but only a handful. You have to distinguish between the real core and the sections of the population that are sympathisers,'[43] my interlocutor told me.

He went on,

The few named individuals the Americans want aren't in camps – as the Egyptians or Saudis would say – but are floating freely. You're talking about a manhunt, and the Americans in the past month have had intelligence that almost led to them going to do unilateral action – twice. The situation is complicated because of a lack of a clear military target. But the Americans haven't caught any of the al-Qaeda people – the security forces that have been built up have been ineffective.

While there are no comparisons to be made between Ireland's Independence War and the aims and methods of al-Qaeda, the task for spies is little different: both events posed the same intelligence challenges, and required similar means by which to meet those challenges.

It would not be until nine years after my discussion that day that intelligence would eventually lead the CIA and a team of US Navy 'Sea Air and Land teams' – or 'SEALs' – to Abbotabad in north-east Pakistan, to a walled compound wherein the al-Qaeda leader Osama bin Laden would be shot dead on 2 May 2011. But on that early autumn day in 2002 a chill seemed even to have gripped the words of the officer with whom I had been speaking, as he went on, 'It's very difficult to predict how this damaged [al-Qaeda] network will behave. But for some time to come what we are going to be dealing with is the remaining networks based on the twenty-eight [Afghan] camps. We will see bits of that unformed network continuing to function.'

Intelligence was never going to stop the IRA of Michael Collins, just as its successes in confronting al-Qaeda did not start to produce results until the long-established practice of 'trading secrets' was acknowledged as redundant, and was replaced – due to the absence of people with whom to trade. Through the prism of intelligence, even the killing of bin Laden is as significant for the fact that he had evaded capture for so long as for the fact that he was eventually tracked down when a courier was identified as his link man to the outside world.[44]

The extent to which he was protected by Pakistan's Inter-Services Intelligence agency – the ISI – is one of that country's dirtiest secrets, explanation of which has still to emerge. But the need to understand *why* bin Laden enjoyed that protection is as fundamental to the intelligence picture as was his address, illustrating as it does how vital it is that intelligence draws not only on the details of the target but also on a full understanding of the environment in which the target is operating. Just as Lord Edward Fitzgerald could live under the noses of the British, so bin Laden lived for six years in Pakistan. But just as the intelligence success of Fitzgerald's capture and death did not put an end to Irish nationalism, nor will that of bin Laden bring an end to the ideas for which he stood. Similarly, just as all intelligence agencies failed to learn of al-Qaeda's most devastating attack until it was too late, so the British in Ireland failed to detect just how strong were the nationalist sentiments which in 1922 would bring an end to centuries of occupation in all but the six counties of what became Northern Ireland.

But despite this mixed record, it is the relationship between Britain and Ireland which then offered a new role for intelligence officers, the onset of the Troubles in 1969 seeing SIS develop what ultimately became one of the most effective roles intelligence agencies have played – that of steering a crisis towards a resolution by creating and managing secret channels to the enemy.

3

TALKING TO TERRORISTS

Fifty years after they had surrendered most of Ireland to its rightful owners, when the simmering conflict in Northern Ireland turned bloody, it shocked the British to discover that much of what had been in the making had passed them by. Moreover, it was only over time – months and years – that they could reasonably assess the potential value of opening secret channels to the enemy. It would be a major leap into unknown territory – but a practice which almost thirty years after the arrival of the Troubles would contribute directly to the successful conclusion of the Northern Ireland 'peace process'; for to be effective in the building of secret channels, the intelligence officers – and the successive governments they served – had to acknowledge the credibility of the protagonists' arguments, and of the motives which underpinned them. With ministers and other public officials condemning terrorist attacks and vilifying the political leadership which ordered them, it was the spies alone who could 'talk to terrorists', seeking out the leaders who might be prepared to 'trade' – in the case of Northern Ireland, to eventually trade the gun for the ballot box.

The need for spies to play such roles has had as much to do with the shortcomings of their own agencies' practices as with the inadequacy – particularly during periods of turmoil – of the conventional means by which democracies seek to resolve conflict.

It is with her characteristic candour – of a kind that would later infuriate her former colleagues at MI5 when, in 2002, she published a memoir of her time as the agency's Director General – that Stella Rimington describes the attempts by MI5 to make sense of what was taking place in Northern Ireland following the eruption of violent protests against anti-Catholic discrimination, which culminated in the 'Battle of the Bogside' between 12 and 14 August 1969: 'At that time MI5 had practically no sources of information and very little intelligence was available.'[1] She goes on to describe MI5's Irish Section as a 'small affair', consisting initially of herself and one other, who 'were supporting a small group who had gone to Northern Ireland to work with the [Royal Ulster Constabulary, the RUC] and to assess what MI5 should do…It was largely assessments of the situation on the ground, reports of meetings and newspaper cuttings.'[2]

Until it became the overall responsibility of MI5, intelligence gathering in the province depended on the combined efforts and resources of the RUC, the Army and the Government Communications Headquarters – GCHQ – while MI5 operated as the collator and disseminator of what had been gathered. Although MI5 would – over the following three decades – develop an effective intelligence-gathering operation within Northern Ireland, the UK mainland and continental Europe in its efforts to contain the Provisional IRA[3] – the 'PIRA' – the shortcomings of the UK's intelligence machinery were as evident in the early years of the Troubles as they had been between 1919 and 1921. Moreover, the reasons for these weaknesses were startlingly similar, and were rooted in some of the same attitudes as had prevailed when Britain had found itself moving towards the loss of Ireland following the War of Independence. Rimington provides a crisp assessment that resounds – although she makes no reference to them – with what would have been the lessons of 1919–21 had anybody been around to learn them. With specific reference to the lack of preparedness for the Troubles, she writes,

> It is a feature of a democracy that a security service will *follow* a new security threat rather than foreseeing it. Of course, resource is devoted to assessing likely new threats but before an investigation can be mounted, using the full panoply of covert resources – interception of

communications, covert surveillance and agent sources – it has to be demonstrable that a serious threat to national security exists. Stated baldly that sounds ineffective, and indeed it does mean that at the beginning of any new threat, intelligence lags behind and takes time to catch up.[4]

It should be noted that MI5 was at that time more of an 'assessing' agency – except in its counter-espionage role against the Soviet Union – than an operational service, which was the role of the Special Branch, so it was not expected that it could swing into action in response to the growing instability in Northern Ireland. Even so, among the officials sent by Whitehall in the wake of the violence of August 1969, a view developed – and prevailed – that the Government at Stormont Castle which had ruled Northern Ireland since 1922 had been permitted to practice systematic anti-Catholic discrimination on a scale that had been largely ignored by the British Government, and which shocked British officials when they experienced it first hand.

When direct rule by Westminster was introduced in Northern Ireland in 1972 and William Whitelaw was appointed as the first Secretary of State for Northern Ireland, it became evident that the complexity of what had been taking place in this corner of the United Kingdom had largely passed the Government by, as a long-serving official who was an early arrival in Belfast at that time told me:

> The situation in Northern Ireland took the Government completely by surprise. The Northern Ireland civil service were not trusted by the inner circle of the British civil service, because they had presided over a situation of extreme discrimination against the nationalist population. They had not governed fairly.[5]

As a consequence, the officials on the ground found that they barely knew who they should speak with to try and gain a sound understanding of the issues that underlay the violence.

The intelligence aspect of the British presence in the early 1970s was limited. SIS wasn't running agents of any significance in the province at that time, the primary concern then being to try and manage the escalating violence. It was with this aim in mind that Frank Steele – a former colonial official who was by then a highly regarded SIS officer, and who had been sent there in both an intelligence capacity and as political advisor to Whitelaw – brokered what was supposed to have been a *secret* meeting between Whitelaw and the PIRA leadership. It was held on 7 July 1972 at the home, on Cheyne Walk, Chelsea, of the then Minister of State for Northern Ireland, Paul Channon. The meeting – for which the future Sinn Féin President Gerry Adams had been released from prison to attend – was led by the PIRA Chief of Staff Seán Mac Stíofáin, and included Dáithí Ó Conaill, Martin McGuinness, Seamus Twomey, Ivor Bell and Adams. Discussions ended in failure, and it was decided that no similar attempts would be made. An official involved at the time explained: 'There was so much distrust. The 'B Specials' (the reserve force of the Royal Ulster Constabulary) had been a problem; internment [of activists, which had been introduced on 9 August 1971] was an albatross,'[6] he told me, acknowledging what a weight the heavy-handed security measures had by then become. Against this bleak background British officials had 'firm instructions not to talk to the IRA'.[7]

However, before leaving at the end in 1974 of his tour of duty in the province, Steele mentioned to his successor from SIS, Michael Oatley, the names of some individuals who might nevertheless be worth approaching.

Oatley had spent his early years in Africa, and a decade later would go on to oversee the service's Middle East and European operations. The intelligence service had deployed first Steele then Oatley as a means of putting SIS skills at the disposal of the Secretary of State and his team, rather than to launch intelligence operations. Despite the failure of the Cheyne Walk talks, Steele had organised the Army's unopposed deployment in the previously 'no go' area of Derry's Bogside in what was called 'Operation Motorman'. Seen as probably his key success, as part of the lead he took in seeking to move the political agenda forward, he had also gained the confidence of leaders of the republican SDLP, a relationship which laid the groundwork for what turned out to be the shortlived power-sharing agreement signed at Sunningdale in December 1973.

In an extensive discussion about the role and activities of Steele and Oatley, a former senior member of Whitelaw's staff who arrived in Northern Ireland early in 1973 explained to me how at first it was Steele who:

> made an enormous contribution, far too little recognised, to the UK Government team's ability to understand the situation and react creatively to it in the early days of direct rule and the period leading up to it. He combined the skills of a very able and experienced intelligence officer and diplomat with those of his early life as a Colonial Service district officer in Africa. He was a big man in every way, highly intelligent, independent and brave, and with a good deal of cheerful charisma. He made friends and contacts everywhere, his unexpected arrival in troubled areas where no government official had been seen for many months giving encouragement to community leaders trying to resist violence.[8]

With Steele's departure from the province, Oatley took up the task of 'exploring the grass roots, while acting notionally as deputy to [the Foreign Office official] James Allan, who took over Steele's role as political advisor, operating on the overt political level', the former Whitelaw official told me. Of Oatley and Allan vis-à-vis the team of UK officials, he said: 'These two acted as its eyes and ears beyond the [Stormont] Castle walls. Oatley seems to have recognised, as Steele evidently had, that there was no scope or need for him to attempt to engage in actual espionage.' The opportunities to manipulate events on the basis of intelligence seeming non-existent, he explained, '[Oatley's] opportunity – exploiting the connections left to him by Steele – was to understand, and to try to influence the situation towards a lessening of violence, using SIS ways of contact-building, and drawing on the support available to him from London.'[9]

Though not unique, this role was extraordinary. In the Northern Ireland of the early 1970s it was the benefit of anonymity coupled with a freedom of action not afforded to other public servants which allowed an understanding of the complex political currents to develop; there was little or nothing to spy on – just raw and brutal truths to try and understand. By the early 1970s the crisis had developed too far for the two sides to be manipulated. Influencing Oatley's activities was the view – which eventually became clear to his colleagues – that insufficient attention was being paid to understanding the Sinn Féin/ PIRA programme and leadership and trying to bring influence to bear on them. Consequently, the official explained,

> Oatley embarked on an extremely dangerous – even foolhardy – programme of visiting hardline republican areas, to which the Army went only in armoured vehicles. He did it without telling anybody, in order to talk with people who could bring him closer to his objective. Frankly, he was extraordinarily lucky to get away with it, and would certainly have been stopped if anyone [in government] had realised what he was doing. He later told of being mildly disconcerted by a Sinn Féin contact who had once said to him rather earnestly, 'For God's sake don't tell us when you're coming. Then we can't be blamed when they kill you.' At the time he thought the man's use of 'when' rather than 'if' a little pessimistic, but with hindsight it probably wasn't. I don't think he found these lonely expeditions very enjoyable.[10]

By late 1974 Oatley had established three potential channels of communication to the PIRA leadership – one through Belfast, one through Derry, and one direct to Dublin. The most promising of these seemed to be Brendan Duddy, a Derry businessman to whose fish-and-chip shop the young Martin McGuinness had at one time had the job of delivering food supplies, but who also had the contacts that would allow messages to reach the top level of the PIRA.

It was through Duddy – who was keen to see the secret channel of communication opened – that 'the Link' was created.

Having decided that this would be the channel which he could pursue, Oatley spoke with Frank Cooper, the Permanent Under-Secretary of State at the Northern Ireland Office in 1973–76, and reported what he had done. Cooper – an RAF pilot during World War II – was seen by some in Whitehall as tough and ruthless; these were traits that worked to Oatley's advantage, as the former official explained to me, recollecting a discussion he himself had had with Cooper:

> I asked Frank, some time after he had retired, about his method for managing a large department. He told me – and I well recall it – that 'it's no use working through the hierarchy. It's too cumbersome and you have to ignore it if you want to get anything done. People outside the group won't like it, and may resent you for it, but you have to choose a small group of able people and you work through them. It becomes recognised

within the department that what they are saying will have your support. So, after a while, people will accept that and not bother to come to you to check.' And this is what Frank did in Ireland; he was a real leader, and quite original – an anti-bureaucrat who played the bureaucratic machine.

Just as would be the case under later governments, Oatley's efforts to seek out and communicate with the PIRA leadership via the Link were in defiance of government policy, which forbade all such contact. It was to get around this hurdle that the dialogue was conducted at one step removed, via Brendan Duddy, Oatley making his own interpretation of the rules, and judging what he could get away with, while seeking to minimise the risk of creating political embarrassment if his efforts were revealed to the public.

Aside from seeking ways around government directives, the nature of the Link was also dependent on Oatley – who was the sole force behind it – being left to his own devices to see how far it could be taken. According to one official, Maurice Oldfield (head of SIS, 1973–78) told Oatley, 'Do whatever is helpful to Frank Cooper.' Acting alone, Oatley made his own decisions as to how far to go, and informed his superiors of what was in train only after the opportunity for dialogue had been set up. As a former senior official told me,

> It wasn't really an SIS operation. Oatley had been lent to the Northern Ireland Office, and in practice was only answerable to Frank Cooper, who in my view was a wonderful person to work for – he would give instructions, but he wasn't specific about how they should be carried out. And [Prime Minister Harold] Wilson simply told Cooper, 'Keep me informed [of the contacts being made].'[11]

The official continued,

> Wilson had an instinct for this kind of thing, and [SIS Chief] Maurice Oldfield was very supportive. But in the end Oatley was able to take personal decisions, the main one being that he would try to get to the [PIRA] leadership and try to bring about a ceasefire. So he went as a personal agenda to develop lines of communication with the leadership. He wasn't being told what to do. It was a completely unusual situation. The SIS contribution was to send some of these skills to the province. Having established the Link – though having yet to conduct any dialogue

through it – Oatley then operated the channel under the control of Cooper, who also kept the Prime Minister informed.'[12]

While keeping Oatley on a 'long leash', the former Whitelaw official said,

Cooper trusted him (Oatley) to push the limits while not going too far. He thought the back-channel route was worth a try and took responsibility for it, clearing the initiative personally with the Prime Minister. At each stage he (Cooper) saw Oatley on his own, discussed the next step, encouraged him as he would have done a young fighter pilot, and fired off a staccato account of developments to [Harold] Wilson – on whose instructions the Secretary of State, by this time Merlyn Rees, was left in ignorance.

Steadily, Oatley cemented the ties to Duddy, by now meeting either at the businessman's home in Derry or at a hillside safe house outside the city.

For Duddy the meetings were an opportunity to educate Oatley about the thinking within the PIRA leadership, while Oatley would use the opportunity to put forward suggestions and gather responses as to what might be considered by the leadership as possible ways out of the violence. But what was also insisted upon at an early stage was that the Link would be secret, a condition to which Duddy responded by telling his SIS interlocutor: the IRA shoots people who are indiscreet, so there's no question of them being indiscreet.[13] And underpinning their discussions was the view that those within the PIRA who were steering it further down the path of terrorism should have their eyes opened to the possibility that their goals could be realised through politics.

This was the possible 'trade' that could be made; it would not be a 'trade in secrets' – Oatley was sharing ideas not intelligence, and Duddy was nobody's spy – but a possible trade-off with regard to the means of achieving goals. It would be twenty years before the deal with the PIRA leadership was sealed, the terrorist campaign coming to an end in return for respectability being accorded by Britain to those who had once led that campaign. Without the Link the peace process would undoubtedly have taken far longer – with more deaths in the meantime – and would have involved a far more painstaking initial stage, during which the negotiators would have had to familiarise themselves with the background knowledge which the Link had already provided.

While Oatley was not in a position to make any offers to the PIRA leadership – and did not seek to – he was able to gauge what the possibilities might be, in anticipation of the day when the political leaderships would be able to talk directly with each other. In their conversations during 1974–75, Oatley and Duddy sought material to pass down the channel of communication to the PIRA leadership which might encourage the latter towards political thinking. After some considerable time it became clear to Duddy, however, that the PIRA side was beginning to feel the discussion lacked direction, and so arranged to introduce Oatley to representatives of the Provisional Army Council. From then on a direct dialogue developed between Oatley and the PIRA, with the latter's team being joined and effectively led by Provisional Sinn Féin President Ruari O'Bradaigh. Meetings were held under secure circumstances in Derry, managed by Duddy, who, though not taking part, was very much the stage manager. In the latter stages Oatley was accompanied by the political advisor James Allan, on the instructions of Frank Cooper, who had – according to an official familiar with the process – 'rather brutally stood back and left Oatley to make his own defence of what he was doing, until he put in James Allan to back him up in the talks and act as an independent witness, by which time a heavyweight cabinet committee was vetting every move'.[14]

The result of the process – which on the PIRA side was described as 'negotiation of a truce', and on the British side as 'explanation of the consequences of a cessation of violence' – was the ceasefire that came into effect on 9 February 1975.

But the halt to the violence was tenuous. Agreement was reached on a cessation of PIRA activity in return for assurances on the withdrawal of the British Army from certain areas, and a general lowering of the security forces' profile. Accounts differ as to what else – if anything – was agreed, the PIRA later claiming that a truce was negotiated in which they received substantial concessions. However, the Government position remained that there was no negotiation, simply an explanation of what would follow as a logical response to a cessation of violence. As the official aware of the process explained, 'What seems to have happened on the Sinn Féin/PIRA side was that those who were looking for a political future chose to make the most of a rather insubstantial situation – with some embellishments – in presenting it to their colleagues.'[15]

When the ceasefire collapsed on 23 January 1976, the new Secretary of State for Northern Ireland, Roy Mason (1976–79), adopted a very hard line, and decreed that no contacts with paramilitary groups would be held in the future. The trade was off.

However, it became apparent later that Oatley and Duddy had decided to ignore Mason's instruction. It seems that Oatley did not tell his superiors about his next move, because they would naturally have adhered to the Secretary of State's order. He and Duddy agreed that the personal trust which had been built up – and the possibility of direct and secret dialogue – was too valuable to throw away. Although there now seemed little to talk about, and there might not be for a long time, they concluded that the Link should be kept in existence. They put this suggestion to their PIRA contacts, who accepted it: Duddy was to be the man holding the key, and Oatley – wherever in the world he happened to be – would be immediately available to him, and able to communicate with the Government at the highest level.

Between 1976 and 1991, the Link was used only once, in an effort – which failed – to bring an end to the October–December 1980 hunger strike of prisoners held at the Maze Prison in Belfast. Few in Whitehall seem at that time to have questioned why the Link existed and how or why it was available for use on that occasion despite the prohibition on contacts with the PIRA; on learning of it, however, Prime Minister Margaret Thatcher immediately authorised Oatley's pursuit of an attempt to have the hunger strike called off. Even her later prohibition on 'talking to terrorists', notably in the aftermath of the PIRA's bombing of the Grand Hotel in Brighton on 12 October 1984, when it sought to kill the entire British Government, did not close the channel down. Throughout the 1980s the Link remained in place, the onus being on the PIRA leaders who knew of its existence to keep it a very closely guarded secret – which they did.

But Michael Oatley was far from being the only intelligence officer active in the province; others were using their skills to fight the war Oatley's efforts seemed intended to stop.

Although it is not widely discussed among the intelligence professionals who focused on Northern Ireland following the eruption of violence in 1969, secret intelligence has made the difference between policy success and policy failure throughout recent Anglo–Irish history. As with many intelligence operations that have had the most lasting effect, the most significant Army intelligence activities in Northern Ireland benefited – at least in their early stages – from the readiness of senior officers to pursue 'maverick' ideas if they appeared worth a try.

These initiatives were taking place against a background of what seemed – for much of the 1970s and 1980s – to be a relationship of tension between the different branches of the intelligence machinery which was operating in Northern Ireland. These conflicts and rivalries were manifested most startlingly in the decision within the Army to operate intelligence-gathering operations that were ultimately as maverick as the Link with the PIRA, as a former senior official with detailed knowledge of intelligence operations in the province told me. When asked about the emergence of what became the Army's Force Research Unit – FRU – he explained, 'The Army got bored with the failure of the intelligence agencies. So it went private, and created the FRU. It was not that there had been a change in the rules. But clearly the Army was running operations that – if they had been civilian operations – were illegal.'[16]

But it was not so much the 'muddling through' approach which inspired the Army top brass to go 'private' and start running its own agents within the PIRA. The reasons were far more serious, as a former long-serving senior Army officer who experienced the shortcomings of the 'intelligence machinery' in Northern Ireland at first hand told me:

The core problems were a lack of coordination of the intelligence gathering, and a routine refusal [by the intelligence agencies] to share it with the Army. There were examples of single sources who were providing intelligence to different agencies – to both the RUC Special Branch and to MI5 and perhaps to us (the Army) as well – who would give different accounts of the same event or issue to different intelligence officers. Sometimes – and it happened on a number of occasions, leading us to assume there was more to it than 'cock-up' – the RUC would arrest sources they knew were Army sources.[17]

He went on, 'People had realised in the early days that the RUC had no valuable intelligence. Initially their intelligence was tainted, though it got better. But they were reluctant to share – the fact that the Army was there at all was a sign of their (the RUC) failure.'

The failure of what was on offer – and the Army's decision to create the FRU in 1980, despite doing so being 'wholly improper', as a senior Army officer closely involved in its activities told me – exposed how vulnerable those in the military front line in Northern Ireland felt they had become.

Then new problems on the intelligence front emerged. A senior Army officer who did a tour of duty in the highly volatile area of South Armagh in 1980–81 explained: 'During that entire tour of duty I received not a single piece of "contact" intelligence – that is, intelligence that would enable soldiers to be placed in a situation where they could legally engage terrorists.' Martin Ingram, a former FRU officer, explains in his account of FRU agent-handling that the intelligence agencies in Northern Ireland during the 1980s and 1990s – comprising the RUC Special Branch,[18] the Army's 22 Squadron SAS and 14 Intelligence and Security Company,[19] as well as MI5 and the FRU (which was disbanded in 1991, to be replaced by the similarly named Force Reconnaissance Unit) – faced a major problem, which was 'little or no co-ordination, due mainly to the intense distrust between various agencies'.[20] Ingram asserts that the Army's prized spy within the IRA – 'Stakeknife' – was even approached by the RUC Special Branch, which 'made a number of hostile attempts to lure him away from the Army to the Branch'.[21]

Stakeknife's recruitment in 1976 gave the Army – and later the FRU, which took over the handling of him – access to intelligence on PIRA activity which senior officers, who were at that time also grappling with an already difficult relationship with the RUC Special Branch, to this day regard as having been of unique value to the overall intelligence capability during the Troubles. The manner of his recruitment was in itself revealing of the important role the Army had, in being the most visible interface between the 'Brits' and the Irish population. While Royal Corps of Signals officers were bugging PIRA communications and passing their findings directly to GCHQ in Cheltenham, MI5 and SIS were liaising directly with their offices in London. Meanwhile the RUC was regarding these British 'blow ins' as interlopers on their territory. So the thousands of British troops who passed through the province on their tours of duty sought other ways of communicating with the population. A former officer who worked closely with the FRU explained: 'Soldiers were told to say "good morning" to everybody they passed on the street, and this approach fed directly into what the FRU did.'[22] Such was the case when a young soldier in plain clothes found himself chatting with the man later codenamed 'Stakeknife', as a senior officer who knew the soldier and who met Stakeknife many times told me:

> Stakeknife liked the Army. He hated MI5 and SIS – he said it: he saw them as 'poofters'. Within the Army it irritated us that you could rarely raise MI5 at the weekend, because they took the flight back to London on Fridays, while there was no point in trying to speak with the RUC when *Match of the Day* was on.
>
> We in the Army were alert all the time during our tours of duty, and Stakeknife's handler first met him in a bar in Belfast. Initially it wasn't a question of 'recruitment'. They just chatted – that's what soldiers like him were: 'chatter-uppers'. Getting to know people in bars, on the street, was vital. With Stakeknife no money changed hands. His motives for talking to us – for more than two decades – were, I suppose, that he was rather taken by the idea; it was extremely lucky for us that he was promoted within the PIRA. It was he who would be responsible, for example, for hiding weapons caches, and who put trackers on weapons so we could know where they were. And as for the arms dumps, he would have the responsibility for creating them, and would then tell us where they were.[23]

The intelligence successes born of chance meetings like that between a soldier and Stakeknife could not, however, dilute the impact of the mistrust, lack of cooperation and failure to coordinate, which plagued intelligence gathering in Northern Ireland. Moreover, similar shortcomings existed around the world – and were only brought to an end in the wake of 9/11. While it was the failure of the CIA and the FBI to cooperate and coordinate with each other which contributed directly to the failure to identify the 9/11 suspects – even if such identification would not necessarily have led to detection of their plans – the territorialism, occasional disdain and undercurrent of competitiveness which also characterised relationships between agencies on other Western countries, was ubiquitous. The structures of the agencies, the backgrounds and ambitions of their staff, their differences of style and approach, had been allowed on occasion to evolve into rivalry, at least with regard to the jealous guarding of their sources; the rivalries in Northern Ireland were a microcosm of a much wider reality.

It would be wrong to suggest, however, that the 'intelligence machinery' in the key global intelligence-gathering states, which was forced into overdrive in the wake of 9/11, had by then become dysfunctional; the shortcomings in the relationships between agencies within the leading intelligence services were – in different ways – compensated for by inter-agency bodies such as the UK's Joint Intelligence Committee, wherein what has been learned is pooled and then shared with the appropriate ministries.

But as with so much that has changed since 9/11, while it was acknowledged as vital that the practice of spying be transformed – once it was realised that the new threat was unprecedented – what that transformation should entail remained for many months little short of a mystery. The realisation that al-Qaeda was not staffed by people prepared to trade secrets, dawned only slowly; only with spies on the inside of the terrorist structure could the long-established methods of intelligence gathering be practiced. But the agencies – constrained by structures formed during the Cold War – could not transform overnight their methods for 'making spies'.

4

MAKING SPIES

The Anglo–Irish relationship of the past two centuries has spawned an intelligence role with a depth and variety which has overshadowed that of any other single 'target' – in many aspects including that of the Soviet Union. While the Cold War seemed to be the *sole* axis about which the post-colonial world was revolving – most tumultuously in disparate locations across the decolonising world – it was in many ways an overarching 'theme' which occasionally united what were in fact very distinct upheavals.

And while political leaders packaged the world into often startlingly simple phrases, the spies were entangled in an often very different set of circumstances.

For much of the Cold War era those within the intelligence machinery of the West were living in a different world from that of their own political leaders. The two sides did not meet often; it is illustrative of the British case that – according to one senior official – the Chief of SIS rarely had regular *informal* meetings with the British Foreign Secretary (to whom SIS is answerable) until Sir Richard Dearlove (Chief, 1999–2004) started to have a monthly breakfast with Jack Straw (Foreign Secretary, 2001–6). More recently, while visits by Foreign Secretaries to the SIS headquarters – located at Vauxhall Cross in South London since 1994 – were extremely rare, the Foreign Secretary in the newly elected Conservative–Liberal Democrat coalition, William Hague, took SIS by great surprise when he 'was there within 24 hours' of the Government being formed on 12 May 2010, to meet with the SIS Chief, Sir John Sawers.

For decades prior to the recent – though varied – transformations in relations between political establishments and intelligence communities, the community of spies saw a world dominated by shades of grey; the political leaders who came and went by necessity saw much in terms of black and white.

Lying at the heart of the difference between the two is the role of ordinary people.

It was at a lunch at the Portrait Restaurant that I first met Antony. Overlooking Trafalgar Square, it is reached through the corridors of the National Portrait Gallery, its walls lined with the silent portraits of the great, the good, the bad and the ugly. In the confidential calm of the top floor, the restaurant keeps its secrets well. Looking west across the square and down Whitehall, the Union Jack seems to flutter from every rooftop. Nelson – almost on a level from there – observes sanguinely the passing of the ages that his early efforts forged into history and etched onto the nation's mind, and Antony sat opposite me, apologising for having taken so long to arrange our lunch – a delay caused by a bad back, he explained.

It was late 2002. We could have talked of the weather – warm for autumn – but I instead asked him what 'KGC' stood for. The letters were written on his tie, beneath what looked like two crossed hockey sticks but which were in fact golf clubs.

'Kabul Golf Club,' he said.

What Antony said was often as captivating as the way this long-time SIS officer said it. It seemed that he was used to speaking very quietly but with a determination to be clearly understood, which led to him mouthing words as if talking at the top of his voice. In public – a coffee bar at Victoria Station, a café at the Royal Festival Hall, atop the National Portrait Gallery, on the Centre Court at Wimbledon where we once spent a hot afternoon, and in the numerous other London haunts in which we met and which have never seemed the same since – he actually spoke barely above a whisper.

The more time I spent with him the less I felt I knew him, at least in the terms that had prevailed before I started to cross paths with spies. I was a newspaper reporter looking for explanations; I had by then lived for seven years in sub-Saharan Africa, two years in the Maghreb and almost four years in the Middle East. I had met rebel leaders, kings, presidents, dictators, fundamentalists, terrorists and freedom fighters. I had even written books about this cast of characters. But still there always seemed to be some other story going on – a story beneath the surface.

'I don't remember the golf club,' I replied, casting my mind back to a winter's day in 1996 when I had taken a taxi out of Kabul and headed north to see where the front line lay. 'Where was it? Close to the road out to Charikar, out near the King's summer palace?' 'Around there', he told me continuing,

> It was a place to meet with sources. I had a caddy who would carry my clubs for the first eight holes. Then at the ninth the caddy would change, and the new one would be from the *Mujahideen*. He would carry my clubs for three holes, when the original caddy would reappear and take over. It really was an excellent way of keeping up with what the *Muj* were up to: who was where, who had fallen out with whom. The Russians never seemed to suspect anything, despite their best efforts. After all, Kabul was small; we knew who the KGB officers were, and they thought they knew who we were. And I never had to carry my own golf clubs. Then the club chairman himself gave me this tie, just before I left, which I am extremely proud of.
>
> 'And did the club wonder about the change of caddy?' I asked.
>
> Well, there were small hills behind which the changes would take place, which meant it could all be done rather discreetly. But the Club officials were all on one side or the other. By then it looked as though the Russians had lost it; the *Muj* were in disarray, but Najibullah was so heartily despised that I could probably have entertained the *Muj* in the clubhouse and nobody would have objected, except the Afghan secret police, who were pretty much everywhere. Everybody was on one side or the other, so recruiting people to help us was easy, if you kept your wits about you. There were plenty of people who wanted to help us.

Antony had seen Kabul fall into the hands of the Soviet Union as it sought to satisfy the imperial ambitions which – overstretched – would bring it down on 26 December 1991; I had been in the city as it fell under the winter freeze that accompanied its fall to the Taliban in 1996. He and I had seen different ends of the same story. The Cold War came to an end just as I was setting off into the world. By the time my reporter's journey took me to Kabul in 1996, the golf course greens that Antony had strode across, lay beneath thick snow. But even as political earthquakes continued to rumble, real knowledge – of why and how what had happened had happened – remained hard to come by. On the surface, the Berlin Wall had come down and democratic elections were taking place in countries that had never before known them. Meanwhile, beneath the surface, there were other currents at work. New 'Great Games' would emerge and new rivalries evolve, as the losers of the defeated 'old world order' strove to take their places in the 'new world order' the victorious West sought to lead.

Antony's journey to Kabul had begun when he decided – for reasons he never told me – to change his career path and terminate his job selling lingerie at an upmarket department store in Singapore. He – like many others – seemed to be a part of a tradition of seemingly ordinary people thrust into extraordinary circumstances. The motives of the spy, the intelligence officers and agents without whom – at least until bugging devices, telephone taps and other 'signals intelligence' became as sophisticated as they now are – there would be no secret intelligence, have remained rooted in the widest imaginable range of motives, from the crude, instinctive, humane or greedy, to the idealistic or vain.

Today, it is their understanding of people which has been vital to developing comprehension of the 'non-state' terrorist threat. A world away from Antony's – though their paths would come close to crossing – the story of Séan O'Callaghan is a case in point.

On a mid-April day in 1975, O'Callaghan had been making tea for the PIRA's then adjutant-general and later head of its Northern Command, Kevin McKenna, at a safe house in Monaghan, a town in the Republic just south of the border with Northern Ireland. As he prepared the tea, O'Callaghan writes in his memoir *The Informer*, the attention of the gathered PIRA activists was drawn to a news report of a bomb explosion in Bangor, north of Belfast, which had killed a policewoman. O'Callaghan relates how McKenna, 'the man I respected so much, the man who was to become my boss' had 'turned his head slightly in my direction and said, "Maybe she was pregnant and we got two for the price of one."'[1] O'Callaghan slowly made his way to the upper floor of the safe house and 'burst into tears and lay down on one of the mattresses on the bedroom floor' – an emotional response to McKenna's comment, which was followed later that year by him reaching a conclusion: 'I realised that joining the Provisional IRA had been the biggest mistake of my life.'[2]

It was the moment of turning point, of revelation, without which the intelligence community would be deprived of the core ingredient necessary for it to function: betrayal.

What Séan O'Callaghan heard that day turned him for the very best of motives into one of the most significant spies the Irish police – the Garda Síochána na hÉireann – were to have within the PIRA. The same drift which saw the former lingerie seller of Singapore become the gatherer of *mujahideen* secrets on a Kabul golf course and this 'wild and a little reckless'[3] Tralee teenager become a key spy within the PIRA's Southern Command, acted no less on Stella Rimington, as she recounts in the story of how she became Director General of MI5. While hinting that her real motive for joining the Service – after a stint as a 'diplomatic wife' at the British High Commission in Delhi – was her sense of 'romantically dreaming about the Great Game',[4] the future DG describes her feelings as she arrived for her recruitment interview at the Service's office in Great Marlborough Street, London in July 1969, as follows:

> Certainly my motives were nothing like those they look for in recruits nowadays. I did not feel a particular urge to serve my country, though I was averagely patriotic, nor did I have a strong sense of dangers to the state to be tackled or wrongs to be righted…The truth is that I had not seen enough of the dull side of the [intelligence] work to be put off; I thought it would be interesting and that I would get some amusement and fun out of it…I saw this just as a job, something I might do for a time…hopefully until I had a baby, but possibly until something else cropped up.[5]

As for Antony and Stella Rimington, Séan O'Callaghan's life as a spy became his life. Illustrative of what *intelligence* is, however, he was only one of several – perhaps many – whose information seemed all-important and definitive to them, but whose scraps and fragments of intelligence were in fact only part of a much larger picture.

The tale of the *Eksund* places the life-changing experiences of a lone Kerryman into a more worldly context.

Loaded with 150 tonnes of weapons, ammunition and Semtex explosive, the Panamanian-registered ship set sail from the military port area of the Libyan capital Tripoli on 15 October 1987 for what was intended – by those members of the PIRA Army Council who were aware of the cargo – to be the 'Tet Offensive' that would turn the war against British rule in Northern Ireland definitively in their favour.[6] It would be the fifth cargo provided by Libya to be delivered to the PIRA in just over two years; four smaller cargoes delivered since August 1985 had successfully brought AK-47s, ammunition and other equipment to waiting dinghies off the Irish coast at Clogga Strand in County Wicklow, south of Dublin.

But the story of the *Eksund* was different, for within hours of steaming out into the Mediterranean – the only one of the consignments to have been loaded in Tripoli, the others having been transferred mid-sea off the Maltese coast – the ship was being trailed by an unmarked spotter plane. Then, in the Bay of Biscay, the vessel developed engine trouble. A short while later the PIRA's Director of Engineering, Gabriel Cleary – the man sent to Tripoli to oversee the smuggling of the consignment – noticed that wires connected to explosives he had rigged up around the ship that would be used to scupper it in the event of its interception, had been sabotaged. Then, as the ship drifted towards the Brittany coast having failed to resolve a steering problem, the spotter plane passed overhead and French coastguard vessels sped across the water towards the crew of smugglers and their deadly cargo.

But what the hapless crew could see on the surface was not all that had been tracking the ship. Soon after it steamed out of Tripoli and into the Mediterranean it was also being trailed first by a French submarine and subsequently – as it went north along Europe's Atlantic coast – by a Royal Navy submarine, a senior British Army officer confirmed to me.

The seizure of the *Eksund* was an intelligence coup for which neither the British nor the French sought to take credit. To this day it remains uncertain who within the upper echelons of the PIRA Army Council passed on details of the smuggling operation, still less to whom that information was passed. O'Callaghan's account provides the kind of fragments out of which the broader picture may have emerged: on deserting from the PIRA in 1985 he lived for a year in Haarlem, the Dutch town west of Amsterdam, where he was debriefed every few weeks by 'John', an MI5 officer. When news of the seizure of the *Eksund* was reported, O'Callaghan writes, 'My delight was quickly to turn to disbelief and anger as it became clear that the IRA had in fact already succeeded in landing three shipments (in fact it was four)...I had told the Gardaí, Scotland Yard and MI5 that the shipments were due and MI5 were aware of where they would be landed.'[7]

But the role played by people like O'Callaghan is twofold: not only was intelligence sought regarding plots, but the clear message was sent to the PIRA that its ranks had been infiltrated. Although in the short term the arms seizure – and others like it – was all-important, in the long term the impact on PIRA morale of realising there were traitors in its midst, was of equal import due to its eventual role in edging the organisation towards negotiations.

Although he recognises Séan O'Callaghan as the informer who reported the arrival of weapon supplies from the United States, the well-informed writer on the IRA Ed Moloney does not cite him as the source of intelligence regarding the *Eksund*. This tends to suggest that the PIRA – within which Moloney clearly has excellent contacts, and from within which a part of his view of O'Callaghan's real significance will have been formed – did not regard O'Callaghan as likely to know in detail of the Libyan supply line following his desertion from the organisation a few months after the first shipment had arrived. The scenario is common: a piece of intelligence from one agent provides a lead; his 'handlers' – in O'Callaghan's case the Gardaí and later MI5 – may have other elements to put together with what he tells them. The fragments were drawn together, and – as I was told by an influential British Army officer in a position to know because he did several tours of duty in Northern Ireland between the mid-1970s and the mid-1990s, and who had access to secret intelligence during those periods –

> The PIRA was so heavily infiltrated that they began to realise it. They knew they could not 'win' – they knew that the British Army wasn't going to leave, and at the same time began to realise that one of their operations after another was going wrong. Arms dumps would be

discovered, their people would be picked up, and their plans would be thwarted, in one way or another. Then they realised that it must be because of the degree of infiltration that had taken place. My view is that the driver for the IRA to come to the peace talks was the fact that they knew they had been infiltrated.[8]

He added, 'The events that were crucial in this were Gibraltar[9] and Loughgall. I sensed that they knew they were penetrated.' In Gibraltar on 6 March 1988 three unarmed IRA members – Danny McCann, Sean Savage and Mairéad Farrell – were killed by the SAS on suspicion that they were planning to attack British troops on the territory; at Loughgall on 8 May 1987, eight PIRA members were killed in an SAS ambush as they prepared to attack an RUC base, further pointing to PIRA plans having leaked.

Meanwhile, Libya was not the only country to have created ties with the PIRA, Antony told me when we met again some weeks later, at the same restaurant overlooking Trafalgar Square, he – like many long-serving intelligence officers – having found himself embroiled in the affairs of Northern Ireland despite Asia having been his major focus as in SIS officer.

It was following the shaky start to the Northern Ireland peace process in the 1990s that SIS decided to give an additional boost to the dialogue with the PIRA by seeking to bring an end to its contacts with Tehran. A year-long intelligence-gathering operation had focused initially on meetings between PIRA operatives and Iranian officials that had taken place in the German towns of Dortmund and Münster. The surveillance had then been extended to Athens, where SIS officers and the Greek authorities had discovered and followed a consignment of drugs estimated to be worth £19 million, reckoned to have been provided by Iran, intended to aid PIRA fundraising.[10] On 28 April 1994 the British Government summoned the Iranian Chargé d'Affaires in London, Gholamreza Ansari 'to convey our concern and to request an assurance at senior level that contact would be immediately and conclusively severed' between Iran and the PIRA.

The context in which the diplomatic request was delivered was characteristic of SIS: information about the drugs consignment had been leaked to an Athens newspaper – *Eleftheros Typos* – with allegations of the Iran–PIRA link prominent in the article that appeared on 25 April. Thus, when the Foreign Office Minister Douglas Hogg made his *démarche* to Ansari he was able to cite 'press reports' of the allegations: despite the Athens newspaper referring to the SIS role, 'intelligence' remained conspicuous for its absence in their discussion.

But intelligence was – and remains – central.

As part of the ongoing focus on external support being provided to the PIRA – which had at one point allegedly led to Iran asking the PIRA to assassinate exiled opponents of the Iranian regime in return for weapons supplies (a request the PIRA turned down)[11] – the combination of fresh hopes for the peace process and the challenge to the republican leadership of reconciling republicanism with the Iranian regime's core ambitions, meant a risk was worth taking that might terminate the PIRA–Iran link altogether.

The first outward signs of the operation began when parents at the primary school south of London at which Antony would drop his two young children on the mornings when he was not travelling abroad, began to wonder why this conventional-looking parent who worked in the 'foreign service' had started to grow a beard. It drew some comments, but turned to marked concern when his skin appeared to be becoming a few shades darker. Then the other parents began to make polite inquiries as to his health. All was fine, of course, though it was decided after a few weeks that he should change his domestic routine, and focus on the plans then being developed.

Within six weeks he had become what any passing or even close observer could see was a member of the Iranian political establishment, a medically darkened complexion complemented by the neatly cropped beard characteristic of Iran's political leadership. This was followed by contacts then being made – not via the Link – with the PIRA leadership, and a meeting was arranged.

Suitably dressed in the attire of the regime, and equipped with a range of items that could attest to his fake identity, Antony made his way to the first meeting with the PIRA, accompanied by a large, armed bodyguard. Several meetings took place, all of them in continental Europe, with the purpose of first assessing the state of relations between the PIRA and the Government in Tehran, and then bringing that relationship to an end. It is not known who it was Antony met from within the PIRA leadership; however, at that first meeting and those that followed, he appears to have succeeded not only in convincing his PIRA interlocutors that he was a representative of the Iranian regime, but that in the view of Tehran the relationship was one that should be terminated.

As the food on our untended plates grew cold and the Union Jacks fluttered in the breeze that passed over Whitehall, Antony, a fluent Farsi speaker, told me,

> My bodyguard had been taught two words – 'baleh' and 'nah' – 'yes' and 'no'. It was all that was needed, because he was under instructions to do one thing – shoot if they did. But it wasn't necessary. The aim was to let the PIRA know that 'we in the Iranian Government' no longer felt that our causes were common, and that we wish to bring it to an end. Which we did.

'And how many meetings did you have with them?' I asked.

'There were...several.'

'Where?'

'In...Europe.'

'And wasn't there the risk that between meetings they would somehow be able check whether you were who you said you were?'

'Certainly,' he said, a wry smile breaking out across his face. 'But even now, it seems, they never worked it out.'

'So they really did think that the Iranians were ditching them?'

'Pretty much.'

'And how many meetings did you have?'

'You have already asked me that.'

'Well, how many?'

'Three.'

'And where were they?'

'You have asked me that too. I am afraid I can't tell you. But they were in Europe, in a third country. Not in England, nor in Northern Ireland. Nor in the Irish Republic.'

'And there was never any suspicion on their side that you were not who you claimed you were?'

'Nope!'

'And since then has it ever emerged that it was an intelligence operation?'

'No.'

'So, nobody outside the Service knows about it?'

'No. Well, they do now. Don't they?'

'Who knows?'

'*You* do,' he said.

While the fight against terrorism – specifically the thwarting of plots, which was and today remains MI5's top priority – was the immediate intention of gathering intelligence in Northern Ireland, using it to try and identify avenues that could contain the violence in the long term followed closely behind. From 1991 it was central to MI5 activity, following the decision – unknown to MI5 until after it had been taken – by the SIS officer Michael Oatley and the Derry businessman Brendan Duddy, to revive the Link that had existed with the PIRA since 1975.

Despite having lain dormant since the failed efforts to use it to bring an end to the hunger strikes at the Maze Prison in Belfast in 1980, the Link was regarded by those who knew of its existence as being of undoubted value. This was explained to me by the former member of the team sent to Northern Ireland with William Whitelaw:

> In practice, although dormant, the existence of the Link was prized by the PIRA leadership, chiefly Martin McGuiness and Gerry Adams. They recognised that they might one day need it again, and were impressed by its effectiveness. This gave Brendan Duddy a status and special significance, which helped him in his lonely efforts to canvass the attractions and opportunities of a non-violent political programme for the republican movement. It was Duddy's intimate connection – based on the Link – and his own extraordinary determination, which eventually produced practical results.[12]

Duddy and Oatley had kept in touch over the years, as Oatley moved from London to Hong Kong to Zimbabwe, and then on to run SIS operations in the Middle East and finally in Europe, from which last post he was about to retire at the beginning of 1991. He and Duddy agreed that news of his impending retirement might offer an opportunity for renewed dialogue. The aim was to let the PIRA leadership receive the message: 'The Link is going. What do you want to do about it, and might the time be ripe for making progress?' As one of those familiar with Oatley's role and the significance of the Link explained,

> Duddy suggested to Martin McGuiness that a meeting without commitment might be worthwhile, before Oatley – whom they knew and had trusted – disappeared from the scene. So McGuinness and Oatley met and had a long and productive talk in a safe-house in Derry during Oatley's last week as an SIS officer.[13]

Oatley's meeting with McGuinness – the first they had ever had – happened entirely without the approval of any of the British Government officials from whom assent would normally have been sought. However, according to a former senior official who was aware of the response of Sir John Chilcot – at that time Permanent Under-Secretary of State at the Northern Ireland Office – Oatley visited Chilcot after the meeting and told him, 'This is what I have done, and I have done it without telling you because I knew you would not approve.'[14]

The events which followed served to illustrate how conventional diplomacy can fail to work when the most crucial element is the building of trust. The trust that lay at the heart of the Link had endured years of apparently lost opportunities to turn the secret dialogue into public action. But this time things were very significantly different, because this secret channel would slowly but steadily feed more directly into conventional diplomacy and the making of history. This began when Oatley handed over responsibility for the Link to a long-time intelligence officer seconded to MI5, who is referred to by all those who know him simply as 'Fred'. The former official cited earlier explained: 'Fred was put in to pursue what Oatley had arranged with Martin McGuinness. He had the back-up, but he did somewhat lack the experience. And he made an ambitious leap.'[15]

Fred's role in what eventually became the peace process that led to the Good Friday Agreement of 1998 marked an end to the role of mavericks and the beginning of a far more structured methodology overseen by MI5. It culminated in the writing of a note purportedly from the PIRA leadership which eventually arrived on Prime Minister John Major's desk. The note began with the line, 'The conflict is over but we need your advice on how to bring it to an end. We wish to have an unannounced cease-fire in order to hold dialogue leading to peace.'[16]

The true provenance of the note has never been revealed, though Fred's 'ambitious leap' was one that leaked to the media and led to a strong denial from Martin McGuinness that he had written it. Indeed, given McGuinness's great caution over many years, it was unlikely that he would ever have committed such sentiments to paper; more likely, according to several sources familiar with the issue, was that he held these views and shared them with his closest confidantes within the PIRA, and it was these views – which may have *appeared* to have come from McGuinness – that filtered through to Fred, who then took the 'leap' of assessing they were views McGuinness held and upon which action could be taken.

What thus began as an extremely high-risk game of chance was to become a part of the foundation for the agreement that followed half a decade later.

Jonathan Powell, Chief of Staff in Prime Minister Tony Blair's office, 1997–2007, and the official who deserves most credit for drawing Northern Ireland's rivals to the negotiating table, said of the Link and of the message passed on by Fred, 'Thank God. If you don't have a channel to the terrorists you don't have that communication.'[17] Although Powell said of the Link that – due to negotiations having failed to bring results – it had 'completely broken down by the time we came into office [on 2 May 1997]. There wasn't a lot of trust,' he nevertheless recognises that the Duddy–Oatley channel had been essential, in part as a way of ensuring that nobody forgot that in the end negotiation was the only means by which the conflict could be brought to an end. The character of the negotiations that were eventually overseen by Blair and Powell was determined, Powell told me, by Adams's and McGuinness's longer-term plan, which was focused on winning political respectability: 'Sinn Féin reached a very clear view that they wanted to negotiate with a public figure [not an intelligence officer]. It all took so long because of the need to build trust.'[18]

At that point, the early efforts of maverick intelligence officers became more directly tied to the negotiations that first John Major and subsequently Tony Blair steered towards the accord that exists today.

In the context of the Northern Ireland peace process intelligence is seen within the agencies as having contributed to the readiness of the political players to take risks, by giving them a flavour of the internal dynamics of the PIRA. But while intelligence was always a central part of day-to-day security operations, it was in fact in the political process that it was ultimately at its most successful; it allowed the British Government to 'know more about them than they do about us'. As a result of its operations very often being betrayed by touts, the PIRA leadership could not fail to conclude that even though the conflict could be continued – perhaps forever – the superiority of British intelligence meant that infiltration would prevent it from winning the war.

Thus it was that intelligence – the knowledge that it was being gathered, and the betrayal of trust its collection revealed to those who became increasingly aware of their own vulnerability – came to operate as a weapon in its own right. The exposure of plots and the discovery of arms caches clearly had a directly practical benefit, by saving lives; but the uncertainty, mistrust, tension and paranoia which the process of spying created – as well as the violence of the punishments meted out to touts by the PIRA, and the consequent disgust such measures engendered within Northern Ireland's nationalist population – were powerful weapons in themselves. The PIRA leadership could never feel comfortable, aware as it was that those within its ranks might actually be working for the other side.

Intelligence thus became a destabilising force, fear of it hampering the enemy's plans and thereby limiting the activities of those who would carry out attacks, due to their worry that they might be betrayed. The view – expressed above – that ultimately the PIRA sought a political solution due to the leadership's awareness that infiltration meant it could not ultimately 'win' the armed conflict, is an extraordinary one. But the suggestion – made back in 1920, with regard to their capacity – that spies can 'do anything' was a powerful myth. As with all myths it was vulnerable to exposure. That exposure would arise when the rules of 'the spying game'[19] were overturned, when the enemy could no longer be bought, when there could be no more trade. By then, however, it had become the modern world's most powerful myth, having fed – in very real and direct ways, as well as by way of romance and mystique – into the spy-craft of intelligence agencies around the world as the Cold War intensified.

5

GAMES WITHOUT FRONTIERS

I caught the tail-end of the Cold War when in September 1989 I left a job reporting from Westminster and started a new life in Abidjan, Côte d'Ivoire. It was a time when West Africa's dictators were beginning to feel the reformist heat being generated by the rapid collapse of the regimes in Eastern Europe on which some had sought to model themselves for much of the previous thirty years.

I soon learned that while Europe had been portrayed as the heartland of the East–West rivalry, it was really the countries emerging from colonialism wherein the 'heat' of the Cold War had been felt. Although there was no Berlin Wall in Africa upon which slogans could be daubed, or along which victims could be shot while trying to cross, nor a 'Checkpoint Charlie' or equivalent symbol, there were hundreds of thousands of victims scattered across the battlefields of conflicts that were part-imported and part-indigenous.

Antony, the spy with whom I would later lunch at the window overlooking Trafalgar Square, had spent his early childhood in Africa. The son of colonial parents, he had grown up running barefoot through a village in Malawi. For those like him, whose first sense of the world was dominated by decolonisation and the new geopolitics that emerged from it, one of the great dividers within his profession was that between the old colonials of the intelligence services and those who had no sense of what that disappearing world had been like.

But perhaps more stark than this generational divide was the national one: Africa's former colonial powers generally saw the 'superpower' rivalry that emerged in the Congo in 1960, then in Angola and Mozambique in 1975, as a complex mix of local – often tribal – rivalries that were then catapulted onto the new, global geopolitical stage. For the United States and the Soviet Union – states lacking the experience of close proximity to the 'other' that colonialism had afforded the Europeans – the battle was a rather different one. Even though Britain, France, Belgium and – at least for a time – Portugal despatched their spies to Africa with briefs to assess who among the new generation of post-colonial leaders should be courted, opposed or considered for assassination, it was the United States and the Soviet Union – with occasional forays being made by China – that took up a notch or two the opportunities offered by this new world; what happened in Kolwezi, Mogadishu or Algiers came – for a short while – to be regarded with almost as much seriousness as what might be going on in Warsaw, Budapest or Havana. And as they sought to gain influence, promote their favoured candidates for power and discredit their critics, the entire African continent fell 'like a plum' into the hands of the CIA and the KGB.

The phrase is that of John Stockwell, one of what he himself described as those 'foot-soldiers of foreign policy',[1] a CIA officer tasked with leading the fight against the Soviet Union in those parts of the world wherein most of the population would have been hard pressed to pinpoint Washington or Moscow on a map.

The Cold War threw up some dramatic myths about spies and spying, when in fact most of what the world's intelligence agencies engaged in was covert diplomacy and dirty tricks. The exotic tales of daring – while very real when they happened – were overall far less common than the extensive use of intelligence-agency structures and methodology to pursue deniable, covert means of gaining influence, supplying weapons, making secret payments and thwarting the enemy's plans through the effective use of propaganda, forgery and misinformation. As a former senior SIS officer reflected,

> During the Cold War thirty-three percent of SIS resources were focused on the Soviet Bloc. My belief is that they spent thirty-three percent of their resources over thirty years and achieved very little more than

attracting the defection [of Soviet informers]. It was completely futile [trying to make contact with Soviet officials while they were still in their roles] because they were so well protected. The only way to do it was to go through third countries. But that wasn't the mentality. From the moment of recruitment we were told to only think about the KGB.[2]

He – like others within the intelligence profession on both sides of the Atlantic – refers to the same two individual Russians as examples of those extremely rare successes in making such in-roads into Moscow's intelligence apparatus. One was the Soviet military intelligence (GRU) officer Colonel Oleg Penkovsky – codenamed 'Agent Hero' – who passed secrets to SIS and the CIA, most significantly regarding the details of Soviet plans to site missiles on Cuba which led to the Cuban Missile Crisis of October 1962. The other was the KGB Colonel Oleg Gordievsky, who spied for SIS from 1974 until the KGB became suspicious of him, summoned him to Moscow for interrogation, but then astonishingly failed to prevent him in 1985 from being smuggled by an SIS officer, out of the country into Finland, in the boot of a car.

Both Penkovsky and Gordievsky – about whom much has been written that it is not necessary to repeat here – hated the Soviet Union, and this hatred was what drove them to treachery. Both were vital at crucial moments in the Cold War: by informing his go-betweens with SIS – the businessman and SIS agent Greville Wynne and the British diplomat Janet Chisholm in Moscow – of how *un*developed the Soviet nuclear arsenal in fact was, and later of Moscow's nuclear plans on Cuba, Penkovsky's information was at the time regarded as a vital part of President John Kennedy's approach to the Cuban Missile Crisis (though the real value of his information has since been questioned).[3] Likewise, without the intelligence provided by Gordievsky, British Prime Minister Margaret Thatcher and US President Ronald Reagan would have been denied insights that were valuable in forming their strategies for bringing the East–West conflict to an end in the 1980s.

The significance of these spies is thus specifically tied to these – clearly extremely important – episodes in the drama of the Cold War.

While it may seem too obvious to be worth stating, a point widely expressed by intelligence professionals in countries ranging from China to Sudan is that the value of intelligence lies essentially in knowing what is *really* taking place; it may not be the case that intelligence agencies can respond, or that Governments can take immediate action in response to what they learn, but it is better to know than not know, if only to avoid any unwelcome surprises, as Sir John Scarlett – SIS Chief in 2004–9 and Gordievsky's former 'handler' – said of Cold War espionage:

> What nobody wanted was to be surprised. And that intelligence knowledge, intelligence base if you like, gave knowledge which greatly reduced that fear of a surprise attack. And, as the Cold War developed, more confidence developed that the other side was understood, and that helped manage the situation and was a key reason why we got to the end without a blowout.[4]

But what Western Cold War espionage rarely did in anything like as effective a way was cast light on the political, diplomatic and ideological *intentions* of the Soviet Union.[5]

It is an awkward truth for the leading Western intelligence agencies that the era which created their modern image was in fact one during which success rates were – if the views of the former SIS officer quoted above are to be regarded as accurate – low, when seen against the abundance of resources deployed. It should of course not be overlooked that achieving success in these activities is an extremely difficult task, not least when considered against a background – like that described as prevailing within the PIRA – of concern that one's own side may actually be riddled with traitors. Such concerns were very real, and lives were lost as a direct result of these treacheries. But for intelligence agencies on both sides of the Iron Curtain, the Cold War role of preventing their Governments from being 'surprised' was really only a small part of the picture; similarly, John Scarlett's assertion that intelligence contributed to the world reaching the end of the Cold War 'without a blowout' is debateable. Why so?

Central to the East–West conflict was an understanding – of course unwritten – that the rivals were engaged in a conflict in which the stakes for both had similarities. Both possessed nuclear weapons, and thus faced the risk of a devastating attack; both had spheres of influence which they saw it as vital to retain; both had a global intelligence-gathering capacity, and were prepared to deploy it globally. But similar 'balance' was also discerned by spies on both sides as to how these 'games without frontiers' should be played, as was explained to me by a long-serving intelligence officer whose career straddled the era of decolonisation, the intensification of the Cold War and the emergence of al-Qaeda. Asked to reflect on the changing environment in which spies were operating, he – in 2003 – told me, 'In the Cold War, espionage was in some ways a gentlemen's game, where the worst consequence could be that you were declared *persona non grata*. Now, agents could be executed. It's become significantly more dangerous.'[6]

In essence, the Cold War rivals primarily saw themselves as engaged in a high-stakes competition to outwit, demean and demoralise the other side. Counter-intelligence was as much of a preoccupation as was intelligence gathering, in part due to the evident difficulty of recruiting genuine 'insiders' at the senior levels of each other's agencies.

These exploits – and the occasional, 'tit-for-tat' expulsion of diplomats – acclimatised successive generations of Cold War spies to a world in which the trading of secrets was essentially manifested in the form of a trade-off between superpowers who were acutely aware that their rivalry must at all costs not be permitted to escalate into direct armed conflict. It was a battle of nerves, which it was only possible to prevent from escalating by using intelligence to spread the load: instead of a mushroom cloud being permitted to rise from the ruins of Moscow or Washington, numerous armed conflicts would be stoked around the world. It was a strategy which would leave Western intelligence agencies ill-prepared for what would come after the Cold War, when al-Qaeda emerged with a new set of 'rules' – in fact no rules at all.

This ill-preparedness can be traced back to those early Cold War moments, when instead of seeking to use intelligence to understand an adversary's true intentions, devise strategies on the basis of reality, and use subtle means to steer events in a certain direction, it was used to manipulate, misinform and manufacture truths. Most potent in this regard were the largely exaggerated claims attached to Moscow's plans for world domination in the Cold War zones which became the hot military conflicts of the developing world. Often profoundly misunderstood, such conflicts were equally often misrepresented in order to justify Western – usually US – action to 'halt the spread of communism', in the form like that explained in words that clattered onto the teletype in the office of the CIA Congo desk officer in Washington DC on 18 August 1960:

EMBASSY AND STATION BELIEVE CONGO EXPERIENCING CLASSIC COMMUNIST EFFORT TAKE OVER GOVERNMENT. MANY FORCES AT WORK HERE; SOVIETS [section blacked out] COMMUNIST PARTY ETC. ALTHOUGH DIFFICULT DETERMINE MAJOR INFLUENCING FACTORS TO PREDICT OUTCOME STRUGGLE FOR POWER, DECISIVE PERIOD NOT FAR OFF. WHETHER OR NOT LUMUMBA COMMIE OR JUST PLAYING COMMIE GAME TO ASSIST HIS SOLIDIFYING POWER, ANTI-WEST FORCES RAPIDLY INCREASING POWER CONGO AND THERE MAY BE LITTLE TIME LEFT IN WHICH TAKE ACTION TO AVOID ANOTHER CUBA.[7]

This message was followed on 27 August by a second cable, sent by Allan Dulles, the CIA Director, to the CIA Chief of Station in the Congolese capital Leopoldville (later renamed Kinshasa), Larry Devlin:

IN HIGH QUARTERS HERE IT IS THE CLEAR-CUT CONCLUSION THAT IF LLL CONTINUES TO HOLD HIGH OFFICE, THE INEVITABLE RESULT WILL AT BEST BE CHAOS AND AT WORST PAVE THE WAY TO COMMUNIST TAKEOVER OF THE CONGO WITH DISASTROUS CONSEQUENCES FOR THE PRESTIGE OF THE UN AND FOR THE INTERESTS OF THE FREE WORLD GENERALLY. CONSEQUENTLY WE CONCLUDE THAT HIS REMOVAL MUST BE AN URGENT AND PRIME OBJECTIVE AND THAT UNDER EXISTING CONDITIONS THIS SHOULD BE A HIGH PRIORITY OF OUR COVERT ACTION.[8]

The character 'LLL' was the Congolese Prime Minister Patrice Lumumba, whose three-month premiership (24 June 1960–14 September 1960) created the ground rules by which the Cold War would be fought in Africa for the next thirty years. The 'HIGH QUARTERS' referred to was President Dwight D. Eisenhower, whose approval – and what seemed like his suggestion – of an attempt to assassinate Lumumba, was only revealed publicly in 2000 when the proceedings came to light of the US Senate Select Committee to Study Governmental Operations with Respect to Intelligence Activities.[9] The Committee, which had met in 1975, was looking into assassination plots hatched by the CIA. Among those interviewed was Robert Johnson, a senior State Department official who had been a note-taker at the National Security Council during the Eisenhower presidency (1953–61). Johnson was present at the meeting during which – he told the Senate Committee – Eisenhower turned to CIA Director Dulles and was heard 'in the full hearing of all those in attendance and saying something to the effect that Lumumba should be eliminated'.[10]

The preamble to the Committee's report – almost apologetic in tone, while also seeking to be justificatory of American actions in the early 1960s – reflects how the United States had become driven by fear of the Soviet Union (a fear which clearly had not diminished by the time of the 1975 Committee hearings), explaining these plots as understandable in the circumstances, as follows:

> The fear of Communist expansion was particularly acute in the United States when Fidel Castro emerged as Cuba's leader in the late 1950s. His takeover was seen as the first significant penetration by the Communists into the Western Hemisphere. United States leaders, including most Members of Congress, called for vigorous action to stem the Communist infection in this hemisphere. These policies rested on widespread popular support and encouragement. Throughout this period, the United States felt impelled to respond to threats which were, or seemed to be, skirmishes in a global Cold War against Communism. Castro's Cuba raised the spectre of a Soviet outpost at America's doorstep. Events in the Dominican Republic appeared to offer an additional opportunity for the Russians and their allies. The Congo, freed from Belgian rule, occupied the strategic center of the African continent, and the prospect of Communist penetration there was viewed as a threat to American interests in emerging African nations. There was great concern that a Communist takeover in Indochina would have a 'domino effect' throughout Asia. Even the election in 1970 of a Marxist president in Chile was seen by some as a threat similar to that of Castro's takeover in Cuba.[11]

Across the South Atlantic these sentiments had little currency among the new, ill-prepared Congolese political leadership, as it sought to respond to the irrepressible nationalist fervour driving public opinion as colonialism came to an end.

Within a week of independence from Belgium on 30 June 1960, the Congolese Army had mutinied, while the new Government of President Joseph Kasavubu and Prime Minister Lumumba was incapable of bringing calm. As Madeleine Kalb makes clear in her remarkable study of US policy during this period, *The Congo Cables*,[12]

[US Ambassador Clare] Timberlake believed that anarchy in the Congo would have repercussions far beyond the immediate crisis: it would play directly into the hands of the Russians by providing an opportunity for radical forces to take over and undermine Western interests in this rich and strategic part of Africa. At the same time he realised that the only action capable of preventing anarchy – intervention by Belgian troops – would also play into Soviet hands: it would antagonise the new Congolese government and give the Russians an excellent opportunity to stress their anti-imperialist solidarity with the new African states.[13]

But for the CIA Station Chief in Leopoldville, Larry Devlin, the motivation was even more black and white, as he subsequently wrote in his own memoir of the period:

The Cold War, like it or not, had come to a hot country and the battle lines were rapidly being drawn in the streets of Leopoldville and across this enormous, fragile country. It was my job to do something about it, and the first task was to create a network of agents and then mount clandestine operations against the Soviet Union and its allies, which were clearly setting their sights on influencing, if not controlling, Lumumba's fledgling government.[14]

In fact it was the CIA that was taking the lead, the cable message of 27 August going on to tell Devlin that expenditure of $100,000 had been approved to pursue the plan to 'remove' Lumumba. It ran:

TO THE EXTENT THAT AMBASSADOR MAY DESIRE TO BE CONSULTED, YOU SHOULD SEEK HIS CONCURRENCE. IF IN ANY PARTICULAR CASE HE DOES NOT WISH TO BE CONSULTED YOU CAN ACT ON YOUR OWN AUTHORITY FOR TIME DOES NOT PERMIT REFERRAL HERE.

Thus the CIA began to plot the assassination of Lumumba, bringing poison provided by the Agency's in-house 'chemist', Dr Sidney Gottlieb, a man known within the world of the CIA as 'Joe from Paris', a later CIA 'Memorandum for the Record' dated 14 February 1972 stating that 'poison was to have been the vehicle' and that the officer involved had 'been instructed to see Dr Sidney Gottlieb in order to procure the appropriate vehicle'.

The view – as expressed above by John Scarlett, long after the Cold War had ended – that 'What nobody wanted was to be surprised' remained an enduring reason throughout the Cold War, and still is today, for retaining and expanding an intelligence-gathering capability. However, Scarlett's view that 'as the Cold War developed, more confidence developed that the other side was understood' is far less evident. While the need to prevent plans like that to station Soviet missiles on Cuba from being 'surprising' is evident, far less so is the evidence that intelligence-gathering really did mean that 'the other side was understood'.

But it took a Soviet spy – Vasili Mitrokhin, a KGB archivist who copied 25,000 pages of KGB material between 1972 and 1984, which he later passed to the British – to reveal just how little of the Soviet Union's aims and attitudes had really been understood in the West – and then only after the 'War' was over.

It is the Cold War in Africa – and specifically Congo in 1960 and Angola in 1975 – which provides much evidence of what can happen when intelligence regarding the political landscape and the players occupying it is poor. The issues the intelligence services' experience in Africa created are seminal, with the turmoil experienced in the Congo (today the Democratic Republic of Congo) and Angola two of the most vivid.

It is one argument in favour of greatly expanding the capabilities, powers and influence of the intelligence community that when intelligence is poor it can have catastrophic effects. On the other hand, placing intelligence and the agencies that gather it closer to the heart of policymaking – rather than retaining them as a somewhat distant *part* of the overall input into the governmental assessment of global issues – creates the danger of intelligence being 'politicised'. The range of activities in which intelligence officers are involved – from their often crucially important role as practitioners of covert diplomacy, as in Northern Ireland, to that of devising and planting propaganda in the hands of gullible newspaper reporters – has tended to draw certain kinds of people into the agencies; their characters will often set them apart from conventional diplomats, the readiness of some of them to engage in the 'craft of cheat and imposter' tending to illustrate the worst rather than best of human beings. To bring them closer to the conduct of foreign policy may thus seem far from attractive.

The results for the Congo of the politicisation of intelligence – and of its being placed at the forefront of policymaking in the 'heat' of the Cold War – were stark.

To this day the country has lived with the consequences. It really does not seem to have mattered to the Eisenhower Administration that the 'CLASSIC COMMUNIST EFFORT TAKE OVER GOVERNMENT' referred to in the 'Congo Cables' was really nothing of the sort. It did not matter that – at least in the African context – no such 'classic' practice even existed, certainly not at that time; by 1960 there had been no 'communist takeovers' of governments in the newly independent states of Africa. Despite the left-leaning policies of leaders like Sekou Touré in Guinea and Kwame Nkrumah in Ghana, even these regimes were essentially nationalist in their outlook, and regarded the Soviet Union as a potential source of financial and other aid that would help them unburden their countries from dependence on the former colonial powers. Nor was it the case that the Soviet Union had any evident capacity to mount such 'takeovers' – in the context of Congo, there is no evidence to suggest that it was the hope or plan of Patrice Lumumba to have the newly independent country 'taken over' by anybody; his only wish was to see the Belgians leave, so as to free Congolese from the colonial yoke under which they had suffered more extremely than most African colonies, since 1884.

Moreover, evidence of how unfocused Moscow actually was on Congo, and thus how great was CIA misunderstanding of Soviet intentions there, emerges clearly in the vast archive of secret KGB material that Mitrokhin painstakingly copied from the Service's foreign intelligence archive and passed to SIS when he defected to Britain in 1992.

There is little doubt that the Mitrokhin Archive[15] is unequalled as a source of publicly available information on KGB activity throughout the Cold War; it is likely surpassed only by the archive still held by its successor agency, the FSB, at the Service's Yasenevo headquarters outside Moscow. As Oleg Kalugin, the KGB's most successful Washington-based agent handler during a 31-year career, said when he first read Mitrokhin's carefully copied notes, 'I was stunned by the accuracy of his descriptions of many intelligence operations I had been personally involved in … Ever since, Mitrokhin's book has become for me an encyclopaedia of sorts, a treasure trove of information about the cold war times.'[16]

It was due to the KGB's office move to Yasenevo that Mitrokhin – who was tasked with overseeing the relocation of the files – had the opportunity to copy many of them by hand, hide them in his *dacha* outside Moscow, and eventually find a foreign intelligence service that would be interested in seeing what he had in his possession.

But one of the many fascinating aspects of this treasure trove is what is *not* in it – the absence of evidence of Soviet activity in select countries is as revealing as what the archive *does* include.

In light of the CIA's focus on Congo in 1960 – and its readiness to take the confrontation with communism even to the point of plotting to kill Lumumba – one would expect Mitrokhin's notes to provide abundant evidence of Soviet plans to 'take over' the country. But Congo barely figures in the archive. This may be because it is understandably incomplete as a source, being the product of a grand-scale theft of information in the pre-Internet age. However, given the enormous significance of the Congo crisis of 1960 as a Cold War 'theatre', for it to be almost completely absent from the most comprehensive Soviet archive available to us, strongly suggests that the CIA had misread Soviet intentions. The similar lack of evidence of Moscow's focus on Africa evident from the important memoir of the defector Oleg Gordievsky casts further doubt on whether the CIA was getting it right.[17] The sense meanwhile from the declassified CIA 'Congo Cables' is of a conviction that the Soviet Union *must* have been up to something, and that Lumumba was 'Moscow's man'.

The chaos which reigned in the immediate aftermath of Congolese independence can barely be said to have had a definable political direction. The variety of programmes that existed within the fragile coalition of interest groups the Lumumba Government sought to lead, rendered it largely powerless. Its credibility in tatters, it severed diplomatic ties with Belgium and appealed to the Soviet Union to consider intervening – a move that inevitably played into the hands of Lumumba's critics in Belgium, who led the charge in claiming that he was 'pro-Soviet'.

Lumumba's appeal to Moscow is seen to have 'increased the pressure on Premier Khrushchev and probably forced him to become more deeply involved in defending Lumumba's interests than he had originally intended'.[18] However, it was enough to lead the Eisenhower Administration to seek alternative leaders for reasons starkly explained by the US Ambassador to Belgium on 19 July 1960 in a cable to the US State Department, in which he wrote,

Only prudent, therefore, we plan on basis that Lumumba government threatens our vital interests in Congo and Africa generally. A principal objective of our political and diplomatic action must therefore be to destroy Lumumba government as now constituted, but at the same time we must find or develop another horse to back which would be acceptable in rest of Africa and defensible against Soviet political attack.[19]

Essential to any understanding of what kind of a threat Lumumba *really* represented is an understanding of the real *intentions* of the Soviet Union, and it is the issue of *intent* which in the post-Cold War world has been most significant in defining the ability of Western intelligence agencies to limit the prospect of 'surprise'; for it was the failure of some within the US intelligence community to accept fully that those around Osama bin Laden had the intention of turning thoughts into actions, and the failure of the CIA and SIS really to understand the Iraqi leader Saddam Hussein's intentions with regard to the development of weapons of mass destruction, which have been responsible for the biggest intelligence catastrophes since Nazi Germany failed to learn in advance that the Allies intended in 1944 to land on the beaches of Normandy. Understanding *intent* – and, by implication, getting inside the minds of those who represent the threat – has long been the challenge; meeting the challenge has thus far been met with far greater failure than success, and the legacy of the Cold War mentality has been singularly responsible for hampering the shift in mentality necessary to meet the terrorist challenge of today.

Vital to successfully making the 'leap' is an *understanding* of what is motivating the target.

In her record of how the CIA, the State Department and the White House framed the Congo Crisis, Madeleine Kalb's account of the variety of reactions by US policymakers reveals the extent to which responses to Lumumba and the reality of the Congo on its own terms evolved entirely through the prism of superpower rivalry. Lumumba's emergence on the political scene was increasingly viewed in Washington as being the result of deliberate Soviet manipulation of the chaos. But to attribute such success to Moscow's strategists in itself betrayed the extent to which the United States had failed to read correctly the influence and capacity of its superpower enemy, to which was added 'the limited understanding on the part of both Soviets and Americans of the determinants of [Congolese] internal politics'.[20]

Defenders of US support for the man then put in place by the CIA – the army chief Joseph Mobutu, who later remodelled himself as the leopard-skin-hat-wearing dictator Mobutu Sese Seko, Maréchal of Zaïre – drew upon some of the most spurious arguments. One such emerged in a 1984 verbal exchange between William Colby, CIA Director in the mid-1970s, and John Stockwell, the former CIA officer stationed in the southern Congolese town of Lubumbashi, who later became head of the Agency's Angola task force before resigning and publicly criticising CIA actions in Africa. During this exchange, Colby asserted,

> The question we faced in the Congo was whether that country, which had just gained independence from Belgium, would be run by some toadies of the old Belgian mining companies or by men aided by Che Guevara and supported by the Soviet Union. The CIA found a midpoint between those extremes – it helped Joseph Mobutu, then a nationalist member of the Congolese forces, become the third alternative.[21]

His argument was neat but disingenuous, failing to take into account the fact that even though Lumumba had requested assistance from the Soviet Union there was no real evidence that it would be forthcoming, nor that the Russian leader Nikita Krushchev saw Lumumba as a reliable ally, one American academic condemning the CIA's misrepresentation of Lumumba thus:

> Lumumba's appeal for Soviet military aid to counter a much larger Western intervention in Katanga may have been unrealistic given the US's violent reaction; but it was not the result of Soviet-exploited 'personal instability'... Nor were his actions guided by 'pro-Soviet' advisers as the Americans charged. For example, two of his most trusted counsellors... opposed Lumumba's decision to accept Soviet aid. The Prime Minister's most influential colleagues were other [Congolese] nationalists.[22]

Generally, the view among scholars is that advanced by the US academic Michael Schatzberg, who wrote,

> With the clarity of hindsight... Lumumba was probably no more than a populist and nationalist politician, albeit with increasingly radical tendencies. It is doubtful that Soviet ideology or academic Marxism

influenced him... We should also remember that Lumumba appealed to the West for assistance in terminating the Katanga secession and in removing Belgian troops from his country before requesting Soviet aid. Indeed, Lumumba's travels in search of assistance took him to the United States, but never to the Soviet Union... But these initiatives did not, and perhaps could not, alter official Washington's strong prevailing perception of Lumumba as a tool of Soviet interests. If Lumumba was, in fact, sending signals to Washington, they were drowned out by international static.[23]

For the CIA in Congo the wish was to be seen to be fighting communism – even when there were no communists to fight.

On 25 April 1974, 14 years after the birth of the independent Congo, when Portugal underwent its *Revolução dos Cravos* – the 'Carnation Revolution' – that ended the 48-year dictatorship of António de Oliveira Salazar and his successor as President of the Council of Ministers, Marcelo Caetano, it was the turn of Angola to face the Cold War music. Its fate would be closely linked to what had taken place in Congo, which Mobutu had renamed Zaïre on 27 October 1971.

On 16 July 1975 US President Gerald Ford approved a CIA plan submitted to him via the Executive's '40 Committee' (which reviewed US covert actions) by which $6 million – to be supplemented by $8 million on 27 July – was to be provided for arms supplies to the Frente Nacional de Libertação de Angola (FNLA) led by Holden Roberto (to which the CIA had already channelled $265,000 between January and July 1975) and the União Nacional para a Independência Total de Angola (UNITA) forces of Jonas Savimbi,[24] in their conflict with the leftist Movimento Popular de Libertação de Angola (MPLA). On 29 July a C-141 military transport aircraft left Charleston, South Carolina bound for Liberia's Robertsfield Airport. At Robertsfield it refuelled, then set off across the Bight of Bonny and along the coast of Central Africa to the Zaïrean capital Kinshasa. It was met under cover of darkness by a convoy of trucks provided by Mobutu's army. The hold of the C-141 opened, the 25 tonnes of weapons were disgorged, loaded into the trucks, and the aircraft left for the United States.[25]

Thus began the CIA's next effort – in the view of the 40 Committee, and as recounted by John Stockwell, who would manage the Agency's Angola Task Force in Washington – to establish a military balance and discourage further resort to arms in Angola. Such covert financial assistance, it [the 40 Committee report] continued, would prevent the quick and cheap installation in Angola of what Mobutu and [Zambian President Kenneth] Kaunda would regard as a pawn of Moscow on their borders.[26]

Meanwhile, what was the Soviet Union doing to inspire this elaborate arms-supply system that was indeed intended to bring about the 'quick and cheap installation in Angola' of a government that would be their 'pawn'?

Broadly speaking, Soviet policy in Angola was responsive rather than proactive. When a vacuum appeared the Soviets would offer assistance,[27] the political historian Fernando Guimaraes writes, adding, 'In the face of its diminishing influence, Moscow [after Khrushchev] began to streamline its policy towards the [African] continent. From that time, it was to consist of concrete relations with African regimes, relations not solely based on ideological affinities.'[28]

What is evident from the Mitrokhin Archive, however, is that with regard to Angola the KGB – as the implementer of what the Politburo transmitted to the Service's First Directorate, responsible for foreign intelligence – was far more engaged in deception than it was in furthering any ideological ambitions Moscow may have had.

It is no exaggeration to suggest that at some point in the mid- or late 1960s – after the first flush of radicalism among Africa's newly-independent states had died down – the Soviet Union became rather tired of Africa. Certainly, others within the Soviet orbit – notably Che Guevara, who was heard to say that 'Sub-Saharan Africa had a long way to go before it achieved real revolutionary maturity'[29] – steadily became disillusioned with the prospect of Africa becoming the 'continent of revolutions'. Outside South Africa – which had been a key focus of the Communist Party of the Soviet Union since the days of Vladimir Lenin – Moscow had little expectation of establishing long-term influence at the leadership level in the most important African states that had by then emerged. Thus it was left to the KGB's 'Service A' – responsible for disinformation and covert action – to perpetuate the Cold War by other means.

So began a long period of elaborate deceptions, all intended to discredit the United States, as well as Britain, France, South Africa and other states as the occasions arose, in an effort to irritate the West with pin-pricks.

Service A's forgeries were – the KGB officer Vasili Mitrokhin states – 'one of the staples of KGB active measures',[30] along with the deployment of security advisors, who arrived in considerable numbers to assist in the creation of the security apparatus in Ghana under Kwame Nkrumah, Algeria under Ahmed Ben Bella, and – to a limited extent – during the short-lived premiership of Patrice Lumumba in Congo. A crucial element in the KGB's strategy was to engender paranoia in the minds of the African governments with which it was seeking to cement ties. To this end, Service A created forged documents aimed at encouraging Ben Bella in 1962 and Nkrumah in 1964 to believe that the CIA was planning to overthrow them; it later did the same in Guinea and Mali,[31] even managing to plant documents with Ben Bella which he then passed on to the Malian President Modibo Keïta, in which details based on a 'CIA document' purportedly revealed a French plot to overthrow Keïta.

However, the activities of Service A – while having potentially appalling consequences, in view of the violent tendencies of those leaders, who might seek retribution for these 'plots' – were ultimately more of a nuisance than a serious effort to roll the Soviet empire out across Africa. As Mitrokhin makes clear, 'Despite the success of KGB active measures (specifically, propaganda and deception) in promoting anti-American conspiracy theories in Africa, the Soviet Union was powerless during the 1960s to prevent the overthrow of two of the African regimes with which it had closes relations,' namely those in Ghana and Mali. And as Moscow's expectations waned, the 'threat' it posed – if indeed it was a threat – became narrowly focused on channelling support to the South African Communist Party and the armed wing of the African National Congress, Umkhonto we Sizwe – support for which, in Mitrokhin's informed view, nevertheless 'posed no significant threat to the South African apartheid regime'.[32]

Then, in 1975, Angola provided an opportunity for the KGB to regain some lost credibility.

In 1961 a KGB officer in the then Congolese capital Leopoldville, Oleg Ivanovich Nazhestkin, had first made contact with Angola's then exiled MPLA leader Agostinho Neto. Nazhestkin later wrote how Neto – the supposed 'Marxist' – asked him during their discussion, 'And what is communism? Help me to come to grips with this question. After all, you're a communist and you must understand it well. Help me to obtain the necessary literature.'[33] Further visits by KGB officers to the 'Marxist' leader of the MPLA proved equally unsettling and, according to Mitrokhin, by 1973 'Soviet support for the MPLA was reduced to a trickle',[34] and only resumed in 1975 after the 40 Committee in Washington had recommended to President Ford that arms supplies to the MPLA's rivals – the FNLA and UNITA – be stepped up.

But even as American weaponry reached the hands of their enemies, Neto and the MPLA were being urged by the Soviet Politburo to unite with rather than fight with the FNLA and UNITA.[35] Only when it became clear that the MPLA – which retreated to Luanda in October 1975 – appeared to be on the verge of annihilation, did Moscow agree to escalate the supply of arms, while Cuba sent troops to fight alongside Neto's forces. It was then, on 13 December, that the scale of the CIA's support for the FNLA and UNITA was suddenly revealed in the American media, and the US Congress demanded a halt to the military assistance.

Even after the MPLA survived the threat of destruction, Neto 'continued to be distrusted in both the [Soviet] Foreign Ministry and the International Department [of the Communist Party of the Soviet Union, the CPSU]', leading the KGB to cultivate 'Agent Vomus' – an MPLA official who was Neto's political assistant in Luanda – as a spy[36] to keep the KGB's Luanda *residenz* informed of the MPLA leader's activities.

Something of a fresh effort by Moscow to win over Africa came in August 1976 when Yuri Andropov, the KGB chairman who would later be CPSU General Secretary for fifteen months between 1982 and 1984, issued a directive urging 'residences' in select African countries to 'obtain reliable prognoses concerning the situation in the country and the region as a whole, and on the activities of the Americans, the British and the Chinese, and to carry out wide-ranging measures against them'.[37] While Moscow consequently despatched technical, military and other advisors to assist the regimes in Angola and Mozambique as well as the 'Derg' junta in Ethiopia, much of this additional effort simply involved operations intended to discredit the West and instil further paranoia in the minds of these countries' leaders, and were aimed first at creating then sustaining and intensifying their suspicion that the West was seeking to overthrow them.

Despite the focus – according to Mitrokhin – of KGB activity being on the deception of African leaders as well as of the West, it would be wrong to diminish the Cold War in Africa to merely a game between the superpowers. The large number of real-life victims of the conflict, who littered the battlefields, died in the prisons, and were tortured in the dungeons of regimes that may never have been born and in many cases would not have endured had the Cold War not taken them in its embrace, are sufficient testimony to the brutal reality. It would, however, be accurate to assert that the role of intelligence within the African Cold War 'theatre' was for the most part a game of cat and mouse, in which one side would create a lie, spread a rumour or engender a suspicion, and the other would assess whether or how to respond. The 'CLASSIC COMMUNIST EFFORT TAKE OVER GOVERNMENT' alleged by Larry Devlin in his infamous 'Congo Cable' of 18 August 1960, did not take place. Nor was it likely to have taken place. Within a few years of believing that Africa was ripe for such takeovers in the 1970s, Andropov's 'optimism had evaporated',[38] for perhaps the reasons that Che Guevara had identified somewhat patronisingly almost fifteen years earlier. What had been envisaged as about to happen in Africa, did not; and to anybody who was able to see the emerging continent through eyes not tainted by the antics of 'Service A' or the warrior mentality of Larry Devlin, reality was staring them in the face: after empire, Africa sought to be left to find its own way. The wish to ally with another imported way of life – even by choice – was weak, as Nelson Mandela would write of the time when the fledgling ANC was considering how to manage its relations with the political left in the 1940s: 'We were extremely wary of communism … which many … including myself, considered a 'foreign' ideology unsuited to the African situation.'[39]

The 'African situation' was evident on the streets of Luanda, as I arrived there early one morning in 1993. The military checkpoints were gunmens' shadows; the blackened buildings rose leering as blank as the devastated faces of the people in the darkness against the starlit sky; a brazier glowed beside the road to the airport. It was August and the southern summer. Luanda bore the scars of its pain, its destruction exposing the depths of its calamity. Even so, it had been months since there had been any fighting, I was told by Vladimir, the TASS correspondent, one of the four hundred Russians remaining from a previous Soviet presence of five thousand. He sat, half-naked and hunched over his desk in a dingy apartment block, bemoaning the fact that his wife and child were forbidden by Soviet-era rules to accompany him to such a place, as he tapped out his reports and sent his telexes to Moscow, a chronicler of the last days of the defeated Cold War power's African adventures.

False hopes lay ruined in the doorways, where families huddled for shelter, and everywhere at night shadows lingered in the shadows – gunmen, thieves, police, all trapped in the hopeless spiral of twenty years of war, then twenty-five years, war forever threatening to crash into streets which for now were deserted. I had the overwhelming sense that the city and the country were little different from the days and weeks in 1975 when the war, whose third or fourth chapter I was witnessing, had begun. Thirteen years of war against the Portuguese colonisers had ended on 25 April 1974, when the dictatorship was ousted in Lisbon and Portugal rapidly quit its African colonies. 'I remember the wooden crates the Portuguese made to take their possessions back to Europe,'[40] said Katia Airola, the resilient Finnish woman who at that time ran the government press office.

> The line stretched from the port all the way up the hill. There were so many crates because the Portuguese knew they couldn't spend their Angolan currency in Portugal, so they bought anything they could here, in order to sell it when they got home. They emptied the shops. There was nothing left. The shelves only filled up in 1991, during the peace. But now they're empty again.

Years earlier I had passed more than two hours in a luxurious, sprawling villa almost hidden by the thick trees covering a slope on the edge of the rich Cocody suburb of my then home city of Abidjan, Côte d'Ivoire. A telephone call and a summons had interrupted the calm prevailing that Sunday. The villa had been the gift to Jonas Savimbi of Felix Houphouët-Boigny, the Ivorian president and one of UNITA's stalwart African supporters. The surrounding streets were quiet and empty as a large gate swung open onto a drive cluttered with gleaming Mercedes. Paratroopers languished on chairs near the back door.

John Marques Kakumba, Savimbi's impeccably dressed resident representative in Abidjan, approached, and welcomed me and two other reporters with equally impeccable grace. We waited inside until suddenly a door opened, and in the forthright style of his wife's brother-in-law – Mobutu Sese Seko – Savimbi strode into the large reception room, swinging a carved cane, an enormous diamond glittering in a gold ring on his finger. The smiles were as for old friends, or at least acquaintances, though neither I nor my colleagues had met him before. The charm was gushing, the image intended to confound rather than confirm, the theatrics beginning with the offer to conduct our discussions in whichever language we cared to name.

Savimbi had by then passed through many phases – some of his own making, others the result of plots hatched in Washington, Langley and Pretoria. US policy in the mid-1970s had been led by the CIA and the Secretary of State Henry Kissinger, with barely any reference to other policymakers until after the US commitment to the anti-MPLA forces had become entrenched. Kissinger's efforts were thwarted not by Soviet and Cuban power, but by congressional resistance to his warmongering, which led to assistance to the warring parties being terminated following the passage of two congressional amendments.[41]

But the polarisation the US role in the conflict had created during the bitter war of 1975–76 was just the beginning. Following the fall of Richard Nixon and the unremarkable term in office of Gerald Ford, President Jimmy Carter admitted in 1976 what most already knew when he said that 'We should realise that the Russian and Cuban presence in Angola, while regrettable and counterproductive of peace, need not constitute a threat to United States interests, nor does that presence mean the existence of a [Soviet] satellite on the continent.'[42] But largely due to its concern not to be seen within the United States as 'soft on communism'[43] the Carter Administration nevertheless refrained from recognising the MPLA Government, and by 1981, when President Ronald Reagan strode onto the world stage with a desire to stoke the fires of the Cold War in Africa and elsewhere, Angola was ripe for a return as the target of the same destructive policy as had been practiced six years earlier. This time, however, US support for UNITA was more complex.

The Clark Amendment – which had prohibited direct US military assistance – was the hurdle Reagan sought throughout his first term to have removed. It was not until 11 June 1985 that he achieved this goal, congressional advocates of repeal asserting that Angola 'was a place where we can achieve victory, a psychological victory, which will give strength to free men across the world'.[44] The amendment was repealed by 63 votes to 34. While diplomatic ties between the United States and the MPLA Government were at that time years away, Luanda terminated all diplomatic contacts with the United States in response to the American move. This put on hold the strategy of 'constructive engagement' which Chester Crocker, Assistant Secretary of State for African Affairs during Reagan's first term, had attempted to put in place, and which it had been intended would lead to both Cuban and South African forces withdrawing from Angola, as well as bringing independence to Namibia, which had been occupied by South Africa since 1915. With the repeal of the Clark Amendment, pressure mounted for military supplies to be sent to UNITA, and Reagan signed an order permitting $13 million-worth of assistance, despite some in the Administration arguing that doing so would limit the chances of successfully pursuing Crocker's multilateral strategy. The US media, critical of a resumption of military aid, also argued strongly that such assistance would ally the United States too closely to the apartheid regime in South Africa, with which the CIA had anyway long worked intimately and whose interests Crocker's 'constructive engagement' policy were intended to protect in pursuit of regional peace.

At odds with Congress, the Reagan Administration ignored the critics. In 1986, the CIA provided UNITA with TOW and Stinger anti-aircraft missiles, anti-tank weapons, 106mm recoilless rifles, ammunition and fuel. In 1987 the value of this assistance increased to $30 million, and to

$50 million by 1989. Destabilisation of the MPLA was the intention of the UNITA–South Africa–US strategy, and claimed a sickeningly high level of success, with the deaths of 435,000 people – including 331,000 children – in 1981–88, anti-personnel mines alone killing 40,000 Angolans, lost revenues to the Angolan economy during this period amounting to $40 billion, and the total value of physical infrastructure destroyed between 1975 and 1988 eventually being put at $22 billion.[45]

More than in 1975, the Angola of the late 1980s and beyond was a theatre of the Cold War which was totally removed from the roots of any indigenous conflict, while – as we now know from the Soviet-era records which have since come to light – the destruction was not justifiable on the basis of intelligence suggesting that Moscow had designs on the country. Moreover, the implementation of the 1988 accord – which saw Cuba and South Africa withdraw their forces from the country, and which led to Namibian independence – is widely regarded as not having been the result of the pressure created by the escalation of US military assistance to UNITA after 1985. '[The] main original thrust of constructive engagement – support for the reform efforts of white South Africa – had produced no meaningful progress at all.'[46] In short, more death and destruction was not what ultimately brought the sides to the negotiating table to hammer out a settlement. The shifting positions of sanctions-hit South Africa and the momentous political shifts in the Soviet Union under Mikhail Gorbachev had a much greater impact, against the background of war-weariness among Cuban troops on the ground in Angola. 'If the US had been willing more quickly to distance itself from Pretoria, Moscow was eager for compromises in a region that most Soviet policy-makers saw as marginal.'[47] Set against the long-term background of US involvement in Angola, the posturing and intimidation dominating US attitudes during the 1988–91 negotiations between the MPLA and UNITA, served Washington poorly. Had the United States been a broker rather than a player it may never have got itself into the position of supporting so determinedly a guerilla leader – Jonas Savimbi – who ultimately proved himself completely at odds with the ideals which had, at least for the consumption of US policymakers and their constituencies, been the justification for lending him US support in the first place.

Savimbi's identity as a creature of the Cold War, a protégé of the United States, bolstered by a 'Devil's pact' with the apartheid regime in South Africa, reached the point at which he had no alternative but to negotiate directly with his enemies. The waltz he had danced with successive US governments was over, as Chester Crocker told me when we met in his office at Georgetown University, the snow of winter reminding us of how very far away from the reality of the sun-drenched plains of the 'front line' Western policymakers are able to go: 'I never trusted Savimbi,'[48] he said bluntly, of an 'ally' whose role had by then been crucial to US policy in *the* key 'hot' theatre of the Cold War for almost twenty years.

So, who had been leading and who following? 'The civil war was the result of our own problems. But once the Soviet Union said they would stop supplying the MPLA once there is a ceasefire, the MPLA realised it could not afford not to listen,'[49] Savimbi had told me that Sunday afternoon in Abidjan. Who was listening and who was not was perhaps not the issue. The 1991 peace accord effectively marked the end of US political support for UNITA, leaving both it and the MPLA facing the question of whether for 16 years they had been fighting a war on behalf of the superpowers or a war whose reason was closer to home. The United States and the former Soviet Union were largely immune to the conflict's indigenous characteristics – for them it was a proxy war. But by the early 1990s the real war – a war between Angolans – was about to start, and it was that which I hovered over in an ancient Russian helicopter bearing Aeroflot insignia, which swayed and swung like a huge drunken bird onto the runway at Benguela, barely touching the tarmac, hovering on soft tyres as though always about to take off.

In the darkness at the rear were the anxious young faces of new army recruits to the war, sitting awkwardly in their uniforms as they handled their unfamiliar guns and wondered if this journey might be their last. With the door barely closed, the hulk took off and left Benguela behind, flying low, dodging from side to side as it barely missed the trees. We flew for less than an hour, sliding through the barrage of an imagined battle, the pilot clearly exhilarated, the passengers suffering in the hold.

We touched down at Ganda, and jumped out, the helicopter immediately taking off, leaving us stranded on the deserted edge of a town that had been captured by government forces a month beforehand. We walked along a hot road into the town. There was nobody to see, nor any sounds of war, nor signs of life along the neat streets, which were lined with curbstones and other details of urban existence which made the emptiness all the more eerie. It was as if a wind had swept all the people away, while leaving the town apparently unscathed. Reaching a crossroads, a military vehicle approached us from the direction we had walked. An officer was driven past without acknowledging us. He stopped a little further ahead to speak with some soldiers we had not noticed, and then drove on. We turned up a hill, and ahead of us some children were standing on the street. A boy sped past, pushing himself on a wooden scooter. As he passed, the front wheel fell off and he lay on the road in the wreckage of his broken toy. Further on, at a market, the space between the near-empty stalls had become a sombre meeting place for war victims, limbless men dragging themselves around on rickety wooden crutches and subdued children begging for money and cigarettes. A shoeshine boy dressed in clothes blackened from top to bottom plied his trade hopelessly, while women offered unripe tomatoes, peanuts and small heaps of salt for sale, and men sold twists of tobacco and marijuana.

Colonel José Manuel de Souza, the young officer who had passed us on the street earlier, reappeared. We were driven to the military headquarters, and then drove with him to the edge of town. The men of the FAA – the new national army, the Forças Armadas Angolanas, created by the 1991 peace agreement – would take us on patrol, out into the rural areas they had captured east of Ganda. Our journey had taken us deeper into the country, first to the desertion of Benguela, then by helicopter to Ganda, now onward in a military truck, then on foot through a forested land of rolling hills and fields littered with landmines, which the farmers had no choice but to cultivate as they gambled with life and death. We walked for an hour or more, in single file across the rich earth. We stopped at Vindongo, a hamlet of neat huts, where the people were slowly starving. 'UNITA has complicated our lives,'[50] said Maria N'guare. Malnourished children stared at us as we passed, women offering to sell withered and blackened plantains as we walked on. The villagers were eating manioc leaves, too frightened here to work the fields. 'If we bought maize in the market, UNITA would come and take it from us. They would take our clothes. A lot of people are going to die of hunger. Around a hundred and fifty have already died. The children and the old people are the ones who are dying,' Maria N'guare said, as our military escort walked on, oblivious perhaps, helpless certainly. We walked to Atuke, a village so densely surrounded by minefields that it was impossible to grow any crops. The mud-brick huts had no roofs. People lay on the ground barely moving. A woman suckled a crying baby. The people had left a nearby village because UNITA forces had stolen their remaining food. 'We have nothing,' said Domingues Kalende. 'No money. No food. Nothing.'

With the end of the Cold War, attempts to portray US diplomatic efforts in southern Africa as having brought the end of conflict were being cast into serious doubt:

> It is a logical fallacy to conclude simply from the historical sequence that US aid to UNITA facilitated either the 1988 or the 1991 settlement… [Meanwhile the] Soviet Union in the 1980s, far from pursuing an aggressive expansion of influence in southern Africa, aimed to limit its involvement – without, however, being forced to withdraw or seeing its allies collapse under joint South African and US pressure.[51]

By creating African realities of their own – and for each other – the CIA and the KGB abused the weakness of the fragile new countries into which they injected themselves. From the perspective of their own intelligence spy-craft they also created, developed and refined practices which divorced them from the process of gathering genuine understanding of the societies whose destinies they were seeking to manipulate. While it is evident from elsewhere that it is not a central aim of intelligence agencies to understand the societies in which they are operating, failure to do so usually leads to intelligence failing to produce reliable results – as the intelligence catastrophe that led to the 2003 invasion of Iraq would later show.

When the 'new' threat from al-Qaeda emerged, after the Cold War had come to an end, the ability or wish to get under the skin of a society – as had been done to some effect in Northern Ireland – had come to be seen as little short of eccentric by many within the intelligence sphere. But for the agencies to succeed they would need to be patient, to understand this new threat; there would need to be a readiness to cooperate with the 'bad guys' in order to succeed in confronting the 'really bad guys'. A wish to be noticed – rather than to remain shadowy and at large – would drive this new threat out of the Cairo slums and the casbah of Algiers and onto the world stage; it would happen with a combination of stealth and speed, and would leave the spies asking themselves whether – in the two hundred years since modern spying had been born on the streets of Dublin – an intelligence 'profession' had been created that could be as effective when operating in places into which it had not been invited, as it was when operating among ideological allies or in its own backyard. Western intelligence agencies operated in Congo, Angola and other Cold War 'theatres' in what was essentially a static conflict which was going nowhere; it was a conflict which brought no real victories before it ended, and was one driven not primarily by the need to spy on the Soviet Union and its allies, but by the territorial void opened up by the end of European colonialism.

The 'peace dividend' – that mistaken idea that 'the end of history' had been reached with the end of the Cold War, and that henceforth humanity would coalesce into a single, progressive, like-minded force for good – had been an early example of Western post-Cold War political aspirations clashing with those that had simmered in the global underworld for as long as the East–West conflict had been played out. Just as it had been convenient for 'cold warriors' like Larry Devlin to adopt tunnel vision when assessing what was best for the newly liberated Congolese, so it was that Western governments – and, as a consequence, the spies from whom they requested secret intelligence – had tended to see as peripheral the political and social trends that had emerged in opposition to Cold War allies in Asia, the Middle East and Africa. These trends could not be dealt with on a government-to-government basis, because they involved 'non-state actors'; nor were Western allies in these regions of the world prepared to admit that they were threatened by what was emerging – to have done so would have loosened their grip on power.

Above all, however, these emerging trends could not be seen as ordinarily threatening Western interests.

It is a widely held view that even in the most non-specific terms the world's intelligence services did not see 9/11 coming. It was not simply that they did not notice 19 hijackers board US domestic aircraft on the morning of 11 September 2001. It was that the world which had created these men was one that had emerged largely unnoticed, except by agencies in some Middle East countries, as well as by a limited number of intelligence officers in Paris, London and Washington – a few of whom were seen by their superiors as maverick or wayward, or perhaps even a little racist. Budgets and resources were a part of the problem: in the United Kingdom the 'peace dividend' led to a near-flattening of defence, intelligence and security budgets; for MI5 and SIS the focus was on organised crime, particularly the international trade in narcotics; where Middle East terrorism was an issue in the 1990s it was not seen as 'Islamist' but as related to the Israeli–Palestinian conflict. Moreover, the experience of 'scale' was significant: post-9/11, the proportion of resources devoted by the intelligence agencies to counter-terrorism – which in 2010 was around 70 percent in the UK, with similar proportions elsewhere – almost dwarfs the 30 percent or thereabouts that was devoted annually to the Cold War 'fight' against the Soviet Union.

The experience of a single issue – counter-terrorism against a single, worldwide, multifaceted movement – becoming so dominant, was in itself a new challenge outside wartime. It raised very real concerns within the agencies that allotting such significant resources to one issue would lead to other issues being neglected, under-resourced or even remaining unnoticed altogether. Governmental demands for detailed intelligence on radicalism within the Muslim communities of the Middle East and elsewhere, were not being routinely made before 9/11. Nor were there consistent demands for domestic security services to focus on these communities or on specific individuals within them who were based in the West. As a former senior officer at the CIA's Counter-Terrorism Center told me, 'We were event-driven,'[52] and between the aftermath of the victory over the Soviet Union in Afghanistan and the violent arrival of al-Qaeda in the form of the bombing of the US embassies in Kenya and Tanzania on 7 August 1998, there were no 'events' to speak of. This had decisive consequences when it came to countenancing the possibilities, as the same former CIA officer told me:

It may have been one of the failings of [the Counter-Terrorism Center] that we didn't recruit as well as we might have done, even though we had some very good people. On the whole we had very good analysts. [But] it was an institution, and it became institutionalised. There had been built up a sense of resistance to the idea that an attack could take place in the US.

Struggling with the institutionalised mindset that had set in – or which had perhaps always been there – during the Cold War, was identified post-9/11 as rooted in the ongoing experience of action and reaction which had marked the growing pains of the US intelligence community ever since the 1950s. Both the CIA and the FBI had been the butt of criticism over many years – either they were seen as hamstrung by caution, or as overly aggressive; when action was needed, they erred in ways which seemed logical to some on the inside but inappropriate to the media, public and political leadership; this was made clear by James Woolsey, CIA Director, 1993–95, when he described to me his response to the revelation in 1994 that the CIA officer Aldrich Ames had spent nine years spying for the Soviet Union and had in the process betrayed around a hundred CIA 'assets' within the KGB, ten of whom were later executed:

One of the criticisms was that we didn't fire anybody after the Ames case … I didn't fire anybody. The general feeding frenzy when something goes wrong has led in the past to [a tendency to] thrash around and fire people. And over the years that has caused a very very cautious mindset [which lay behind CIA caution regarding al-Qaeda]. It's not principally a matter of organisation at all. If you look at it case-by-case – at what was not done right – much of what we learn about terrorism in the US isn't going to be learned from foreign intelligence agencies. Most of what you have learned hasn't come from any aspect of traditional intelligence collection. Many of the failures [exposed by 9/11] – between law enforcement and the intelligence community – tend to be more or less one way. There were provisions of law enforcement that barred the FBI from passing on information to the CIA.[53] The FBI had been beaten up time and again for being too aggressive over the years. So they erred on the side of caution. The notion was that the enemy was abroad.[54]

The execution of the spies betrayed by Aimes is proof – if any were needed – that the Cold War of course did not just have its victims on the battlefields of the developing world; the superpowers had their victims too, their deaths nevertheless being more directly linked to intelligence operations than can be said of the landmine victims of Angola. Even so, that the spying game of the Cold War appears in retrospect, post-9/11, to have been a 'gentlemen's game'– one which is now 'significantly more dangerous' – is a change which can nevertheless be qualified; it is not that the number of spies captured and killed has necessarily increased since 11 September 2001, but that the 'game' has been one in which the two sides – at least for the first few years – have been playing by different rules. Aside from the change from peacetime to wartime espionage in 1939, no shift in the recent history of spying has been as dramatic as that from the Cold War to the confrontation with al-Qaeda. Although there have been instances of spies emerging from within – or being infiltrated into – the ranks of al-Qaeda, the most recent example being that of a Yemen-based al-Qaeda bomber who in May 2012 revealed his plans to the CIA – a central challenge to the West's spies has been to change their own mindsets, as the challenge of understanding the mentality of the new target has become evident: while it is clear from the Mitrokhin Archive and other post-Soviet accounts of Moscow's intent during the Cold War, that Western understanding of that intent was deeply flawed, the severity of the consequences was in part diminished by the assumption on both sides that military conflict should be avoided; the opposite is clearly true with regard to al-Qaeda and the groups which have carried its banner into the twenty-first century. With conflict of all kinds now a part of the landscape – whether terrorist attacks, assassinations or full-scale battles – and the intelligence target as evasive as al-Qaeda and its inheritors have proved themselves to be, spies are largely focused on preventing attacks. Understanding the terrorists' strategic intent, mapping the organisation, particularly while Osama bin Laden was in hiding in Pakistan and since his death, and identifying its methods of recruitment, have had to become secondary. In terms of understanding it – as former CIA Director James Woolsey says – the enemy is indeed as alien as if it were 'abroad'; in terms of looking for it, however, it is very much closer to home.

6

THE OSAMA METHOD

Karim Omar stroked his neatly trimmed beard as the rain beat hard on the window of the terraced house in north London. He had returned from Afghanistan two weeks beforehand, back to the European city he called the 'new Peshawar'.

The man known to the intelligence agencies by his real name of Mustafa bin Abd al-Qadir Setmariam Nasar had at first been reticent about meeting me, concerned, he said, that if he talked about his politics it might lead to his expulsion from Britain. We were introduced in January 1997 by a mutual acquaintance in whose house we met, and for two days he told me his story – how he had left his native Syria in 1980, spent two years living between Jordan and Iraq as he deepened his ties with the Muslim Brotherhood, and had then in 1983 visited Saudi Arabia:

> After four months there I went to France. I had problems with the Muslim Brotherhood – differences over direction, so I went to study in France and then went to live in Spain in 1985, which is where I was based until I came to London in 1995. But from Spain, from 1987 to 1994, I was mostly working in Afghanistan, in humanitarian aid, with the Arab groups. I was close to the chiefs. Osama is a close friend.[1]

I had first heard more than just a whisper of Osama bin Laden's name during my many visits to Khartoum in the early 1990s. Then his name started to come up more regularly while I was living in Rabat in 1995,

99

in conversations during the late-night meetings in Morocco, Algeria and Egypt with Islamist critics of North Africa's ruling regimes.

For much of the previous five years I had closely followed the emergence of what would later become known as 'political Islam'. Hours had been passed with the leadership of the National Islamic Front in Khartoum; I had witnessed the 'Black Hawk down' drama in Mogadishu on 3–4 October 1993, which the then Sudan-based Islamists associated with bin Laden claimed as their first battle with the United States.[2] In Kabul, Khartoum, Kaduna, N'Djamena and Kashm al-Girba the message I had heard was that from the late 1980s something was happening in these places that seemed to have little to unify it, but wherein a common thread of ideas occasionally seemed to coalesce into a definable 'movement'. Sometimes I would look for a leader who would have all the answers: in the casbah of Bab el Oued in the heart of Algiers, Abdelkadir Hachani of the banned Islamic Salvation Front shared tea and cakes as I listened to him explain that 'there are two forms of violence in Algeria – and the violence that is not a religious affair is criminal';[3] in the sitting-room beside his Mogadishu mosque, Sheikh Mohamed Moalim Hassan gave me a very fine Koran, which I still have, and which he inscribed with my name; in his cold office Mullah Amid Khan Muttaqi, the Taliban Information Minister in Kabul, wrapped himself tight inside a fine woollen cloak beside a glowing brazier as he told me, 'Islam is Islam everywhere. The only difference is that some people are saying it, but they are not doing it practically.'[4]

Sometimes it would seem as though all I needed to do was to listen, then all the pieces would fall into place.

But long before the ferocity of al-Qaeda erupted on 7 August 1998, and 263 people lay dead on the streets of Nairobi and Dar es Salaam amid the ruins of the US embassies, the potential for a trade in the secrets which would have steered the threat in other directions to those which it took, had been on the table. Sudan had sought such a trade, seeking to use the offer of intelligence-sharing with the United States as a means of casting off its pariah status. Following the US decision, announced on 1 February 1996, to 'suspend our diplomatic presence' in Khartoum, on the grounds that the regime was harbouring terrorist groups and that Americans in the country were not safe, Ambassador

Tim Carney met with Foreign Minister Ali Osman Taha before leaving the country, to discuss US preconditions for the normalisation of ties.[5] The next five years saw the overt and the covert – the public and the secret – intertwine in ways that would lead to the political currents of the Clinton White House flowing in conflicting directions, as intelligence and policy, *realpolitik* and personal agendas, spawned a confusion at the heart of the US Government as to what should be done about al-Qaeda. Underpinning everything was a lack of knowledge: after five years of intelligence gathering, little was really known; infiltration – despite some later debatable claims to the contrary – had been impossible; spying was not working, because the spy-craft of the Cold War – working with allies, relying on defectors, running spies at the heart of the enemy camp – was all but redundant. What was needed was insight from those who knew; that meant talking to the Sudanese.

But just as secret intelligence regarding al-Qaeda would be the key to thwarting its plans, *political* intelligence regarding the countries in which it had taken root would determine the value and timeliness of the secrets that might be gathered and shared. The lessons to all Western intelligence agencies of the experience of the British in Ireland, both between 1919 and 1921 and during the Troubles which erupted in 1969, are a vital precedent – had those lessons been learned, shared with allies, and passed on. The key lesson was, and remains: understand the society from which the challenge is emerging. But the United States was not about to deal with the military-religious junta that had consolidated its power in Khartoum in 1991 and had become the target of America's 'religious right', whatever the benefits might be for the CIA.

Until that evening in the north London home of the man who introduced me to Karim Omar, all I had sensed of the array of characters who were emerging on this dimly lit stage, were fragments. And against this background of fragments, the intelligence tools of the Cold War – the misinformation, the infiltration and the trade in secrets – which had sufficed for forty-five years, would slowly come to prove inadequate. The new target would – it soon transpired – refuse to trade; meanwhile, some of the best sources of intelligence were individuals and regimes with whom the United States either had poor relations or no relations at all. But the enemy was not a state; it was an idea.

These wholly unprecedented conditions took years to become clear and even longer to remedy.

In the meantime, for much of the 1990s the wrong evidence was being sought.

The Cold War had left policymakers and spies accustomed to looking for tangible evidence of the enemy's 'big picture' strategy. But despite being a very vocal movement – in Algeria and elsewhere – the Islamist movement was almost invisible, because so much of what was happening was going on only inside the minds of those who were becoming radicalised, many of them people who were to be found in towns and villages of the Muslim world about which neither policymakers nor spies particularly cared.

Additionally – with the dissipation of the clues available, as the drift from Afghanistan following the Soviet withdrawal gathered pace – few of those who were at the centre of what was taking place in individual countries, possessed a sense of how the links between one Islamist group and another were forming. Karim Omar was, however, one of this few, and was almost alone within the movement that emerged out of the anti-Soviet jihad in Afghanistan in possessing a relatively comprehensive knowledge of jihadi plans. Knowledge of these plans would determine the success of the intelligence agencies in grasping the challenge that became al-Qaeda: but if the spies could not recruit men like Karim Omar they would fail to thwart those who would later turn jihadist theory into terrorist practice.

Even though he would subsequently be arrested in Pakistan in October 2005 and handed over to the United States, Karim Omar's role as a source of intelligence was by then far less valuable than at that time when, on those evenings in January 1997, he and I talked for many hours. Although more than one intelligence officer told me in the years that followed that they were aware of Omar, his kind had not often crossed their paths, still less often been successfully recruited as informers; the true insiders of a stateless movement which saw 'the West' as its enemy, presented the spies with a recruitment challenge of a kind which Cold War practices had left them ill-prepared to meet. While I could sit and talk with such people – offering nothing to trade but a listening ear and page space in a book I would later write – the spies, it seemed, could not.

The results would be disastrous.

The significance and credibility of Karim Omar lay in his role as a theorist. His written account of the Muslim Brotherhood's conflict in the early 1980s with the Syrian regime of Hafez al-Assad was widely read among Islamist groups. It was followed in 1991 by a two-volume work, *The Global Islamic Resistance Call*, which for the first time in the history of the Islamist movement sought to bring together the different trends across the Muslim world, to identify their similarities and common cause, and to explain in detail how much more effective they could be if they coordinated their efforts and found a common enemy.[6]

Having overcome his initial reticence to discuss these issues with me, it slowly became clear from Karim Omar that the apparently disparate trends I had discerned across North Africa, the Middle East and into Central Asia during the previous half decade, were being drawn together. What is more, that fair-haired man sitting on the settee in the bay window of a room in a modest North London home emerged before me as a – perhaps *the* – key player in what was taking place:

> My book was taken up as a revolutionary guide by many young Islamists. Now I have very close relations particularly with the [Algerian] Armed Islamic Group commandoes. But there are great problems within the Islamic movements – between the young and the old. There's a very strong conflict between the two generations of the Islamic movement, between the Muslim Brotherhood – the democrats and moderates – and the younger generation. The conditions in the Islamic world are being pushed to become even more fanatical, and I would say that Osama bin Laden is between the moderates and the armed groups. Osama is important in the past and for the future. He has passed through many stages. Osama represents the method.

He went on,

> The armed groups are opposed to a foreign presence, opposed to dictatorship, opposed to government that has much foreign influence upon it, and opposed to threats like that in Bosnia. Conflict in the Islamic world is against the Americans, and against the French. The countries that are free of that are Britain and Scandinavia. For the French the Algerian war is a matter of life and death; for the Americans it's all

about Middle East oil. Muslims don't have a conflict with Britain – we are in an important period with regard to the relationship between Islam and the UK [a country which was seen by Omar as more balanced in its approach to the Islamic world than were the United States or France]. [But] the problem with the Islamists is that they view all the foreign interests as being the same. I have tried to explain to the heads of all the armed organisations. I write against France and the US. But in the UK there's liberty and the justice is free.

His stress on this left me wondering if perhaps he thought the room had been bugged, and whether these words were being stated for the benefit of MI5.

He continued,

What is bothering the Western politicians is that they [the Islamists who emerged out of the anti-Soviet jihad in Afghanistan] have turned from being individuals into being a school of thought. The next generation of Arab-Afghans has been born – even the third generation, although they didn't go to Afghanistan. This is a serious security issue, because they are not known. People spent ten years there. Now it's ten years later.

From his native Syria to Western Europe to Afghanistan to Algeria and then London, his trail throughout the 1980s and into the 1990s not only allowed him to gain a first-hand sense of what was taking place within the wider world of the Islamists of which he was a part, but also allowed him to develop a theoretical base within which the disparate movements could plant roots. Without Karim Omar the 'global jihad' would have lacked much of the structure, aims and strategy that helped sustain it in the face of the worldwide efforts to destroy it since 11 September 2001. And it was in the 'new Peshawar' of London – where between 1994 and 1997 he moved freely among the exiled Algerians, Saudis and others whose presence in the city incensed the governments of these countries, who wanted their dissidents silenced – that the comings and goings among radicalised Muslims were more visible, active and ripe for infiltration by the intelligence agencies than in any other Western city.

The intelligence strategy practised for much of the 1990s was to let these activists 'run', that is to leave them unhindered so their activities could be observed. Little could be learned from them if they disappeared, so it was far better to keep an eye on them and identify who they associated with; anyway, unless they had committed a crime in Britain they could not be arrested. Additionally, their presence in London provided the British Government with a subtle form of pressure on the regimes from which they had fled – regimes, such as those in Syria, Algeria, Egypt and Saudi Arabia, whose deplorable human-rights records provided Whitehall with occasional ammunition when diplomatic 'missiles' needed firing at the potentates of the Middle East.

At least, that was the theory. But it barely worked in practice.

The global Islamist movement, for which London was the crucial centre in the West throughout the 1990s, was far more clever than the Western intelligence agencies could ever have thought; meanwhile, the agencies themselves were caught between a movement that had yet to raise its head, and government departments which were yet to become a 'market' requesting intelligence on what was taking place. Even up to a few months before the bombing of the US embassies in Kenya and Tanzania on 7 August 1998 the Islamist movement was being seen by some within the intelligence agencies as non-political. Collectively, the West didn't see it coming, perhaps because people like Karim Omar *seemed* to have no secrets, he openly telling me that the Americans and the French were the enemy. There was little conviction – mainly because there was no proof – that radical thought would or could be turned into terrorist action.

Nevertheless, the threat of violence lurked constantly, perhaps largely by implication, particularly when he talked of his association with Algeria's extremely violent GIA, whose terror I had witnessed first hand during my own visits to Algeria in the years before I met him.[7] The clues as to what was forming were ever-present in his comments, in his books and – perhaps most importantly – in the network of which he was a part. What was needed was a coherent analysis of the emerging radicalisation, which might piece these elements together into a form that, while perhaps not leading to 'plots' being discovered, might at least have cast light on the extent, influence and organisational structure of what it was that was really present in that sitting-room on Dewsbury Road, Dollis Hill. At the appointed hour during our conversations a small plastic model of the Grand Mosque in Mecca would illuminate and emit a pre-recorded call to prayer from inside, Khaled al-Fawwaz – the exiled Saudi who lived there with his family, and who had introduced me to Omar – leading them in prayer.

It is now many years since I sat with Karim Omar in that North London house, and heard him recount what had happened during the half decade before we had met. The events of which he and thousands of others were a part in Afghanistan remain the foundation upon which the challenge from political Islam came to be built. Omar has been held incommunicado since his arrest in 2005, possibly in his native Syria; Khaled al-Fawwaz has meanwhile been in a British jail since 1998, fighting extradition to the United States, where he is accused of involvement in the bombings in 1998 of the US embassies in Kenya and Tanzania.

The history of which these two and others are, in one way or another, a part, has dictated the agendas of all the world's intelligence agencies for more than two decades. While US, Saudi and Pakistani support for the *mujahideen* was crucial in ending the Soviet occupation of Afghanistan, it was difficult to predict the 'blowback' that led to those same Western proxies later bombing the US embassies in East Africa and carrying out or organising the attacks which have followed.

For Western intelligence agencies to gauge what the 'Arab-Afghans' might later become, necessitated first knowing what they had been. As Richard Clarke, US National Coordinator for Security under both Presidents Clinton and George W. Bush, wrote during the post-9/11 period of vicious recrimination that prevailed among White House and intelligence officials, 'Although bin Laden's name surfaced with increasing frequency in 1993 and 1994, CIA analyses continued to refer to him as a radicalised rich kid, who was playing at terrorism by sending checks to terrorist groups.'[8] Decades after the Soviet–Afghan war ended there are, moreover, various explanations as to how and why the 'Arab-Afghans' evolved into al-Qaeda; some even question whether it was really all the same people. 'The reality is that the Arabs didn't play a role [in Afghanistan],'[9] Milton Bearden, CIA station chief in Pakistan and the Agency's field officer in Afghanistan from 1986 to 1989, told me in 1999. 'The Arabs were a nuisance, and they numbered about two thousand.' Despite being a highly decorated intelligence officer, Bearden's assertions must be questioned, when compared first with the account of the Pakistani intelligence officer on the ground[10] in Afghanistan, Mohammad Yousaf – who stresses that neither the CIA nor any other US officials had direct contact with the Arab-Afghans or the Afghan *mujahideen* in the country – and second with that of Karim Omar on the issue of how many Arabs went there to fight the Soviet Union: he told me that it was up to fifteen thousand.

While not deterring former 'frontline' intelligence operatives like Bearden from positing figures, the uncertainty within the CIA as to what exactly had emerged out of Afghanistan in the late 1980s is evident when other views are sought from within the Agency, another senior CIA officer with direct experience of Afghanistan during the anti-Soviet war telling me of the Arab presence within the country: 'The trouble is that we don't know how many [Arabs] there were to begin with.'[11] So when an offer of intelligence sharing was made to the CIA in 1996 by Sudan's military-Islamist regime, which would have provided insights into what happened next, the American response would ultimately determine whether or not the intelligence war against the then emergent al-Qaeda was likely to be fought on terms reflecting a real understanding of what that war was all about.

Just as I had been able to seek out well-placed figures like Karim Omar who were associated with the leadership of al-Qaeda and were in a position to cast light on its intentions, so the Sudanese leadership in the mid-1990s was better placed than any other in the world – including by then that of Saudi Arabia – to cast light on how the network at whose centre Osama bin Laden would emerge, was then being formed. But just as the British 'lost' Ireland because it lost touch with popular opinion – losing the 'intelligence war' with Michael Collins as a result – so the United States lost touch with key Arab veterans of the Afghan war, despite its deployment of a redoubtable CIA Special Activities Division and ex-special forces soldier Billy Waugh to carry out surveillance of bin Laden in Sudan from soon after his arrival there in 1991.

Waugh, who had first established contact with Islamists in Yemen, tells of how the CIA Chief of Station in Khartoum pointed him in bin Laden's direction by saying of the Saudi, 'We don't know what he's up to, but we know he's a wealthy financier and we think he's harbouring some of these outfits called al-Qaeda. See what you can find out.'[12]

In the gung-ho manner in which he passed his fifty-year career as a CIA and special forces operative, Waugh tells of how he started his surveillance of the al-Qaeda leader by jogging every evening past his residence in the al-Riyadh district of Khartoum, stirring the suspicion of bodyguards, who occasionally followed him by car as he jogged in the 40-degree heat.[13] The value of Waugh's account of his operations is as revealing as the observations he makes:

> You have to remember, bin Laden was next to nothing at this time (between February 1991 and July 1992). We (the CIA) didn't have any reason to believe he was capable of mass destruction against the United States. We knew he was angry, we knew he hated us, and we knew he was moving a lot of money around. Those facts were enough for the CIA to find out what he was all about... We took a lot of the right steps in following this man. In the early 1990s, though, it was impossible to read his intentions. He was an enemy, definitely, but he was not considered an imminent threat.[14]

Waugh constructed a straw cabin on the roof of a Khartoum villa, from where he photographed bin Laden as he conducted daily noontime prayer meetings in the courtyard of a mosque on South Riyadh Road.

A visual impression of bin Laden's relationship with his followers was built up; the fact that he went daily to the bank where he held his accounts was noted; he was only ever seen driving alone, in a white Mercedes, while his house was permanently guarded. Then Waugh moved on from bin Laden, turning his attention to the capture of Khartoum's at that time far more notorious resident terrorist, Carlos the Jackal, who was seized on 14 August 1994 in a joint US-led operation with the French, and who has been in jail in France ever since.

The Jackal's departure from the Sudanese capital left the CIA plenty of time to come to terms with the uncertain challenge from the man Waugh had photographed so extensively at the mosque on South Riyadh Road, the glaring hole in the available intelligence becoming more worrisome and the difficulty of developing reliable sources within al-Qaeda becoming more evident. This was made startlingly clear when the story of Ali Mohamed began to unfold – a tale illustrating the extent, complexity and structural failings of CIA and FBI intelligence gathering as al-Qaeda started to emerge.

Like Francis Magan in 1798, David Neligan in 1920, and Oleg Gordievsky in the 1980s, Ali Mohamed was the kind of 'asset' that intelligence agencies worldwide dream of coming across. The agent operating on the inside – 'in place' – over a long period of time, is gold dust. And that is what Ali Mohamed had the potential to be when he approached the CIA in Cairo and offered to spy for them.

Three years earlier he had been at Fort Bragg, North Carolina on a special forces training course for foreign army officers. Rising to the position of major in the Egyptian army, Mohamed had grown up in the Egypt of Anwar Sadat when the Islamist movement spearheaded by the future al-Qaeda number two, Ayman al-Zawahiri, was gaining influence within the armed forces.

In 1984 Mohamed had been forced to leave the Army when suspicions grew that he had become sympathetic to the Islamists who were by then forming into the Jama Islamiyya and – under al-Zawahiri – the Egyptian Islamic Jihad.

His relationship with the CIA got off to a rocky start when the Agency learned that he had told members of a West Germany-based cell of the Lebanese Hizbollah organisation on whom he had been asked to spy, that he was working for the CIA. Thus began a tale of bluff and double bluff that would last for fifteen years. The Agency claimed then to have cut him loose, but he in fact managed to enter the United States in 1985 under a secret CIA programme open to such 'assets'. He married an American woman shortly after his arrival, signed up for US military service, and set up a home in Santa Clara, California. From there he renewed his contact with the CIA, as well as with the Al-Kifah Refugee Center in Brooklyn, New York, a charitable institution associated with the Makhtab al-Khidamat, a then Pakistan-based charity whose activities were guided by Abdullah Azzam, a cleric Karim Omar told me had been a key influence on Osama bin Laden.[15]

While keeping his CIA contacts informed of his movements, and acting as an instructor at the John F. Kennedy Special Warfare School, Fort Bragg, Mohamed would stay at the Brooklyn home of an Al-Kifah associate, El-Sayyid Nosair; he also developed a relationship with Sheikh Omar Abdul-Rahman, the exiled spiritual leader of the Egyptian Jama Islamiyya, who was living in New York.[16]

The range of activities, contacts and access with which Mohamed operated, is comparable with that of Karim Omar; but while Omar was the modern jihad's theorist who was not recruited, Mohamed was a practitioner and fixer who was. Such people were rare within the Islamist movement that coalesced into al-Qaeda in the 1990s. The value to the intelligence community of recruiting these people could be incalculable – a fact that was not lost on those within the CIA and FBI who handled Mohamed following his arrival in the United States.

But this handling of an agent exposed the very same shortcomings within the US intelligence machinery that would let 19 young men travel to the United States, train as pilots, and carry out their deadly mission on 11 September 2001.

When, in 1986, Mohamed told his supervisor at Fort Bragg that he was taking a month's leave to go to Afghanistan to train *mujahideen* fighters, his superiors were informed but expressed little concern, despite the fact of his being a serving US Army officer at that time. On his return he resumed the training of his associates at the Al-Kifah Refugee Center, accompanying several to the Calverton Shooting Range on Long Island, basing his lessons on military manuals which it later transpired he had stolen from Fort Bragg. Thus began the preparation of his pupils for the event that would announce the arrival of Islamist terrorism on the US mainland: the detonation of a massive bomb beneath the New York World Trade Center on 26 February 1993.

Long before then – in November 1989 – Mohamed had been honourably discharged from the US Army with commendations for 'patriotism, valour, fidelity, and professional excellence'. He had then been recruited by the FBI's San Francisco office as an informer – and had become a part of the inner circle around Osama bin Laden, his first major role being to organise the future al-Qaeda leader's move from Afghanistan to Khartoum. From then on he came to play a central role within al-Qaeda, with US intelligence officers with whom he had by then been liaising for five years regarding his knowledge of its organisation, network and resources as invaluable.

But his real value as a spy was not what it seemed: because Ali Mohamed was really spying for Osama bin Laden.

The role of this double agent explains more about the intelligence failure that led to the 9/11 attacks than any other single issue. Owing to what the CIA and FBI already knew of Ali Mohamed, even the activities of the 9/11 hijackers themselves – their focus at flying school on learning how to take off and fly aircraft, with no apparent interest in how to land them – are a lesser failure, due to most of the hijackers being 'clean skins' (that is, individuals who did not appear on any 'watch lists' and whose activities had not aroused suspicion).

The years that followed his departure from the US Army in 1989 saw Mohamed became immersed in the formation of the global movement which on 23 August 1996 would crystallise its message in the form of a *fatwa* issued by bin Laden entitled the 'Declaration of Jihad on the Americans Occupying the Two Holy Places'. The intervening years would see him as instrumental in forging al-Qaeda's place within the world of Islamist militancy: on 5 November 1990 Rabbi Meir Kahane, the founder of the right-wing Jewish Defense League, was gunned down in New York, the main suspect being El Sayyid Nosair, Mohamed's former pupil at the Calverton Shooting Range, and in whose Brooklyn home he had stayed. The at that time unexplained name 'al-Qaeda' appeared among the 47 boxes of documents later found by police at Nosair's home, where a videotape of a lecture given by Ali Mohamed at Fort Bragg was also discovered, along with 'top secret' US Army documents, including details of special forces operations. Then, in February 1991, Mohamed oversaw bin Laden's move to Khartoum, and began organising the creation of three camps south of the city to house and train al-Qaeda's fledgling force. There he provided training advice to – among others – bin Laden himself, Abu Ubaidah al-Banshiri, al-Qaeda's first military commander,[17] and Mohammed Atef, its second military commander. A short time later he passed information to the FBI regarding the activities of attendees at a mosque in San Jose, California; in the autumn of 1992 he revisited Afghanistan, providing military training to various military commanders involved in fighting against the Northern Alliance, which had taken power following the Soviet withdrawal – a role that led Nabil

Sharef, a former Egyptian intelligence officer, to say after the 9/11 attacks, 'For five years he [Mohamed] was moving back and forth between the US and Afghanistan. It's impossible the CIA thought he was going there as a tourist. If the CIA hadn't caught on to him, it should be dissolved and its budget used for something worthwhile.'[18]

At 12.17 p.m. on 26 February 1993 a 1500 lb urea nitrate–hydrogen gas bomb concealed inside a Ryder rental truck in the car park beneath the North Tower of the New York World Trade Center was detonated as the climax of a conspiracy that involved several of Mohamed's other charges from the Al-Kifah Refugee Center and his lessons at the shooting range. Two of the conspirators – Mahmud Abouhalima and Mohammad Salameh – had been secretly filmed by the FBI with Mohamed at the range; and while the New York World Trade Center bombers were finalising their plans Mohamed – using the *nom-de-guerre* Abu 'Abdallah – travelled to Bosnia as part of a team which trained and armed Muslim fighters there until June 1993, when he travelled on to Khartoum and was asked by bin Laden to set up the al-Qaeda cell in Nairobi, Kenya.

Ali Mohamed slipped through the cracks in the US intelligence structure. Even after his name had emerged as linked to the February 1993 World Trade Center bombers, and while he was assembling the Nairobi cell – out of which would emerge the plot that would lead to the bombings of the US embassies in the Kenyan and Tanzanian capitals on 7 August 1998 – he was being debriefed by his FBI handler, John Zent. According to the writer Peter Lance in his detailed account of Mohamed's activities, Mohamed informed Zent – for reasons that baffled the FBI, and which remain unexplained – of the training camps he had been involved in establishing in Afghanistan,[19] then informed a team from the National Security Agency (the US signals-intelligence agency) of the location of the camps, and later provided them with a range of details when asked about 'this guy named bin Laden'. The details were collected in an NSA report that was filed with the US Defense Department, not shared with the CIA, and which subsequently went missing, and was 'probably destroyed in a reorganisation of intelligence components' in the Defense Department.[20]

Only in late 1993 was surveillance placed on Mohamed: his telephone calls were monitored, the intelligence gathered leading to knowledge of al-Qaeda's cell in Nairobi. Meanwhile, he remained on speaking terms with the FBI – even as the al-Qaeda plan to destroy the two US embassies was underway,[21] and became one of several al-Qaeda operatives who travelled to Somalia to aid Mohamed Farah Aideed in the fight against the US forces which culminated in the 3 October 1993 battle in Mogadishu which left 18 US Rangers dead.[22] Mohamed then left Mogadishu, flew to California, and returned to Khartoum with a brief to improve bin Laden's security following a 4 February 1994 attempt to assassinate the al-Qaeda leader. Mohamed acknowledged his links with bin Laden to the FBI when they debriefed him again in December 1994 and January 1995, and he was listed as an 'unindicted co-conspirator' in a 24 June 1993 plot to blow up several New York landmarks; the same list included bin Laden's name – but the FBI still did not see fit to regard their agent as a terrorist. It was not until October 1995 that the CIA decided to share its bin Laden files with the FBI, thereby clarifying suspicions about the Nairobi cell and eventually leading in September 1998 to the arrest of Mohamed following the embassy bombings – his wife telling Peter Lance in 2006, 'I really can't say much. He can't talk to anybody. Nobody can get to him. They have Ali pretty secretive… it's like he just kinda vanished into thin air.'[23]

Al-Qaeda learned far more from Ali Mohamed than this double agent told US intelligence officers, his military skills and the secret operational material he stole from Fort Bragg apparently feeding directly into the terrorist capacity of the bombers gathered at the Al-Kifah Center. In October 1997 Mohamed was taken out for dinner by three US officials, including two FBI agents, who made a pitch to recruit him fully as a spy.[24] He took the opportunity to provide them with details of his personal history with bin Laden over the previous six years, and made it clear that he 'loved' the al-Qaeda leader, and that he was himself in touch with hundreds of people he could call upon to 'wage jihad against the United States'. Having rejected the offer to spy for the United States on a full-time basis, he told his dinner hosts that 'I can get out anytime and you'll never find me. I've got a whole network. You'll never find me.'[25]

Despite this brush-off, one of the FBI agents remained in contact with Mohamed, who in a later conversation hinted that a location in East Africa may have become a target for attack. But it was a hint that did not provide the lead that could link what was already known about the Nairobi cell with the bombers who, at 10.35 a.m. and 10.39 a.m. on 7 August 1998, blew up the two embassies. Mohamed told his FBI contacts shortly afterwards that he knew the bombers' names but would not divulge them. A month later he was arrested and charged, but even in 2012 remained to be sentenced, and is reckoned to be 'helping the authorities with their inquiries' from a location of which even his wife is not aware.

7

THE ROAD TO 9/11

Ali Mohamed's game of cat-and-mouse with the FBI, the Bureau's lack of co-ordination with the CIA, the secretiveness of the NSA, the challenge of tracking the legacy and whereabouts of the 'Arab Afghans', and – above all – the difficulty of infiltrating known and trusted outsiders into bin Laden's inner circle, lay behind the CIA's decision in February 1996 to create 'Alec Station', a dedicated unit which would focus solely on gathering intelligence on bin Laden and al-Qaeda. To lead it the Agency appointed the head of the Islamic Extremist Branch of the CIA's Counter-terrorist Center (CTC), Michael Scheuer, who ran what started as a team of ten but which had grown to 40 by 11 September 2001.

The decision to create Alec Station served to demonstrate how ill-prepared the US intelligence agencies were in the face of the threat that was by then well developed, as Scheuer would write – under his *nom-de-plume* of 'Anonymous' – in a post-9/11 tirade entitled *Imperial Hubris*.

In it, Scheuer tore into the intelligence agencies by condemning the tendency of the FBI to see counter-terrorism as a law-enforcement exercise, and derided the CIA, FBI, NSA and others for the 'lie'[1] that there was 'seamless cooperation' between them in the pre-9/11 effort against al-Qaeda. He would conclude,

> Useless computers, obsessive focus on overseas operations, aggrandisement of self and institution, and disregard of al Qaeda leads in the United States – these failures must be attributed to deliberate decisions by FBI

officers, living, retired or dead. A more appalling case of negligence, however, lies in the moral cowardice of my own agency's (the CIA's) leaders, men who were repeatedly briefed on the problems but did not try to correct them. They then compounded this dereliction by falsely assuring policy makers and congressional overseers that cooperation was 'seamless'. Of such things are made the events of 11 September 2001.'[2]

Illustration of how dysfunctional relations between key departments of the US Government had become, would emerge from the pages of the US Senate Intelligence Committee's 7 July 2004 report on the intelligence failures surrounding the war in Iraq.[3] Personal and interdepartmental rivalry dominated decisions regarding what was the 'truth' and what was not.

The Pentagon's rivalry with the CIA – from which the Pentagon emerged victorious when the CIA was roundly criticised for its failings with regard to the intelligence gathering on Iraq's WMD, by both the Senate Committee and the 9/11 Commission – was clear from the testimony of Defense Department officials to the Senate Intelligence Committee. 'The CIA's interpretation [of al-Qaeda ties to Iraq] ought to be ignored,'[4] one Pentagon official told the Senators. The same Pentagon official – a staff member of the department's Defense Intelligence Agency (DIA) – explained how he was asked in July 2002 'to prepare an [intelligence] briefing on Iraq and links to al-Qaeda for the [Defense Secretary, Donald Rumsfeld] and that he was not to tell anyone about it.' The result was a briefing which was as much about how wrong the CIA was in its doubts about the alleged al-Qaeda ties with Iraq – which the Bush Administration so desperately wanted to find – as it was about the alleged links themselves. The briefing was even called 'Fundamental Problems with How Intelligence Community is Assessing Information'. In a slideshow, the briefing concluded that Iraq and al-Qaeda had 'more than a decade of numerous contacts', that there were 'multiple areas of cooperation', a 'shared interest and pursuit of WMD', and 'one indication of Iraq; coordination with al-Qaeda specifically related to 9/11.'

In response to the briefing, the DIA official received a note from Rumsfeld's three most senior advisors, which said, 'This was an excellent briefing. The Secretary was very impressed. He asked us to think about some possible next steps to see if we can illuminate the differences between us and the CIA. The goal is not to produce a consensus product, but rather to scrub one another's arguments.'[5] The Pentagon then decided to give the same briefing to George Tenet, the CIA Director, though with the omission of the slideshow that so roundly criticised the CIA's conclusions on Iraq. Tenet is quoted in the Senate Committee report on Iraq as saying after the briefing that he 'didn't think much of it...I didn't see anything that broke new ground for me,' though he agreed to postpone a new CIA report on *Iraqi Support for Terrorism* until the points raised by the Pentagon had been considered.

It was against a similar background of animosity that Michael Scheuer had for three years run Alec Station between 1996 and 1999. Early on, the unit requested that the NSA eavesdropping agency provide intercepts of calls made by bin Laden, notably to his associates in Yemen, but was refused access to the full transcripts and was given only summaries. Such incidents – as reported by Scheuer – were legion, and became even more frustrating to him when what appeared to be al-Qaeda's 'communications hub' was detected in Sana'a, Yemen in May 1996 by a CIA officer seconded to the NSA – a finding which offered the chance to expand greatly the interception of satellite telephone calls being made by bin Laden from Afghanistan. According to Scheuer, his requests to his superiors within the CIA to pressure the NSA to provide full transcripts of the intercepts were met with inertia, leaving Alec Station with access only to the far less useful summaries of these conversations; it later developed its own listening station in the Indian Ocean, but found it could only intercept calls from Yemen and could not pick up what was being said from Afghanistan.[6] A further attempt to have the NSA provide the Afghanistan-to-Yemen conversations was met with a refusal.

The experience of those involved with Alec Station – an experience which culminated in the intelligence failure of 9/11 – illustrated what it is that must be in place if intelligence gathering is to lead to successful intelligence-led operations. It was – again – the functionality of the trade in secrets which dominated what was taking place in Washington DC and the surrounding suburbs, home to America's spy agencies. But this time the trade was not initially between spies and sources, but between the spies themselves. America's agencies failed to coordinate and cooperate with each other, much as the UK agencies had at points done in Northern Ireland. By failing to trade, share and jointly assess the issues at hand, the fundamental ingredients permitting sound assessment were therefore not combining into a form recognisable as a terrorist structure which could be understood. Intelligence is a cumulative entity – it emerges over time, from different sources; it is rare that one source or agency has the full picture; corroboration is vital; cooperation – between states as between the institutions within a single country – is essential. Not even the most sophisticated electronic intelligence gathering can produce indisputable, actionable intelligence; amid the uncertainties of spying, no single agency has a monopoly of the truth.

In such circumstances, trading is vital – between both sometime enemies and sometime friends, as well as between allies. So it was that from Langley, Virginia to Khartoum, Sudan, the collapse in the trading of secrets denied America's intelligence gatherers the raw material which might have permitted them to identify what was gathering on the horizon.

But it is also necessary to accept that – just as, back in 1920, British officials in Dublin were wholly mistaken in their view that their top spy in Ireland 'could do anything' – even the best secret intelligence on al-Qaeda's intentions might not have averted 9/11. Why so? Because an attack on the United States was not an isolated plan – it was al-Qaeda's destiny. It would happen, because those that wanted it to happen had made it their mission. The US relationship with those communities which had spawned Islamism, was irreversible and irreparable; 9/11 was inevitable, and would happen in one form or another, even if those particular attacks had been thwarted.

It is for this reason that unless secret intelligence is gathered against the background of a profound understanding of the communities from which the specific intelligence targets have emerged, it runs the risk not only of failing to identify threats, but of precipitating events and reactions which may produce more problems than it solves.

It was over dinner in the exclusive surroundings of Washington's Metropolitan Club that I met Michael Scheuer, and began to understand why this long-serving intelligence officer had over time fallen out with John O'Neill, the FBI's highly regarded New York-based head of the National Security Division focused on al-Qaeda, had developed strained relations with the similarly respected Richard Clarke, National Coordinator for Security at the White House, and why it was that personality clashes within the intelligence hierarchy had played such a crucial role in the failure to coordinate the efforts to confront al-Qaeda as the East African embassy bombings approached. Clarke and Scheuer remain at loggerheads to this day, the White House man saying of the CIA man long after 9/11,

> Throwing tantrums doesn't help. Fine that you came to the same conclusion that we all came to, fine that you're all worked up about it, and you're having difficulty getting your agency, the rest of your agency, to fall in line, but not fine that you're so dysfunctional within your agency that you're making it harder to get something done.

To this the CIA man responded, 'Mr Clarke was an interferer of the first level, in terms of talking about things that he knew nothing about. Mr Clarke was an empire builder. He built the community, and it was his little toy. He was always playing the F.B.I. off against us or us against the N.S.A.'[7]

Scheuer – as his writings and interviews testify – is a difficult man, but also one who is aggrieved by the failures that he rightly perceived as having permitted the 9/11 hijackers to carry out their plan. Over our dinner he railed against everybody, condemning 'the Europeans' for their prime responsibility in 'helping' the 9/11 bombers to plot, train and carry out their plans on US soil; it was is if the failure of his own organisation – with which he had by then fallen out – was nothing compared with that of the Germans, the French and 'you Brits'. His anger and aggression were as intense as his sense of regret, as the US intelligence community nursed the wounds that were ripped open by 9/11.

Equally, however, his role and manner were a startling reminder that in the end the ability to grasp what al-Qaeda represented, what – in the words of Billy Waugh – was *really* meant when it was said bin Laden was 'definitely' a 'threat', had been grasped only by the mavericks within the CIA. Just as it was Michael Oatley in the Northern Ireland of the 1970s who had the nous to dig deep into what was driving the PIRA, so it was the case within the CIA regarding the effort to build an accurate picture of al-Qaeda in the 1990s. The problem for Scheuer was that personality clashes prevented decisive action, whereas for Oatley the Link remained in place – however maverick it was – because at the most senior level there was acceptance that it might one day prove valuable.

Scheuer's fury intensified when the CIA Director, George Tenet, rejected a plan – described as 'perfect' by Scheuer and 'well crafted' by the Pentagon – to capture bin Laden in Afghanistan in 1997.[8] In the two years that followed – that is, both before and after the East African embassy bombings – Scheuer would propose ten different plans to either capture or kill bin Laden,[9] all of which were rejected by Tenet, with the White House and the National Security Council often concurring that the intelligence underpinning these operations was not wholly convincing.[10]

In the immediate aftermath of the embassy bombings Alec Station was asked what it most needed to improve intelligence gathering on al-Qaeda, in response to which the request for the NSA telephone transcripts was repeated – a request which produced no improvements in intelligence sharing – resulting in more Scheuer fury, and in his being fired as head of Alec Station in June 1999. He was replaced by a colleague who encountered the same inter-agency rivalry, and whose experience led inexorably to the conclusion that America endured the 9/11 attacks because it was weakened by the failure of its intelligence agencies to look outwards rather than inwards for where the threat might be coming from.

As Scheuer later told me in a calmer moment to that of our first meeting, 'Our [US] Government is so risk averse that they are always waiting to get other people to do their dirty work,'[11] a comment which would resonate across Angola, Afghanistan and those other Cold War theatres in which proxy wars had laid waste to the developing world. For Scheuer, as for the core of the intelligence community – focused as it is on identifying threats and confronting them – the structure and practices of the CIA and its partner agencies, was the main target of criticism. Changes in the structure would have changed decision-making, and a change in practices – in particular, committing individuals to specific issues for several years, and then ensuring that their successors did the same – would have brought with it such deep understanding of the background that the emerging threat would have been discerned. As he told me,

> The American intelligence system as a whole is committed to generalists (that is, officers with no dedicated, long-term expertise in a particular issue). That's the way it worked in the Soviet era. And I just don't think it works anymore. We were fighting a losing battle before 9/11. Tenet didn't get the message across: he didn't tell people that we were in an era where if you were forty percent sure you were going to have to act.[12]

Unsavoury as it would undoubtedly have been, the first place in which it would have been wise to have created a more effective intelligence-gathering operation was in Billy Waugh's old stomping ground, Sudan.

In preparation for the decision to all but close the US Embassy in Khartoum, Ambassador Tim Carney had in November 1995 delivered an unsigned, undated 'non-paper' to the ideological guide of Sudan's regime, Hassan el-Tourabi, as well as to the President, Lt General Omar Hassan el-Bashir, in which it was stated that if the perceived threat to Americans in Sudan led to attacks, the US response would be 'extremely damaging'.

The paper was delivered not long after Clinton's National Security Advisor, Anthony Lake, had been moved with his family from his home in Washington to a safe house in response to intelligence suggesting he might have been the target of a Sudanese assassination plot. It was not until several months later that the threat to Lake was deemed to have been false and the agent who was the source of the intelligence dropped. This was followed in January 1996 by the CIA withdrawing almost a hundred and fifty intelligence reports regarding Sudan, when it learned that the principal source had either been fabricating or embellishing the intelligence being passed on. Two months later, on 3 March 1996, CIA and State Department officials met with Sudan's Defence Minister, General Fatih Erwa, in Washington, to discuss how US–Sudanese relations might be improved. Erwa made an offer: Sudan would assist the United States in 'keeping an eye' on Osama bin Laden, and even offered to have him extradited, though the US officials rejected this on the basis that they did not have sufficient evidence to indict him.[13] As a consequence, bin Laden was instead expelled from Sudan, and relocated to Afghanistan.

Bin Laden's departure from Sudan gave the United States a number of choices: it could learn more about the al-Qaeda leader by following him to Afghanistan and seeking to infiltrate whatever structure he put in place there; it could use a possible thaw in relations with Sudan to obtain whatever the Sudanese External Security Bureau – the ESB, the country's intelligence service – had gathered; or it could combine elements of both. Instead, the White House dithered – due mainly to its reluctance to deal directly with the Sudanese regime, leaving the initiative instead to a New York financier and Democratic Party contributor, Mansoor Ijaz.

On 12 July 1996 Ijaz was briefed – as a private citizen – on US policy towards Sudan, by two State Department officials, and that evening met President Clinton at a White House dinner[14] at which he told the President that he was going to Sudan to 'have a look around and see if there's something we can help with there'. A week later he met with El-Tourabi, El-Bashir and other senior officials in Khartoum, and suggested to El-Tourabi that he write to Clinton with an offer of cooperation and an invitation to send US counter-terrorism officials to Sudan. On his return to Washington, Ijaz briefed Clinton's National Security Advisor Sandy Berger as well as Susan Rice, the Africa specialist on the National Security Council and a strong critic of the Sudanese regime. On 15 October Ijaz again travelled to Khartoum, meeting again with El-Bashir, El-Tourabi and others, including the intelligence chief, Gutbi Al-Mahdi. It was during this last meeting – which lasted almost four hours – that Al-Mahdi showed Ijaz examples of the intelligence files Sudan had kept on various of the radical groups, including al-Qaeda, that had been based in the country during the previous five years. He then offered to provide them to the United States 'if mutual sincerity can be developed on all sides'.[15] Ijaz relayed this offer to Berger and Rice in Washington, following it up on 27 October 1996 with a written memorandum to Berger in which he detailed the names, dates of entry, passport details and intelligence briefs on the individuals identified as being of interest; on 22 January 1997 – after Clinton's re-election – Ijaz again visited Khartoum, and advised President El-Bashir's political aide, Abu Bakr Shingiati, on the wording of a letter that would make the offer of intelligence-sharing official.

This offer was considered by the White House, the NSC and other Government departments between May and September 1997, during which time an FBI officer told Ijaz that the offer would only be accepted if all departments and agencies approved – a move they rejected on 4 November, when renewed sanctions were imposed 'because of Sudan's continued sponsorship of international terror'.

Thus ended Ijaz's role, when he realised that the political will to take the risk of dealing with the Sudanese regime – to whatever end – was not there.

Undeterred by the rebuff, however, Khartoum sought to develop its trade in secrets in return for respectability with the United States, through separate intelligence and security links. On 12 September and 5 December 1997, David Williams, assistant special agent of the FBI Middle East and North Africa Department, met with Sudan's Ambassador to Washington, Mahdi Ibrahim, and on 2 May 1998 the ESB intelligence chief Gutbi Al-Mahdi wrote to Williams 'to express my sincere desire to start contacts and cooperation between our service and the FBI,'[16] and invited Williams to visit Sudan. On 24 June 1998 Williams replied, 'Unfortunately, I am not currently in a position to accept your kind invitation. I am hopeful that future circumstances might allow me to visit with you in Khartoum and to extend a reciprocal invitation for you to visit us here in the United States.'[17]

Six weeks later the US Embassies in Kenya and Tanzania were blown to pieces.

Despite the rejection of their earlier offer from the White House, Sudanese officials retained sporadic contacts with the FBI. On 9 August 1998, two days after the embassy bombings, two Pakistani nationals – Sayyid Nazir Abbass and Sayyid Iskandar Sayyid – arrived in Khartoum from Nairobi and sought to rent an apartment close to the US Embassy building, but were arrested when Sudanese officials became suspicious of them. Via an intermediary, through whom Sudan retained contacts with US intelligence officials in Cairo, they informed the FBI that the two were being held on suspicion of involvement in the embassy bombings. Yahia Babiker, the Deputy Secretary General of Sudan's ESB, told me later that the two men were also thought to have been an advance team sent to organise the bombing of the US Embassy in Khartoum.[18]

But when Sudan offered to make the two men available for interview, the FBI turned them down, for reasons which remain unclear; they were instead handed over to Pakistan's Inter-Services Intelligence agency and permitted to travel back – as it happened – to Afghanistan.

The political pressure in Washington to prevent the FBI and CIA from dealing with the Sudanese bears a striking resemblance to the efforts of successive British governments in the 1970s and 1980s to – at least officially – ban the intelligence services from 'talking to terrorists'. But the CIA was less prepared to defy the Clinton White House than was SIS to defy Downing Street, as a former CIA officer with intimate knowledge of US–Sudan intelligence cooperation told me: 'The Sudanese did everything the US asked for, and they expected there would be some sort of signal from Washington in return. But nothing came.' Other US officials believe the rigid US opposition to Sudan's Government meant that relative moderates within that Government were weakened, allowing hardliners to increase their influence. 'The problem for the moderates was that the US didn't sufficiently respond. There were moderates in Sudan who wanted to meet legitimate US concerns,'[19] said a senior US official with long experience of Sudan.

Frustration with US intransigence was voiced by Yahia Babiker in his dim office close to the railtrack that runs through Khartoum, where I first met him in October 1999:

> We are not going to compromise with everything in order to please the Americans. They are not ready to be pleased. But we are willing to be very cooperative at all levels, and we are ready to talk to anybody and to listen to their concerns. If they are sincere then so are we. There are many important security issues – drug trafficking, terrorism, money laundering. And though we won't be running after them, we are ready to cooperate with the Americans in all these areas.[20]

He added, 'We suggested to the US that if they wanted to send some FBI delegates to check for themselves what was going on in the camps, and even if they wanted them to be stationed in Khartoum as part of their embassy, we would not object.'[21]

By then it had been a year since the East African embassy bombings had revealed just how serious the threat from al-Qaeda had become. At least three of those later indicted for the bombings were associates of bin Laden about whom the Sudanese could have provided intelligence material. One was Fazul Abdullah Mohammed, who was based in Khartoum throughout the planning period, another was Saif al-Adel, who became the al-Qaeda 'number three' in 2001, and a third was Wadih al-Hage, bin Laden's former personal secretary, who had been involved in establishing the Nairobi cell.[22]

For Sudan the price of its past hosting of Osama bin Laden had been high: in response to the embassy bombings, US cruise missiles were launched on 20 August 1998 on a settlement in Afghanistan at which bin Laden had been located, and on a pharmaceutical factory on the outskirts of Khartoum – al-Shifa – in which the al-Qaeda leader was alleged by the US Government to have been an investor even after Sudan expelled him and two hundred of his associates in 1996.

Despite 66 cruise missiles having been fired on six locations, the attack on Afghanistan did little more than turn up some dust; but the launching of 13 cruise missiles on al-Shifa served as proof that the intelligence war against al-Qaeda – then still in its infancy – was being lost before it had really begun. It was intelligence that was cited as justification for the attack on the factory,[23] not only through the alleged association with bin Laden – which the United States later reversed, a former senior State Department official telling me later, 'It was astonishing that Washington didn't know that [the businessman] Saleh Idriss [who had no connection with bin Laden] had bought that factory'[24] – but also an accusation that the factory was being used to produce EMPTA, a precursor that could be used in the production of chemical weapons. This accusation was also found by the investigative agency Kroll to be wrong: soil samples supposedly showing such chemical activity, which I was later told had been provided to the United States by the Egyptian intelligence service, were found to have been collected across the road from the factory, were nothing to do with what was being produced at al-Shifa, and contained no evidence of precursor; earlier evidence of the presence of EMPTA had been presented to the National Security Council, Richard Clarke telling officials that the substance had 'floated away from the plant in the air or in liquid runoff'.[25]

Such flaky assertions barely constituted intelligence, and were the price the United States was paying for closing the door – by withdrawing all its diplomats from Sudan on 7 February 1996 – on the intelligence value that the Khartoum regime could have been providing, as Yahia Babiker told me when we met again after 9/11:

> The normal thing [in the past and elsewhere in the world] is that the intelligence services do retain their relations even if the political ties are not good and even if they are severed. One of the mistakes [the United States] made was that they severed the intelligence ties. This was one of the awkward things that happened. They didn't want to give Sudan any chance. They weren't willing or able to verify anything with us. Being out of the country itself left a gap in their thinking generally about Sudan, which is what led to the fiasco of the al-Shifa bombing. Generally speaking, severing the ties with Sudan created a hole.'[26]

On the road back into the centre of Khartoum, the city's rattling yellow taxis ground their gears and juddered past the acacia trees which cast squat shadows onto the two-storey office on McNimr Street wherein bin Laden's Taba Investment company had once been housed. The office door was locked, the only evidence that this was once the engine room of what later became a sprawling terrorist empire being a faded orange sign on the wall, reading 'Taba'.

In an office on the upper floor of Khartoum's presidential palace, overlooking what were that day the dangerously high waters of the Nile, Gutbi al-Mahdi peered through his thick spectacles and explained what might have been. 'We have to know how a terrorist is born. What happened to make him such a person?'[27] al-Mahdi, the head of Sudan's external intelligence service during bin Laden's stay in Sudan, told me, detailing what intelligence Sudan had been prepared to share with the United States if only the Clinton Administration had been more ready to listen.

> The turning point in bin Laden's life is very important. He left Sudan and he was very bitter. He felt he was doing good work in Sudan. He didn't commit any crime. Then he was thrown into Afghanistan. He left all his wealth here. He is broke. The [Sudan] Government owes him a lot of money. He lost all his money in Sudan, because we confiscated all his property. There is nothing he can do in Afghanistan except fight. When he was expelled we expelled all his two hundred

people with him. These are people who feel they have absolutely no future. All doors are closed. And they are under nobody's control. We think these are the kinds of mistakes which we feel have contributed a lot to this situation.

In the wake of 9/11 the United States reversed its approach to Sudan, and the intelligence sharing began, as al-Mahdi explained:

The intelligence we have been offering the Americans [since 9/11] is exactly the same as we have been offering them since the early 1990s. We have given them profiles of Arab Afghan people who were mainly associated with bin Laden. Their files are complete and up to date. We have been able to understand how the Islamists react in certain situations. We have the same background. We are an Islamist movement. One thing they have come to learn is that [the terrorists in the United States] are in cells rather than a network.

Sudan's acquiescence in the face of US and Saudi pressure to expel bin Laden in 1996, and to then seek to repair relations with Washington, was, however, a major blow to its standing among the radicals it had – under the guiding hand of the Islamist ideologue Hassan el-Tourabi – sought to influence across the Islamic world. Something of a sea-change in Sudanese political life took place in the late-1990s;[28] this ended in El-Tourabi being cast into the political wilderness, and has seen him in and out of prison since 1999. Even so, few senior members of the Sudanese regime acknowledge that the course and cause of bin Laden's radicalisation was probably more strategic than it was simply the result of events. 'Pressuring Sudan to kick out Osama bin Laden left him with no option but to fight. If they had been left in Sudan, they would have been content,'[29] Babiker told me. By then he had become the central figure within the Sudanese intelligence apparatus to be trading secrets with the Bush Administration, as it sought to gather as much intelligence on al-Qaeda as it could:

What we have been doing [with the United States] is to clear our record. We have been trying to show the Americans that the information that they have about Sudan is incorrect and that it's very bad for an intelligence agency to have wrong information. We are opening up our books. When we have information [about something the United States is interested in] we do respond.

He continued, 'We are helping them understand the bin Laden organisation. Not by indicting people. But they have used our records and have met with some people who have helped give them an insight into the way that Osama bin Laden and his people are thinking.'

In fact they were doing much more than that – all of it clearly far too late, the most actionable intelligence – specifically, the identities of those known to be close to bin Laden – having been offered three years before the East African embassy bombings and five years before 9/11.

But what further illustrated how unwise the Clinton White House had been in not taking up the Sudanese offer earlier, was what emerged from the revelations of a 'walk in' al-Qaeda informer who had turned up at the US Embassy in Asmara, Eritrea in 1996. The informer, Jamal al-Fadl, had been a close associate of bin Laden since 1989, and had been one of three initial signatories to the 'contract' by which adherents signed up to al-Qaeda. Having moved with bin Laden to Sudan in 1991, one of al-Fadl's most important roles was to 'vet' would-be recruits to al-Qaeda – a role which entailed his close cooperation with the Sudanese intelligence service, the ESB, and which gave him access to ESB intelligence files on these individuals.

In his testimony to a New York court in February 2001, al-Fadl was asked, 'Can you explain the relationship between the intelligence service in the Sudan and al-Qaeda after al-Qaeda relocated to the Sudan?' Al-Fadl replied by explaining to the court that bin Laden had requested he work with the 'delegation office ... because he tell me a lot of people come under Islamic Group but they try to get information to other country and we want to make sure, we don't want any problem, we don't want anybody come, and he work for other country'.[30] This concern that Sudan's readiness to admit Muslims from across the world exposed al-Qaeda to infiltration, took root among those around bin Laden. As part of an effort to ensure that individuals who might have been sent to spy on what was going on in Sudan – whether within al-Qaeda's camps or elsewhere – bin Laden put in place a counter-intelligence strategy led between 1992 and 1994 by al-Fadl. This – al-Fadl explained to the New York court in 2001, and which he had already explained during five years of debriefing by the CIA since he had appeared in Asmara – necessitated knowing what the Sudanese intelligence service had in its files. Thus when al-Fadl defected from al-Qaeda in 1996 he knew at least some of what Sudan knew, and was in a position to inform the United States of what was in the files that the Clinton White House had refused to allow the FBI and CIA to look at.

As al-Fadl told the court, this relationship was reciprocal. The Sudanese would ask al-Fadl for intelligence about new arrivals in Sudan:

> If [Sudan's] intelligence office they find somebody they don't know, he was in Afghanistan but they don't know him very well, they ask me if I know him, if I saw him over there, and sometimes we make interview for him, we ask him about jihad, about fatwah, when he began which group he work, if inside work over there, which company he train. After that, I make report and I put my analysis, if what he said is correct or wrong, and if I say this guy problem guy.[31]

The fragments which coalesced into al-Qaeda continued to be seen only as fragments in part because the Western intelligence community all too often appeared to deny itself the capability to piece it together. Friction within the CIA, as well as between the CIA and other departments of the US Government, prevented an understanding emerging of the trend within political Islam and the communities in which it had taken root, which would be al-Qaeda's recruiting ground. A better understanding of the trend is unlikely to have led to the 9/11 plot being exposed, but it would likely have led to a greater sense of urgency as to where intelligence resources should be deployed; the 9/11 plot might have been stumbled across as a result, if only by preventing the hijackers reaching the United States, on grounds of suspicion.

Much that could have cast light on both this political trend and the community in which it had taken root, was available in Sudan in the late 1990s. But it was only a few weeks before 9/11 that the FBI and CIA counter-terrorism teams delivered their verdict that the regime in Khartoum was no longer a supporter of terrorism – a decision that was followed by the FBI then visiting the Sudanese capital to review the ESB's files. What would once have been crucial, actionable intelligence was by then some years out of date, as the 'Global War on Terror' – the 'GWOT' – came to be launched, and Sudan became a part of what would lead to the intelligence catastrophe of 9/11 and the revolution in intelligence operations which has since followed. For instead of 'watching and waiting' in rooftop straw huts and listening posts as the spied-upon went about their business, the spies of the 'GWOT' would then have *carte blanche* to grab who they wanted, transport them to the hidden corners of the globe, and use any means to extract al-Qaeda's secrets. Intelligence gathering would be replaced by arrests, 'drones' and torture.

Thus Sudan, like all other states too cowed to question President Bush's 'either you are with us, or you are with the terrorists' threat made to nations which did not cooperate with his Government's worldwide effort, rallied to the flag that fluttered in the breeze over the citadel of the twenty-first century intelligence community's 'new world': Guantanamo Bay.

8

GUANTANAMO DAYS

Life at Jacksonville naval air station in Florida came to a sudden halt at 8 a.m., as it does each day. 'The Star-Spangled Banner' filled the air, blasting out of loudspeakers at every street corner. Vehicles juddered to a halt in mid-turn as their drivers saluted the flag. Troops in short-sleeve shirts, ill-fitting trousers and patent-leather shoes stopped in mid-stride and stood to attention. The staff at the on-base branch of McDonalds fell silent, hoping the Egg McMuffins wouldn't burn before the last bars of the anthem had been played.

The sun had risen above the cavernous aircraft hangars which surrounded the small terminal building. The murmur of tired voices bubbled up from the orderly queue that had formed at the check-in for the military charter flight that would take me to Cuba. We filed silently out into the glare of the sun, kids holding dolls, mothers shielding their eyes, troops in civilian clothes.

The 737 roared into the clouds over Florida. Marines with elaborate tattoos, army wives dressed as if from the 1970s, and their freckle-faced children, all roared with laughter at the in-flight entertainment. The airline magazine led on an article about a celebrity TV presenter's favourite eateries across America. A flight attendant handed out bland ham sandwiches as 30,000 feet below us the Caribbean swirled and exotic islands drifted in and out of the hurricane season. Then, after a couple of hours, the eastern tip of Cuba rose dry and brown out of the azure waters that lapped its surf-fringed shoreline.

I ambled across the tarmac at the Guantanamo Bay naval base, wondering what would happen next. But not for long. I was quickly taken into the grip of a firm military handshake, then handed a neatly typed itinerary for my visit, had my baggage sniffed by a salivating dog, and was driven in a bus to some military housing on a slope overlooking the sea. In a daze spurred by sudden fatigue and rising heat, I was told what I would do, where I would go, whom I would meet. I was taken to eat deep-fried chicken wings washed down with Corona beer, in a bar where a TV on full volume played baseball and football and basketball and baseball again. The afternoon drifted into evening and as a glorious sunset oozed over the closing moments of my twenty-four hour journey from London, I fell into a deep sleep in the room I had been allotted.

It seemed only minutes later that a loud knock on the door marked the beginning of Day One.

That first journey to Guantanamo Bay, in October 2004, had really begun a decade or more earlier, during the visits I had made to Khartoum to talk long into the evening with Hassan El-Tourabi as he plotted out Sudan's future as the epicentre of a global Islamic movement,[1] the most startling aspect of which I saw in Kabul in the winter of 1996 as the Taliban consolidated its power in the Afghan capital.[2] Anybody who wanted to see and take note of all the events, trends and anger that had ended in the 'surprise' of 9/11 could have known it was no surprise at all. It had been as inevitable as it was predictable.

But neither of these sad facts means it could have been prevented.

At its heart the intelligence failure that preceded 9/11 can only be judged as such if it can be demonstrated that the evidence which should specifically have pointed to what was about to happen had been deliberately ignored or dismissed. But the process of assessing what should or should not be have been done to *prevent* it demands a step much further back than the arrival at Newark Airport, New Jersey of the lead hijacker, Mohamed Atta, in June 2000. Just as was the case in the Ireland of 1919–21, the 'failure' lay in the failure to understand the society from which the enemy had emerged: just as the British failed to understand the sentiments by which Irish opinion was being driven, so the United States – as well as its allies and their intelligence agencies – failed to understand not only how deep and broad was the anti-Western feeling which had coalesced into al-Qaeda, but how far this feeling had been channelled into plans. Above all, the CIA and others simply did not consider al-Qaeda – nor the world of radical Islam more broadly – to have the competence or courage to carry out such an attack. In essence, Western governments and agencies were blinded by their own preconceptions.

When the Sudanese 'walk-in' informer Jamal al-Fadl sat down in the visa office of the US Embassy in Asmara in June 1996, and told the official behind the glass that he wanted to speak with American officials about al-Qaeda, the intelligence officers with whom he subsequently spoke took him very seriously indeed. Five years later al-Fadl appeared as a key witness at the trial – *in absentia* – of Osama bin Laden, the al-Qaeda leader, who stood accused of involvement in the East African embassy bombings of August 1998.[3] In the meantime al-Fadl had provided the CIA and later the FBI with a more comprehensive account of the motivations, general intentions and structure of al-Qaeda than even the double-agent Ali Mohamed. Al-Fadl's value owed much to his having been a relatively more constant presence at the heart of the terrorist organisation, since a day in the autumn of 1989 when a bin Laden associate – Abu Ayoub al-Iraqi – convened a meeting of some of the more long-established 'Arab-Afghans' present at the Farook training camp near the Afghan village of Khowst.

First asked in the New York courtroom in 2001 for a general account of what he had become a part of at that meeting in 1989, al-Fadl was then specifically asked to explain the role of Abu Ayoub al-Iraqi:

> He bring a lot of papers and he give each person three and he say read and we make lecture and we talk about what we want to do…
> He said we going to make group and this is group that under Farook (that is, within the Farook camp), and it's going to be one man for the group and it's going to be focussed in jihad and we going to use the group to do another thing out of Afghanistan;'
> *Question*: 'And did Abu Ayoub al Iraqi tell you what the name of this group was?'

Answer. 'Yes.'
Question: 'Can you tell the jury what the name of the group was?'
Answer. 'Al-Qaeda.'[4]

Al-Fadl was then asked,

> Explain what the al-Qaeda agenda was. Can you tell us what
> those papers [distributed at the meeting] said about the al-Qaeda
> agenda?'
>
> *Answer.* 'The al-Qaeda, it's established for focus in jihad, to do the jihad.'
>
> *Question*: 'And did it indicate – at that time did the agenda indicate what
> the jihad was directed against?'
>
> *Answer.* 'Say again.'
>
> *Question*: 'Was there a particular target that the jihad was directed at
> during that time?'
>
> *Answer.* 'Not at that time.'[5]

While seeming small-scale and apparently vague, the tenor of the
discussions at the Farook camp is testimony to the complexity of what
– even on that very first day of al-Qaeda's existence – was already
evident. Asked to identify the other people at the meeting and the
members of the five committees of al-Qaeda that it was announced to
those present had been established, al-Fadl listed Abu Ayoub al-Iraqi
and other committee members – including bin Laden's future closest
associate, Ayman al-Zawahiri – and was then asked,

> Did you understand whether or not Abu Ayoub al Iraqi had anyone
> that he reported to?'
>
> *Answer.* 'At that time our general emir, Usama Muhammad al Wahal
> bin Laden.'
>
> *Question*: 'After you joined al-Qaeda [at the end of 1989]... When you
> signed the contract, did you have an understanding of how many
> persons had previously signed the contract that you did?'
>
> *Answer.* 'Yes.'

Then later:

> *Question*: 'Were you told at that time what the structure of al-Qaeda
> was, in other words, who belonged and what positions they were
> in?'
>
> *Answer.* 'Yes... It got emir and different committees.'
>
> *Question*: 'Besides the emir, can you tell us what the committees were
> in al-Qaeda?'

Al-Fadl then went on to identify the *Shura* council, which provided overall guidance, the military committee, which was responsible for training, the 'money and business committee', which arranged funding and travel, the *'fatwa* and Islamic study committee', and the media committee, which published a newspaper called *Nashrat al Akhbar*.[6]

It would not be until seven years after the creation of al-Qaeda at the Farook camp that the CIA became privy to what had happened that day, the full story only being told after al-Fadl's appearance in Asmara in 1996. The intervening period would see the FBI follow the leads provided by Ali Mohamed, Billy Waugh taking snapshots of Osama bin Laden in Khartoum for the CIA, the 1993 World Trade Center bombers bringing large-scale terrorism to Manhattan, the attack on the USS *Cole* in Aden harbour in 2000, the creation of the CIA's Alec Station under the leadership of Michael Scheuer, and the CIA, FBI, NSA and other constituent parts of the US intelligence community demonstrating just how ill-inclined they were to share with each other what it was that they were learning.

But even if they had been sharing, 9/11 would not have been prevented.

As he would later do in his February 2001 court appearance, Jamal al-Fadl had been able throughout the late 1990s to make clear to the US authorities that bin Laden regarded the United States with deep hostility. To demonstrate this he cited the issuance of several *fatwas* against perceived US aggression, specifically the stationing of US troops in Saudi Arabia following the 1990 invasion of Kuwait by Iraq, and subsequently the US-led humanitarian intervention in Somalia in 1992. He told the court about a meeting of al-Qaeda adherents after the move to Sudan in 1991: 'They say the fatwah, it say we cannot let the American army stay in the Gulf area and take our oil, take our money, and we have to do something to take them out. We have to fight them.'[7] He then added that among those present there was a concern that the US presence in Somalia might lead to a similar intervention in southern Sudan.[8]

In further questioning, al-Fadl was asked whether there was a discussion at that time of attacks against civilians, and he referred to a conversation between several of the al-Qaeda followers which had included reference to the teachings of the fourteenth-century Syrian scholar Taqi ad-Din Ahmad ibn Taymiyyah, who was regarded by those who had moved with bin Laden to Khartoum as having justified such killing when he said,

> When a tartar come to Arabic war... He said anybody around the tartar, he buy something from them and he sell them something, you should kill him. And also, if when you attack the tartar, if anybody around them, anything, or he's not military or that – if you kill him, you don't have to worry about that. If he's a good person, he go to paradise and if he's a bad person, he go to hell.

He went on to emphasise that 'collateral damage' – that is, the deaths of innocents who were close to 'legitimate' targets – was of no concern to the jihadis.[9]

Beyond the cast-iron determination of al-Qaeda to strike at the United States, other theories have emerged as to why what happened was not averted.

In his otherwise compelling account of the life and role of the double-agent Ali Mohamed, the writer Peter Lance digs deep into the workings of the FBI, the Department of Justice, and the handling of information gathered following the 1993 World Trade Center bombing, but then posits the startling theory that vital clues as to what would happen on 11 September 2001 *were* deliberately 'buried' – because 'FBI investigators and federal prosecutors were desperate to avoid a scandal over an alleged corrupt relationship' between an FBI Special Agent and a mafia 'hit man'.[10] But even though better, more responsible and more astute handling of the intelligence that was being gathered would certainly have provided a fuller picture of al-Qaeda's activities, it is highly unlikely that any of it would have led to the doors of the 19 hijackers.

In their well-informed account of the FBI and CIA failings that preceded 9/11, the journalists John Miller, Michael Stone and Chris Mitchell are as wishful as Lance, quoting an 'intelligence official' as saying, 'Al-Fadl was the Rosetta Stone. After al-Fadl everything fell into place.'[11] But, of course, no such thing happened: what al-Fadl knew would not turn the tide. What did 'fall into place', however, was an unprecedented degree of confirmation that al-Qaeda was well-resourced, extensive and determined. What al-Fadl could not do was provide details of specific future plots – for the simple reason that he did not know about them, his 'defection' from al-Qaeda in 1996 stemming from his disaffection with the rewards it offered, and – as he has admitted to the FBI – from his embezzlement of $100,000 from the organisation while he was running part of its business affairs from the 'Taba' office I had passed by in Khartoum.[12]

Reliance on intelligence whose value was more strategic than operational – that is, intelligence which might cast light on the general aims of the jihadis, but without providing details of specific plots – heightened the need to establish agents *within* the organisation who were prepared and able to spy long term. Without identifying them or identifying for whom they were spying, al-Fadl himself said that three such spies were identified in that role while al-Qaeda was in Sudan in 1991–96: two were imprisoned, the other executed.[13] As Michael Scheuer told me, 'When we were working against the USSR, the hardest person to recruit [as a spy] was the one at the outer edge of the target', where there were individuals who could observe without being noticed. He went on, 'With the Islamist target it's fairly easy to get somebody who is not quite so devout. But as they get closer to the centre' they become more so, and are more resistant to being recruited as spies:

> Getting people inside al-Qaeda was extremely difficult. The senior officers of the [CIA] clandestine service are so unwilling to say that there is something that they can't do, that they say: 'we will do it'. But until you realise that you're working against an ideology you're not going to have much success. And because it's unlikely you're going to have the plans for a 9/11, the type of person you recruit will be someone who can tell you what is in the valley next door and can get you a reading. You are never going to have a one hundred percent Enigma-type intelligence [referring to the Enigma machine which allowed the British to decipher German intelligence communications during World War II].

The response to these changed circumstances was what I saw on a rocky spit of land in the Caribbean. The creation of the prison at Guantanamo Bay was a mark of how far the rules of the intelligence war – which for the duration of the Cold War had been characterised by trading, 'tit-for-tat' exchanges, 'hotlines' and détente – had been overturned. The camps at 'Gitmo' revolutionised the lives of the spies; once the sources had been hunted down, no longer would they be observed, bugged or subtly approached. Instead, in the dead of night or just before dawn the special forces, police units or snatch squads would break into homes, grab slumbering suspects, and within hours be hauling them – blindfolded, bound, shackled – into the bellies of transport aircraft for the long trip to the Caribbean. The spies would bring their sources to them – a captive spy ring, which the Cuban regime would watch through binoculars from the other side of a tall chain-link fence. With al-Qaeda so elusive, the potential to spy on, buy off or 'turn' the inner circle around Osama bin Laden so slight, and the battle, as Michael Scheuer said, being 'against an ideology', the agencies – specifically the CIA – opted instead to capture those they might once have recruited, incarcerate those they might once have permitted to 'run', and brutalise those they might once have coaxed and cajoled.

With the intelligence 'pipeline' to the heart of al-Qaeda all but dry – the 'market' in secrets having effectively closed, owing to the organisation's leadership and those around it having no apparent inclination to make deals – Camp Delta and its constituent prison blocks was intended to re-establish the intelligence war along lines the Western institutions fighting it could foresee as offering the only hope of progress; the trade would be between prisoners and torturers – prisoners would tell their interrogators what they knew, and in return they would be drip-fed rewards, in the form of 'privileges' within the confines of their prison life. The aim was to have a readily available, wholly captive pool of individuals who could be pressed for insights into events taking place around the world; photographs could be shown to them, names could be checked, relationships discussed – in the hope that some of what the captives knew could inform the assessment of the intelligence officers who were tracking events in the countries from which this ever-growing number of captives had come.

Just as the launch of asymmetric war had been heralded most dramatically by the 9/11 attacks, so this revolution in intelligence gathering took place. The CIA brought its assets to the heat and dust of the Caribbean having realised that – with so much of the damage already done – much of what it wanted to know was probably no longer secret; and by holding its intelligence assets incommunicado, it minimised the risk of seeing its aims and interests disclosed.

The difficulties acknowledged by Michael Scheuer in the months and years prior to 9/11 were illustrated by what followed, as first the cages of Camp X-Ray and later the cell blocks of Camp Delta began to fill up.

By 11 September 2001 al-Qaeda's careful vetting of recruits – as Jamal al-Fadl had explained in the context of Sudan – had paid-off: senior-level infiltration by Western intelligence agencies had not succeeded. The challenge facing the agencies was unprecedented. They knew a lot about al-Qaeda from 'walk-ins' like Ali Mohamed and Jamal al-Fadl, as well as from investigations, and from at least some liaison with the Saudi, Pakistani, Egyptian and – finally, in the days before the attacks – the Sudanese intelligence agencies. Even so, the 'Rosetta Stone' which could decipher all the intelligence 'chatter', as it is called, and crystallise it into hard fact, was not within their grasp.

But in addition to the general ill-preparedness of the FBI and the CIA to share and co-operate with each other as they should have done, the *historic* nature of the challenge they faced stemmed from their having gathered as much intelligence as they had done *without* then being able to anticipate what might happen next. The more than forty boxes of material gathered in Brooklyn during the investigation into the 1993 World Trade Center bombing, and the substantial amount of documentation seized during a joint US–Kenyan swoop on a house in Nairobi, were two examples of steps being taken that had added to the overall understanding of the al-Qaeda structure. But plots cannot be predicted; only spying can reveal them. All the signs can be present and can be pointing in the same direction – as they were, in the form of *fatwas* issued by al-Qaeda's Fatwa Committee, as well as intelligence gathered after the East African embassy bombings; but unless there is a spy on the inside, generalised knowledge ultimately has little real value.

It is this that made al-Qaeda such a unique intelligence target. In Ireland, the Dublin Metropolitan Police acknowledged after its defeat in the intelligence war with Michael Collins that the single deepest flaw in the intelligence gathering in 1919–21 had been the failure to *understand* how deep was the nationalist spirit – and therefore how deeply infiltrated by IRA spies it was likely that the British Administration had become. Sixty years later, Oleg Gordievsky's position allowed him to help craft Western responses to Soviet actions and statements as the Cold War wound down, by informing the Reagan and Thatcher Governments about Moscow's fears, anxieties and sense of vulnerability; by enlightening Britain and America as to these surprising realities about the 'evil empire', Gordievsky transformed *understanding* of the landscape to an extent that directly influenced Western responses to *glasnost* and *perestroika*.

But these earlier experiences had not prepared the intelligence agencies for the challenge from al-Qaeda.

The radical sentiments that set the tone of al-Qaeda's *fatwas* were no secret; the evidence of links between different jihadist groups had been well documented from the 1980s; the role of the National Islamic Front in Sudan as a 'state sponsor' of radical groups was common knowledge; the idea of using passenger aircraft as 'guided missiles' had emerged in terrorist 'chatter' about the so-called 'Bojinka Plot' in the early 1990s.[14] So much was not hidden it is small wonder that as the ash from the collapsed Twin Towers was still settling on the streets of Manhattan, the CIA and FBI were being branded as failures. But the failure was less one of intelligence regarding the plot and more one of the lack of readiness of the West in general – and its tough-minded intelligence agencies in particular – to countenance the possibility that what seemed like a fantasy could be turned into such a catastrophically successful reality: despite everything that was known, 9/11 still defied preconceptions and prejudices. The West in general, and the United States in particular, was left reeling because it could not quite believe that people who were operating in the circumstances in which bin Laden had by then found himself – among the mountains of Afghanistan – were technically and organisationally capable of carrying out such an act.

And as the dust settled, the 'Global War on Terror' – 'GWOT' – began.

It began badly, as al-Qaeda dispersed in the wake of US military operations in Afghanistan in October 2001, and the loose and sprawling agglomeration of like-minded veterans of the anti-Soviet war to which its message appealed, took the initiative across the world. The intelligence agencies struggled as they sought first to detect the emerging trends, then to latch on to them, then to see where they led, as a senior intelligence officer at the heart of the UK effort explained to me in 2002, at a time when the 'GWOT' seemed as if it was being lost:

What al-Qaeda people are doing is exploiting the natural flows of people: you used to be able to go to Dubai and move from there. Now, because countries like UAE, Kuwait and Yemen are simply not letting them in, they aren't travelling by aircraft, but are coming across the Gulf by boat. And there are hundreds of them doing it, from Karachi. But I am not even really sure what proportion of these people are al-Qaeda. It's very difficult to predict how this de-merged network will behave. But it is very difficult to imagine that there will be a regrouping, or that there needs to be. For some time to come what we are going to be dealing with is the remaining networks based on the twenty-eight [Afghan training] camps, and we will see to what extent this unformed network will continue to function.[15]

The post-9/11, US-led military campaign against al-Qaeda and the Taliban in Afghanistan meant that the task of mapping how the metamorphosing al-Qaeda structure might re-emerge, would be complicated by a multitude of unknowns. The failure to infiltrate al-Qaeda at a high level before 9/11 meant that the organisation's post-9/11 planning remained a mystery, at the heart of which was the question of whether it actually had any post-9/11 planning. The occasional clues that were thrown up were analysed intensely: when bin Laden issued an audio tape rather than a video tape in October 2002 it was assumed that this was a 'step down', as one European intelligence officer explained: 'He is currently unable to project himself as he wants,'[16] the inference being that the al-Qaeda leader was vulnerable, out of contact with his followers, and

it seems there's been some devaluation of command and control. Previously, he wanted to drive everything. But now he seems to be pushing things out. There's an interesting part of the tape, where he says he will 'be in touch personally' – the suggestion being that at the current time he is not in touch with his followers.

Further inferences were also being drawn by intelligence officers from the fact that bin Laden's key associate, Ayman al-Zawahiri, had issued a video tape at around the same time as bin Laden, in October 2002. The fact of one being audio, the other being video was interpreted as a sign that the two were not on the run together; as the senior intelligence officer told me, 'Zawahiri's tape suggests that he is prepared to take more risks than bin Laden,'[17] adding that the two tapes had 'come via different routes'.

A few days after the issue of the tapes emerged, I was sitting in on a Whitehall meeting as both the scale *and* the uniqueness of the challenge from al-Qaeda were being explained by a senior officer who was frank when he admitted that – whatever could be gathered from bugged telephones and email communications – the only really 'effective way of understanding what's going on is by having someone inside. When you have learned something it's because of human intelligence. It's something in which we have invested very heavily.'[18] He went on,

> The trouble with counter-terrorism intelligence is that it is coming from all sorts of different areas. It's a question of: what is useful? There are market forces operating – people try to sell it to you, and discrimination between good intelligence and rubbish is very difficult. You're in a balancing act the whole time.

When two bombs ripped through several nightclubs at Kuta on the Indonesian island of Bali on 12 October 2002, killing 202 people, the 'balancing act' became even more precarious. Answers as to whether the attack had been instigated by al-Qaeda or was the work of local, like-minded activists acting alone, would provide vital clues as to how the *global* movement was structured, what its capabilities were, and how it could be confronted. But as I was told in the immediate aftermath of the Bali bombing, 'Most of the intelligence is so general as to not be useful. And there's this economic theme running through al-Qaeda targeting. It's almost a weakness in al-Qaeda,'[19] the perception being that al-Qaeda's leadership had singled out 'economic' targets such as the World Trade Center or Indonesia's tourist industry with a view to crippling the West where it most hurt.

For the Western intelligence agencies the Bali bombing nevertheless provided major clues as to what one officer described to me at the time as al-Qaeda's 'transformation', which brought with it an intensification in the intelligence war.

A focus of this aspect of the post-9/11 conflict was on the use of video and audio broadcasts by bin Laden. As I was told, 'Bin Laden isn't interested in communicating with you and me. He goes on air to communicate with people who think like him.' It was on reaching the conclusion that the messages being issued by the al-Qaeda leader were likely to have numerous purposes, that discussions regarding how to handle the growing number of arrests worldwide of al-Qaeda suspects, intensified. A senior CIA officer told me, 'It wouldn't be very surprising if they (al-Qaeda) didn't have a plan for the release of information on arrests.'[20]

The handling of the arrests quickly became a major challenge, as the CIA in particular realised how rapidly the intelligence gathered from detainees could become redundant if the fact of their arrest became known to those still at liberty, as a senior CIA officer explained:

> What is coming out with the arrests is an understanding of the degree of autonomy of the different militant groups. We see now that it would be a mistake to take the 9/11 model – that is, the wiring of money and orders from the centre – because we don't now think that bin Laden's communications are good enough.[21]

But the fracturing of central control meant that the CIA – and more specifically the NSA and GCHQ, the US and UK Governments' listening stations – could not intensify their focus on the channels which had previously led to the centre, because post-9/11 al-Qaeda was diffuse to the point where it had no obvious centre, as its activities spread from Bali to Yemen to Saudi Arabia, to Spain and the United Kingdom. Nor could SIS and the CIA – nor even their allies among intelligence agencies in Pakistan and elsewhere – expect to depend on human intelligence sources to provide a scale of coverage that would meet the challenge. As one example of how uncertain the intelligence picture was in countries in which the threat appeared to be emerging, the US planned and cancelled three times the attack on a Yemeni group associated with al-Qaeda. Only on the third occasion was a Hellfire missile launched – on 5 November 2002 – from an unmanned 'drone', which struck a convoy in Marib Province, killing Ali Qaed Sunian al-Harithi and five others: 'The thing that held them back was the inadequacy of the intelligence they had,'[22] a Middle East intelligence officer close to the CIA told me.

The emergence shortly after 9/11 of first Yemen and then Somalia as draws both for activity by groups sharing a similar purpose to that of al-Qaeda, and as countries within which the fragility or absence of government control allowed these groups to operate largely unhindered

– roles which today both countries are playing even more obviously than in the aftermath of 9/11 – intensified discussion within the intelligence agencies as to where the threat was likely to next come from, and therefore what the intelligence-gathering priority should be. A senior European intelligence officer explained to me at that time, 'Focusing on Osama bin Laden is a real mistake. It's really the fragments of the network that will tell us most. The question is: how do we piece the fragments together?'[23]

But as the agencies sought to discern what the new landscape looked like, governments showed their hand in ways which exposed the gulf in understanding between the intelligence community and ministers. A warning of a 'specific threat' that was issued by the UK Home Office on 8 November 2002 provoked outrage within the intelligence agencies, deeply concerned as they were that even the smallest detail or hint as to how the fight against al-Qaeda was being fought should not be allowed to emerge into the public domain.

The desperation of the agencies – and in particular the realisation that infiltration into the multitude of cells and networks was so challenging that the arrest of suspects was likely to provide more immediate and fruitful leads – meant that action taken to identify and seize suspects was best done by third parties. As early as November 2002 a very well-placed intelligence official told me that 'the Americans are getting other people to do their interrogation – the Moroccans in particular. I don't think there are any American interrogations that are being done in the United States.' By then the go-between who allegedly liaised between the lead 9/11 hijacker Mohamed Atta and the main planner of the attacks, Khaled Sheikh Mohamed[24] – a Yemeni, Ramzi Binalshibh – was in the hands of Moroccan interrogators, while al-Qaeda's supposed 'number three' Abu Zubaydah had been captured in March 2002 and was among the first to be shipped, shackled and blindfolded to that rocky outcrop in the Caribbean, where he has been subject to 83 sessions of 'water-boarding' – simulated drowning – as well as beatings, humiliation, sleep deprivation, and weeks of ill-treatment, which have left him brain-damaged.[25]

9

PRISONERS

As dawn broke over the Bay, the claws of a turkey vulture clattered onto the quayside.[1] It flapped its ragged wings then squatted on the concrete, as the vehicle ramp of the US naval ferry the *R.M. Hunnington* scraped up the slope for the first run of a grey morning. The official history of Guantanamo Bay probably explains who R.M. Hunnington was. I never had time to find out. The vessel plied the swirling currents between the two sectors of the US naval station which surround the Bay. To the south there were a few miles of US-controlled water, where coastguard patrols lingered in the haze before the open sea. The airstrip and the Combined Bachelor Quarters where I had slept the night, were in the east, within the chain-link fence that split America from its communist neighbour.

A large fan, leaning crooked on the sand, blew warm air through the gathering of stiff-backed, crew-cut Military Police who stood beneath a canopy of sun-drenched tarpaulin. 'Honour Bound,' the troops said, saluting. 'Defend Freedom,' was the response, mantras that were stirring and comical in equal measure. Then the mix of bull-necked youngsters and grey-haired reservists who were the gatekeepers to Camp Delta fired their questions at visitors to the camp. Rules were applied, permissions sought, and telephone calls made to obtain 'advisories' on who was allowed entry. Every soldier, sailor and airman who passed through the gate tore a strip off a reel of black tape and stuck it over the name tag on their uniform. I was told that the reservists had been pulled away from

145

jobs or retirement in Utah and Colorado. Some were fire officers, or ran small businesses; others were employees of the US Prison Service. And there they were, bound in honour, defending freedom, donning rubber gloves to prevent contagion as they staffed this barren landscape.

The bolts of the entry gate slid open and I stepped inside Camp Delta.

'They're getting more chatty,' the librarian told me. We were standing in a stuffy, windowless room lined with shelves of books – English books translated into 14 languages, ranging from Uighur to Arabic. Each week he delivered them to the 'deserving prisoners'.

The library was along a bare corridor in an air-conditioned prefab just inside the entrance gate. Doors led off to interrogation rooms on one side of the corridor. On the other, detainees were given the chance, by order of the US Supreme Court, to argue before the Combatant Status Review Tribunal (the CSRT) that they were not enemy combatants, and that they should therefore be released. The tribunals were what I had come to see. 'The Yemenis and Pakistanis are most keen on Agatha Christie,' the librarian continued. 'And one Saudi has become keen on *David Copperfield*. He keeps on reading that one book.'

In a dingy room beside the library I stood next to a man who was wearing headphones, and watched an interrogation through a one-way window. I could see a woman in trousers standing against the door, her hands in her back pockets, while a man seated at a table took notes. Against the far wall, shackled to the floor, a prisoner sat on a chair with his head bowed. After a few minutes I was led along the corridor, where young soldiers sat on wooden chairs, their shoulders hunched as they shifted from buttock to buttock to ease the discomfort of sentry duty.

The theory that lay behind the holding of 'enemy combatants' was put to the test at the end of the corridor. There, the limits to which a democracy can go to defend itself were being redefined. And it was there that secret intelligence was being put on trial.

I sat in a small, windowless room for a few minutes, with only the agitated tapping of an army officer's patent leather shoe disturbing the silence. Expressionless faces glanced at a lone figure sitting in the corner, then quickly looked away. The man's chains clattered as he raised a skinny finger from his orange prison suit and scratched his nose.

'All rise...'

Two men and a woman entered. All in uniform, they had eyes of stone and taut white lips. I will never forget their eyes and lips. The Tribunal President, a US army lieutenant-colonel, sat in the centre. Sitting beside the prisoner was the foot-tapping Personal Representative. His job was to guide the captive through the tribunal process, his identity hidden under the omnipresent strip of black tape. I had even been told to put my identity badge in my pocket, so the accused would remain mystified as to who exactly I was.

Only the chained man, a Kuwaiti, did not stand. His feet were shackled to the floor, and the handcuffs binding his wrists were attached to a heavy chain around his waist. Through an interpreter he was warned, 'If you become disorderly the court will continue to hear the evidence in your absence.'

The captive smiled, asking, 'Do the members of the tribunal have a background in law?'

The Tribunal President replied, 'They are military officers, and one is a judge advocate-general.'

'And the others: do they know anything about the law?'

The President replied, 'We have a general knowledge of the tribunal and the proceedings.'

'I am a civilian, so how can you try me in a military court?' The President told him that it was not a trial but a tribunal, and then asked for the charges to be read.

The Recorder, another officer, presented the evidence against the detainee in the form of a summary of a classified dossier, which the accused was told he could not see, so he would never know the full details of the case against him. The Recorder also had the task of providing his defence. The charges against the Kuwaiti included the accusation that he was a 'member of al-Qaeda' and that 'one of his aliases was on the hard drive of a computer belonging to a senior member of al-Qaeda.'

Then the detainee was asked if he had prepared a statement or comments in response. Breaking off at one point to apologise for the ever-present smile on his face, which he described as a 'long-time habit', he then took the rest of his life in his bony, shackled hands. Like all the detainees, he had no right to a lawyer to present his case.

The President interrupted his statement: 'We can offer the Muslim oath.'

The Recorder, who had read out the charges, declaimed in English, 'In the name of Allah the compassionate, the merciful...'

The detainee repeated the oath and then continued calmly,

> Regarding the accusation that I am a member of al-Qaeda. This accusation does not have anything to support it. It is merely words, with no evidence to prove it, as if monetary records were found on me to support that I had given money to al-Qaeda. Or that I was arrested in a place that is associated with al-Qaeda. Or that it was found that I had a strong relationship with Osama bin Laden. Or that at the time of my arrest I was found with a weapon. So, on what grounds have I been associated with al-Qaeda, when none of these things have been found?

He went on to deny that he had any aliases, and rejected the accusation that his alleged links to al-Qaeda could be proved by a false name on a computer: 'Let's assume that the name found was my name. I can't prevent anybody writing my name if they want to. It's out of my control. If Hitler wrote my name I wouldn't go to him and say, "Why did you write my name?"'

The tribunal listened in silence. He handed over a written testimony that the President said the three-member panel would 'take into consideration'. He was then asked why he had travelled without his passport from Afghanistan where he had been working, to Pakistan, and why it was 'inexplicable' that his name appeared on a computer said to belong to an al-Qaeda leader. The Kuwaiti responded by insisting that the wrong conclusions were being drawn, and that he had only been told after his arrest at the Pakistan–Afghanistan border that his name had been found on the computer, and that the accusation could not be used as retrospective justification for his detention.

Almost three hours had passed.

'All rise.'

Everybody stood but the prisoner, and the three panel members left the room in a line. The shackled man sat staring at the floor, waiting for the room to empty and for the arrival of the Military Police whose task it was to unlock his chains and guide him with their gloved hands back to his cell.

'In cases where they are found to be an enemy combatant, the classified material seals their fate,' an army colonel sitting in the room next door told me. Although the accusations read out to the detainee are 'derived from the classified information', the detainee has no chance to respond to the classified evidence, because it is not given to him. The detainees can call witnesses, 'and we say that the witness is someone who can provide information that is relevant'. Irrelevant witnesses are simply not called. Around half the witnesses have been other detainees. For numerous other witnesses deemed 'relevant' by the tribunal authority, 'we just couldn't find them,' the officer said. 'I personally think it's fair. It's a reputable process.'

But his voice was tinged with uncertainty. His gaze shifted from me to a row of television screens along one wall, some displaying images of empty rooms and others overlooking more shackled prisoners waiting to hear their fate: 'This is the first time in history that an enemy combatant has had the right to go in front of the accusers and contest it,' he said, as we walked out of the prefab.

In the searing Caribbean heat, soldiers greeted each other with a salute and the 'honour bound, defend freedom' mantra. Ahead of us, two gloved Military Police officers were holding a shackled prisoner at the wrists and shoulders as they shuffled him through the maze of mesh and wire. We stood aside. Speaking quietly enough to remain out of earshot, I asked him why the military had been given responsibility for the legal process. He paused and grimaced awkwardly. 'I don't know why it's in the hands of the military. As soldiers, we are not allowed to dip into that area. Aspects of it are moving towards the courts. It's an issue of: it's never been done before. It's new turf. Where it will end up? Who knows?' But then, perhaps aware that he was throwing doubt on the cast-iron certitude of his political masters in the Pentagon, he added,

I don't think anybody after September 11 knew how these things were supposed to be done. We had to take steps. There's a learning curve. How do you protect the American people and our allies in a human-rights- and civil-rights-compliant regime? How do you do this? They struggle with the answers to these questions in Washington.

Then the bolt closing the gate to Camp Delta slid shut behind me, as we stepped outside and onto the road that rises up the along coast.

Despite on-the-ground intelligence – such as that which had led to the missile attack in Yemen in November 2002 – having led to military operations, arrests and actions to thwart plots, the years after 9/11 saw all that might have worked in the past thrown out, in favour of methods and purposes which showed just how devastating a blow the actions of al-Qaeda had been. Gone was much of the careful, stealthy, covert surveillance; gone was the anonymity; off came the mask; off came the gloves; intelligence – and the agencies that embodied its role within the armouries of governments – was no longer a thing to be whispered about; in the post-9/11 world it was almost public property. Everybody had an opinion about it; the carefully honed methodology, the faces of its practitioners – and above all the methods used by agency officers to gather what they were now able to learn – overturned much that had been proven to work in the past. Bloodied by the accusation of 'failure' to either detect that 9/11 might be about to happen and – more – to prevent it, the CIA went to war.

But instead of spying it opted for that vengeful, generally unreliable and utterly outrageous method employed by desperate failures throughout history – torture.

Guantanamo Bay became the torture cell of the global intelligence effort, its 'resource' being dipped into by all the world's intelligence services, as was made clear to me by a senior intelligence officer whose service made frequent visits to the Camp Delta complex around which I had been wandering:

> The overwhelming block of intelligence information on terrorism in circulation today is American. When, for example, the Australians do an assessment, a very high proportion of that is based on American material which is circulated to intelligence allies. It's all the same stuff, and it's a question of analysis and then it's a question of political judgment. You have professionals who are given something about al-Qaeda, and they make an assessment and then a report goes to senior officials and ministers – and they then make a judgment.[2]

The CIA – like the 'foot-soldiers of foreign policy' its agents had been daubed in the 1960s and 1970s – sought ways of marrying the 'old' and the 'new', as a senior Agency official told me in November 2002 when I asked him specifically why it was that torture had become the routine means of extracting information from the detainees at Guantanamo Bay: 'Each kind of source of information has its own thing to contribute. Intercepted communication can be more timely. On the other hand, in terms of the comprehensibility of the sub-source, a detainee who talks can tell you a whole lot more than the intercepts. You need both.'[3] Concerning the by then 'broken' al-Qaeda 'number three', Abu Zubaydah, whose torture had been strongly justified by President Bush,[4] he said, 'The general assessment of the detainees is that some who have talked have talked a lot. But even they aren't telling all. I don't think that what we have found out from the detainees has given us enough of a sense of whether there is a [al-Qaeda] strategy.' Nor was it the case that 'walk-ins' like Jamal al-Fadl and Ali Mohamed could add much to an understanding of the 'strategy'; instead, al-Fadl was shown photographs of around seventy of the detainees being held at Guantanamo, and was useful in providing information regarding two of them.[5]

But other intelligence agencies remained divided over what was being learned from the interrogation of the detainees, a senior French officer telling me, 'Very little has been learned from them. The people they have [at Guantanamo] are mostly just foot soldiers who don't really know anything about the bigger picture of al-Qaeda. There's really been nothing learned about what al-Qaeda may be planning to do next.'[6] But a UK official said very much the opposite, telling me, 'The Camp X-Ray prisoners are giving information of interest.'[7]

At Guantanamo's 'Windjammer' restaurant, Major General Martin Lucenti was chatting freely about the legal status of the prisoners. Over steak and salad he told me frankly that most of the detainees would eventually be released because 'we don't have a level of evidence to feel that we can be confident to prosecute them [all].'[8] I asked him to repeat what he had said, and to confirm that his admission was on the record, which he did.

The Windjammer is Guantanamo Bay's upmarket eatery. It hummed with the murmur of voices, the clatter of knives and forks, the chatter and laughter of the senior ranks.

TRADING SECRETS

'We like to compare what we do here as being like a pitcher and a catcher in baseball. The interrogator is like the pitcher. The catcher is the one who sets up the questions,' a smiling, bespectacled, slightly overweight interrogator told me, the day after I met Lucenti. He was leading me along the network of concrete paths open to the sky and bordered by the fifteen-foot chain-link fences topped with razor wire that make up Camp Delta. 'Everything that we do we have to do in accordance with the Geneva Conventions. If you tortured, you wouldn't trust the information that we got. We are here for the long haul, and everything has to be ethical,' he asserted with a grin. 'There are some who have been very resistant, but after two and a half years they begin to talk. Gitmo (the military abbreviation for Guantanamo Bay) provides a unique place where we can do strategic interrogations. I want to keep these guys safe. We know a lot more about them than they think we do. We are just waiting for them to tell us in their own words.'

Intelligence was all that mattered. And it was not only the unearthing of plots and details about strategy. The creation of Camp Delta and all its constituent parts was the biggest single challenge to its identity the US had created since the days of 'segregation' in its southern states; at Guantanamo Bay the right to a legal hearing – *habeas corpus* – had been dispensed with; torture was routine and had been approved by President Bush; the vengefulness of a bloodied state had exposed the vulnerability and youthfulness of a 'superpower' that had been forced to come to terms with the fragility of national principles which it had assumed were inviolable but which now seemed eccentric; America was on the rampage, its Generals now seeming the last line of defence against an apparently imminent and unstoppable plunge into moral crisis, as Brigadier Jay Hood made clear to me when assuring this 'Brit' reporter that 'what we are doing is treating them consistent with each of the Geneva Conventions. This means every aspect of the human treatment and every aspect of investigation: we are operating in accordance with the Conventions. There are provisions for PoWs in the Geneva Conventions.'[9]

He went on, 'The people here are of tremendous intelligence value.' But as he did so I became convinced that it was not just terrorist plots and plans that the CIA interrogators and the Defense Department top brass were seeking to gather from the illegally detained extremists and others languishing on the spit of land against which the Caribbean lashed in fury. America was looking to learn about itself – and it neither liked nor understood what it was being told; so the military men and the torturers were given the run of the place, largely out of sight of lawyers, while the spies and soldiers sought to establish what it was that had really struck the United States on 11 September 2001. Hood went on,

> When we first established Camp X-Ray we had a long process of sorting out who we had. That sorting-out process took months. As we looked at the population [of prisoners], there was a group that we saw as of very low intelligence value. Within the remainder of the population we have a number of detainees who have been cooperating with camp rules and have been cooperative with us in our intelligence gathering. Others are clearly of significant intelligence value, and have been trained in counter-interrogation techniques. They have been extremely resistant to our efforts to get intelligence from them. In that group there is still a significant amount to learn. That piece of the population is significant. The greatest portion of that hard-core population are very clearly recorded al-Qaeda members – mid- and upper-level al-Qaeda. There's a small group of people at the top end from whom we haven't succeeded in getting that intelligence that we know they have. Intelligence has been gathered here that provided information on aspects of terrorist operations worldwide. Actions have been taken by European countries based on intelligence gathered here. What is shared with them, they may not even know that it came from here.

Then he paused, before adding,

> No American would tell you that the ends justify the means. If we are to carry out this mission for an extended period, we have got to make sure that we have got it right and that the rest of the world can see that we have got it right. I think it's worthwhile at least understanding that this is a conflict like no other that any of our countries have been involved in, against an enemy that is utterly different in terms of character and method. That's what steers the debate.

We were walking across a stretch of gravel that had been baked by the sun. Ahead, two Military Police officers gripping a stooping, shuffling, shackled prisoner approached us through the maze of wire mesh. Bolts slid open. An order was given to open the next gate. A bolt clanked shut as another opened. Between each gate was a holding area where the prisoner stood, held at the arm and shoulder by the MPs. Only one gate could be opened at a time. A bolt slid open, and the prisoner shuffled forward, his shackles scraping the ground. The gate slammed shut behind him. He was moved on until stopped again, and then passed through into the next holding area.

'To get them to be cooperative, we try to find something that is common between us,' a second interrogator, a woman, told me. 'There are several decent chess players among them. Another interrogator went into the meeting and made tea rather than begin questioning.' The banality of her comments was chilling. Her fellow interrogator interjected with the assertion that this job 'is the most rewarding thing I have ever done'. He appeared to be on the verge of giving me a rundown of everything else he had done in his career when I was summoned back to the prefab cabin that housed the library, the interrogation rooms and the tribunal hearings.

The Kuwaiti's tribunal had been dominated by the detainee's assertive and articulate defiance. This next one would be different.

The prisoner was a Turkish national who had been living in Germany. At the time I saw him I was bound not to divulge his name; but now his name is so widely known and his case so well documented in his own book[10] that it seems unnecessary to conceal that he was Murat Kurnaz.

Before I saw him, there was already a lot about him on the Internet, where photographs taken before his arrest showed a young, fair-skinned, clean-shaven individual with a slick haircut, wearing a smart zippered jacket. Nearly three years later his brown hair was a mass of frizzy locks that fell down his back. He had grown a beard that was so long it covered the heavy chain around his waist. He seemed a broken man. Unlike the Kuwaiti, this prisoner had never been to Afghanistan, but according to the Recorder – who listed the accusations – he had joined Jama'at Tabligh, an Islamic group accused by several countries of supporting terrorist acts. He had studied Islam with Jama'at Tabligh in Germany. At the age of 19, two weeks after the 11 September attacks, he went to Pakistan; there, he received lodging and schooling from the group and then travelled to Karachi, Lahore and Peshawar. In addition, the Recorder said, he had planned to go to Pakistan with a man 'who later became a suicide bomber'.

'What explosion was this person responsible for?' Kurnaz asked.

'I can't answer this,' said the Recorder, adding, 'Anything remaining on this is in the classified section,' meaning it would not be revealed to the detainee, even though it could be a major part of what the tribunal members took into account when reaching their conclusion as to whether Kurnaz was an 'enemy combatant' whose continued incarceration could be justified.

Kurnaz told the Tribunal that he had been arrested by Pakistani police after being hauled off a bus in the third week of November 2001, and that he was eventually handed over to US officials. They took him first to Afghanistan, and then transferred him to Guantanamo Bay. He said that when he was 16 he had met the would-be suicide bomber – Serçuk Bilgen – in Germany, but had had little contact with him during the last year in which he had known him: 'I never thought he experimented with bombs,' Kurnaz said, adding that he believed Jama'at Tabligh was a peaceful group, which was why he wanted to study Islam with them in Pakistan. 'In Pakistan I could study in two months what would take three years in Germany.'

After the initial statements, the Tribunal President ordered that the panel members read affidavits submitted by a lawyer known to the detainee and another written by the detainee's family. The room fell into silence, except for the occasional humming of the air conditioning and the rustling of paper.

I was sitting a metre from the detainee, bursting with questions I was not allowed to ask him, bound by the rules not even to make eye contact. I was part of the stony-faced bureaucracy, and felt complicit in the judgement by failing to do any more than listen and take copious shorthand notes. I despaired that my report of the hearing would make no difference, bound as I was to consider the possibility that everything the detainee had said might be a lie. I was left not knowing who was guilty or innocent, whatever decision the Tribunal might reach.

'Do you wish to make a statement to the Tribunal?' the President asked Kurnaz, breaking the long silence.

'Yes,' the detainee replied. He then told them his story all over again, ending it by saying,

> That is all my history. I was 19 years old when I went to Pakistan. I am sure it was a wrong time to travel to Pakistan. But I couldn't know that Pakistan would arrest me because of my colour and because I am from Germany. That's all I have to say. I hope you guys will judge the truth. I am not an enemy combatant. I want my freedom back, because I am not a terrorist.

He paused while the panel members asked him questions about his relationship with Bilgen, and responded with calm though firm denials that he was aware of Bilgen's plans. 'If I go back to Germany I will do anything to prove that I am innocent. I will cut off my big beard, and will do anything to show that I am not supporting terrorists. I will do everything for the German Government to show that I don't support terrorists, so that I can sleep well.'

I left Guantanamo Bay on a hot morning five days after my arrival. The departure hall at the airstrip was brimming with people awaiting the early flight, this time to Fort Lauderdale.

Long, immovable benches faced a wall from which hung a mega-sized plasma screen, so passengers awaiting departure had little choice but to sit and watch the only entertainment available. Engrossed and expressionless, the unflinching crowd sat and watched Mel Gibson's *The Passion of the Christ*. I pulled my newly acquired 'Guantanamo Bay' baseball cap over my eyes and played a Bob Dylan CD extra loud on my Walkman, but could not escape the ghastly extremism of a movie that seemed to have become a focus for America's fundamentalist soul-searching. Children popped sweets into their mouths while the blood of the Messiah gushed across the screen; all of this at seven o'clock in the morning. I was reminded of a week I had spent in Iraq a year earlier with a unit of US and UK soldiers who were scouring the country for weapons of mass destruction. Our days were spent living and breathing the military life. Then, for entertainment, they would produce a war film on DVD. It seemed an odd way to relax, having heard guns going off all day, to spend the evening reliving *Black Hawk Down*, desperate to know more when I told them that I had been in Mogadishu the night that famous battle took place.

When I published the comments regarding likely prisoner releases which had been made to me by Lucenti, the Deputy Commander of the joint task force that ran Camp Delta, the Pentagon issued a stiff denial, saying my report was completely untrue, that the General had not said these things. The top brass at Guantanamo then made it clear that they would not welcome me on a return visit to the camp if I were to request one. Though objections softened after a few weeks, it was not until 18 January 2005 that I joined a queue of travellers on the tarmac at Fort Lauderdale to board a small twin-prop ten-seater aircraft that would take us on the journey south.

A warm winter breeze swayed the mangrove as the *R.M. Hunnington* cut through the water. Creole voices mingled with the southern drawl and mid-western slang of the Americans and the chatter of the Filipinos. The naval station workforce seemed a microcosm of the larger America lying to the north. The lure of big bucks had drawn the foreigners to work in the Cuban Club, the Windjammer, the construction sites, the shopping mall, the McDonalds, and in the military housing in which I was staying, where the staff seemed to do little more than doze into the early hours of the morning in front of an apparently infinite number of badly copied action movies. The Filipinos earned $1.60 per hour. A portion of their salary was taken by their Government before it even reached them. The Jamaicans did much better: $6 an hour. They were all living off America, sending their remittances home to families in Kingston or the polluted sprawl of Metro Manila where I had spent some time a year earlier, on the trail of Khaled Sheikh Mohammed, the mastermind of the 11 September terrorist attacks.

From the landing stage on the eastern side of the bay we followed the winding road to the rocky promontory where the tin roofs of Camp Delta gleamed in the sun. My military guide joked that he might not be let past the bull-necked Military Police patrolling the entrance. 'If I ain't back in fifteen, come and get me ...' But he soon emerged, spinning a ring of triangular copper keys around his finger, flicking his thumb against a white plastic tag which bore the words 'X-Ray keys' in slightly smudged felt-tip pen.

We drove along a deserted road across the hills that crowd around Camp Delta, passing military homes set in bland residential developments named Iguana Terrace, Caribbean Circle and Hibiscus Hollow, and then went further out, beyond the parched greens of a golf course. On the edge of the naval base, white picket fences surrounded the villas that line Nob Hill Road. The Stars and Stripes hung motionless from poles in shady gardens. Children's toys lay strewn across neatly cut lawns. Large cars and SUVs gleamed in double garages. Families were gathered at lunch tables. A way of life that had been shattered when the hijacked aircraft slammed into the World Trade Center was recreated daily up the garden paths of Guantanamo Bay.

Beyond the villas of Nob Hill Road we dipped among the cacti and leafless grey trees and joined Sherman Avenue, which snaked through the base and led eventually to the crossing point with the Republic of Cuba. A watchtower at Gate 17 – once the 'Checkpoint Charlie' of the Caribbean – was only inhabited these days when US Marines took reporters up into the observation post to view the fading symbols of the twentieth century's political landscape.

A short distance from the border, just past a metal-processing plant, a rough track led off into a wilderness of rubble and wire cages: Camp X-Ray.

The first prisoners were held at Camp X-Ray immediately after the invasion of Afghanistan in October 2001. Although it was only home to the blindfolded and shackled detainees until April 2002, when they were moved to Camp Delta, where less primitive facilities had been established, the film and photographs of their treatment became the symbols of the 'GWOT'. We did not need the keys for the now-deserted camp. The locks had been sawn off the metal gates, though nobody knew why. A long central path gave on to prison cages which now lay silent and empty within their wire-fenced compounds. Banana rats the size of cats crouched among the mesh walls and within the coils of razor wire that topped the maze of fences. Weeds had engulfed the place since the prisoners and their guards had moved. The sun had beaten the moisture out of the wooden watchtowers along the perimeter. Heat cracked the ground and the warm breeze rustled dead, grey grass that lay on the gravel. Long-dormant floodlights, buffeted by the wind, peered blindly down at the dereliction. White butterflies fluttered among the glittering razor wire and rusting mesh. It is easy to forget that these cages had been built years before 9/11, in the days when America was a hallowed refuge: the Haitian refugees they had then housed had been guarded just as rigidly, and even rioted when their living conditions became intolerable.

Back along the coast at Camp Delta, to which the X-Ray detainees had been moved, a metal sign across the entrance to the main interrogation block read, 'Do not allow children to play in gate area or operate gate.'

The concrete building called Camp Five is modelled on a maximum-security prison in Indiana. The officers accompanying me didn't see the irony of the sign – I never saw any children at Camp Delta. They shuffled, slightly embarrassed, when the automation of their hi-tech showpiece failed: the closure of the outer perimeter gate was supposed automatically to trigger the opening of the inner gate. But it did not, and for a while we stood as the prisoners of a failed switching system. Sergeant Major Berger then led the way. We all set off a metal detector at the entrance, but nobody paid any attention to the squawking alarm. A heavy metal door crashed shut behind us as we stepped into the octagonal atrium at the centre of the building. In a glass-panelled control room, TV screens relayed real-time pictures of every prisoner's incarceration. Solid metal doors gave off onto smooth concrete corridors lined with maroon-painted cell doors.

This building was my worst nightmare; it left me frozen by the fear of confinement.

'These doors don't just open. It's all a choreographed visit,' Berger said. One hundred people could be held at Camp Five, every minute of their lives controlled by two Military Police officers who watched the detainees from the control room. They had downloaded the Muslim call to prayer from an Internet website, and now piped it via the intercom to each cell, five times a day. 'What we are trying to accomplish here is the minimising of the amount of movement of detainees. We have decreased the amount of daily manpower needed. Our normal manpower would be four per block. But we have reduced it. All the automation is run through there.'

Berger pointed to the control room, from where every door in the building could be opened and closed, allowing each prisoner out individually, to the shower room at the end of the corridor, or into a mesh-encased courtyard of rough concrete where they were permitted one hour of exercise every two days. Footballs were 'not permitted by the Standard Operating Procedures', so the prisoners could only jog around the twenty-foot-square cages, in one of which a large iguana sat hunched and blinking in the pounding sun. How the creature had got through the maximum security cordon, nobody could tell me.

Berger, like many of the Military Police officers at Camp Delta, had worked in the US penal system. He listed the amenities as if showing a prospective buyer around a new home.

> If we ever lose power, the doors lock in a default position. The showers are on timers – so they get ten minutes to shower. The towel hangers rotate on eyeballs, so they can't do any harm to themselves. The windows are frosted for force protection issues: so the detainees can't get an idea of how many Military Police are on duty.[11]

A row of screens flickered inside a small room off one of the corridors where the cells were empty of prisoners. A detainee in an orange suit that identified him as 'high value' or particularly dangerous, was speaking animatedly with his interrogators. Perhaps as long as three years into his incarceration, what did he know that he had not already told his captors? I had no idea whether the image was live, or recorded for the benefit of this visit by an outsider.

'Some people want to be in Camp Five: they don't want to be in social situations,' said a stylish woman wearing high heels who was introduced as the Chief Defense Department Interrogator. She told me she had 25 years' experience. We watched the detainee on the screen, standing alongside a man wearing headphones whose role was to prompt the interrogator with questions posed by experts and linguists who were listening remotely, and who could research the detainees' information as the interrogation progressed. The effectiveness of the system depended on the detainees' compliance. What happened when they kept silent?

'They develop their own counter-interrogation techniques to counter our techniques,' said the woman in the high heels.

But for others, after a couple of years they start cooperating. These are very different dynamics. We all trained for the Soviet-era interrogation. To switch from the Cold War to the asymmetric war, we have to understand where they are coming from. It's been a big challenge. We are getting better at it every day.

Across the road outside Camp Five, beyond the fence and the sign that warned children not to treat the place like a playground, Company Sergeant Major Anthony Mendez tried hard to persuade me that all this was not just to do with terrorism, security and intelligence gathering; it was also designed to turn the prisoners into better people.

Outside the intense mechanical regimentation of Camp Five, which was intended to break the prisoners down, the intention was to cajole, tame and – only if necessary – force the inmates into submission. In cages set along corridors in Camps One, Two and Three some prisoners even had 'comfort items' – shampoo, pens and paper. For all of them, the ultimate comfort was a place in Camp Four, where they lived communally and could wander around the dormitory and courtyard for most of the day. 'The basic items and comfort items for the most part are non-negotiable. But if they try to use their trousers to kill themselves or break camp rules, they can lose the comfort items,' Lieutenant Colonel Bryan Jahnke told me. 'This is where we work the behaviour modification. There's a big split between those who want to cooperate and those who don't.'

Mendez elaborated on the process of 'behaviour modification' and the extent to which the breaking down of the inmates involved letting them know of the benefits and attractions of good behaviour. 'If they're compliant with the camp rules, they're moved up. To get into Camp Four, we have a vetting process that is chaired by the Deputy Commanding General.'

A volleyball net had been strung up between two poles in the courtyard of Camp Four. Heavily bearded detainees eyed us as we wandered across it. The rules of the camp had been written on a large board in several languages:

You will not mistreat each other, visitors or guards.

You will not have an item you can use as a weapon.

You will not be permitted to do any hand to hand combat or martial arts training.

Your compliance with these rules will positively affect your quality of life.

Being in Camp Four is a privilege, not a right. Failure to comply means you can be moved back to Camps One, Two or Three.

Alongside the final warning was a poster showing Afghans voting in the 2004 elections that had sought to legitimise the Government of President Hamid Karzai. It informed the detainees that ten million people had voted in the country's first democratic election. The message to the Afghan detainees was clear: your country is moving on, and you are being left behind.

Behind the wire which separated me from them, men called out in Arabic, French, and in other languages I did not recognise. Theirs were the stories I wanted to hear, though the rules forbade me from responding. I didn't know whether to feel sympathy, anger, suspicion or horror. They stood or sat, staring at me from behind the mesh. Some were old, fat, grey men. One was struggling to use a walking frame. Others were younger. Could their behaviour be 'modified'? Was this the place to turn them into democrats? As we wandered through, I learned that a new facility – Camp Six – was to be built beside the pre-cast concrete of Camp Five, in which several hundred detainees would be permanently incarcerated. 'Ping-pong is very big,' Mendez was telling me. It seemed an indescribably banal alternative to jihad. Would the attraction of the sport encourage these alleged Islamist extremists to find other ways of satisfying their inclination to change the world? 'What we try to do is to provide board games that will involve more than one player. And they get one roll of toilet paper per week, whereas in Camps One, Two and Three, they get toilet paper when needed.'

The lure of communal board games and toilet paper were clearly part of the effort to make those who had graduated to Camp Four feel they had achieved something worthwhile. Mendez was sure of it. 'Detainees strive to get up here to Camp Four.'

Sitting around a large oval table in a prefab in the main Camp Delta complex, Steve Rodriguez gave a blunter account of what was, what was not, and what might be going on there.

The big, bearded, unsmiling Director of Intelligence-gathering Operations was unflinching when I asked him whether the exposure of detainees to extreme temperatures, or sexual advances, had been used during the interrogations which were the main part of his remit.

> I haven't, since I have been here, requested any of these types of techniques. If I felt that there was something above and beyond the techniques available, I would request them. What I am talking about is a simple thing: using a 'fear-up' technique. How do I instil some state of fear that you're in imminent danger of some sort? In order to do that I would have to get information from the Secretary of Defense. But I haven't asked for that.[12]

I asked him whether – in his wider experience as an interrogator – information gained forcibly had proved reliable, in the expectation that if he said yes it would at least imply that force had been used. 'It varies. There has been information gained forcibly [historically, though not specifically at Guantanamo Bay], and it's accurate. I don't know of any real study that has looked through history that has looked at the reliability of information. By and large the direct approach is the best approach.' He meant direct questioning rather than physical violence or the threat of it.

The officers accompanying me were motionless as he spoke. Was he going to admit to anything that would bring America's virtue into further doubt? What about sexual arousal as an interrogation technique?

'It's not happened since I have been here.'

'Is it a technique?'

'Yes, it is a technique.'

'Is it approved?'

'No, not by the Secretary of Defense. We all know in history, you obtain information in many different ways.'

So there we were, chatting about violent torture and squalid sex, as he explained the 'art' of interrogation. He watched me like a hawk, perhaps trying to discern from my reactions whether making himself available to the media was likely to pay off. Which points was

I taking down in my notebook? Was I grabbing at soundbites or taking a verbatim note of his words? He wouldn't be able to ask to see my notes, but he could try to deduce from my reactions what I had found most revealing. In fact I wrote down every word he said, and asked my questions as blandly as possible. I asked him about the allegation made by an FBI agent to his superiors that a prisoner had been draped in an Israeli flag during an interrogation; the accusation had been released under the US Freedom of Information Act. Rodriguez's response to my question about it revealed more than everything else he had said. 'I have a frustration. What I have angst over is the fact that there are many, many things going on in many countries. And there are all kinds of abuse and people's heads being cut off on television, and you and I are talking about an Israeli flag?'

With that, our meeting was over.

I walked in silence, accompanied by my military minder, back to the prefab block where one of the last of the Combatant Status Review Tribunals was about to start.

In the control room beside it, an Air Force Major was chatting with the Army Captain in charge of the proceedings, seemingly oblivious to who I might be: 'There is a rebuttable presumption in favour of the Government's evidence.'

The Captain's verbal contortions failed to conceal what he was really acknowledging, that the Tribunals were loaded against the detainees from the start. He went on to tell me that the witnesses permitted to be called by the detainees 'go through a relevancy test'. But then he added – with a hint of a smile, as if in acknowledgement that detainees' friends or family might not have faith in American 'due process' – that despite the military being prepared to transport witnesses to Camp Delta to give evidence in support of the detainees 'no off-island witnesses have come to the island to give testimony'.

Then the two officers began discussing the case of the Afghan who was about to appear before them, whose Tribunal I was about to see.

'He is innocent. I have had his file on my desk for two and a half months, and he is innocent,' the Major told the Captain, still unconcerned that I might not be bound to keep his secret. 'This guy was just an Afghan in his own country. He was one of those who had the choice of joining one side or the other. It must have been difficult for people like him. He was caught after the combat was over.' And as he spoke, the Captain strode across the room and guided the Major out into the corridor.

They reappeared moments later. I adopted an attitude of nonchalance, as if ignorant of the implications of what had just been said. But it was clear from the Major's outburst – delivered in a tone that betrayed a sense of real concern for the accused – that the Tribunal process was a farce and that this use of 'intelligence' as evidence amounted in this case and probably many others to a grotesque abuse.

The two men changed the subject. Pointing to the row of TV screens, the Major told me how he had once been mesmerised by the image of a shackled prisoner awaiting his Tribunal. The prisoner had asked for some water, and was helped by his Personal Representative to drink it from a bottle. Then the Personal Representative put the bottle on a table and left the room.

> The prisoner wanted some more water, and I watched him as he edged his chair across to the table, picked up the bottle in his shackled hands, leaned his head forward, and was able to bite onto the bottle. Then he tilted his head back with the bottle in his mouth because his shackles prevented him from holding the bottle any higher. Then he put the bottle back. He didn't spill a drop.

The door opened and I was ushered inside.

The Afghan was innocent and should not have been sitting there, shackled to the floor.

It was one of those rare occasions during my visits to Guantanamo Bay when I knew something more than was being officially revealed. The purpose of the Tribunals was to give the impression that there was a system at work: decisions had been made, rules drawn up, standards established, intelligence gathered, verdicts delivered. 'The tribunal is rigorous, professional and repeatable,' the Captain told me as we walked to the hearing room. His words rang in my ears. I was sickened by my own complicity. The Afghan prisoner might stay here forever, and perhaps in the end because I abided by the rules to which I had agreed before setting foot in that place.

The Recorder listed the charges:

The detained is associated with the Taliban. On 27 March 2003 a Red Cross convoy was attacked in Afghanistan and a member of the Red Cross was murdered at the scene. Prior to the 27 March 2003 incident, authorities in the Shawali Kot area of Afghanistan were informed of a group operating in the area with the intent of doing harm to Westerners. The detainee lives in the Shawali Kot area. The detainee is suspected of being a bodyguard to the individual responsible for the killing of Red Cross personnel. On 3 April 2003 an individual known as Abdelgaffar was known to possess a satellite phone. The detained was captured in a creek bed by US forces on 21 April 2003.

For two hours the detainee spewed out his denials.

I am not aware of the Red Cross members and convoy. I didn't see it. Nobody saw me doing anything to that convoy. I have never had a gun in my hand. All of the people in my country are aware that I am a man with a shovel in my hand. If I was a bodyguard it should be evident from a knife or gun that proves my identity as a bodyguard. When I was arrested I never had such a thing on me to prove that I was a bodyguard. If they arrested me and I had such a thing [as a satellite telephone] on me, I would accept that responsibility. I never had such a thing in my hands. I have never used one and I don't know how to operate one.

By the time the Tribunal process came to an end on 1 March 2005 the stony-faced panel members had declared that 22 of the then 558 detainees were 'non-combatants'. Nineteen of these had been found 'innocent' in the last three weeks of the eight-month process. I have no idea whether the Afghan I saw on that final day was among those freed; their names remained confidential. But I'll never forget his parting words.

With the Americans coming to Afghanistan, it should have helped us. But I can see that it's worse than the Taliban. Why do Americans want to be mean with me? For what crime was I brought here? I don't know. America, instead of helping the poor people and the innocent people, has brought these innocent people to this hell.

He was – as the two officers I had overheard knew, and who had mistakenly made clear to me – there because of 'intelligence'. That intelligence was wrong, though nobody had the power or courage to admit it.

But this was not because they did not *feel* a lack of power or courage. It was because intelligence *was* power. The abuse of that power was part of the revenge the Bush White House was taking on an enemy that had shocked the American nation. Power became something to abuse as much as to exercise – the brazen pursuit of the former was a part of what the wounded superpower sought to portray itself as capable of, in 'defence' of the latter. It soon lost its way, truths and lies losing their distinction, the US approach being reflected on in this way by a senior European intelligence officer with long experience of the US intelligence community: 'The CIA strategy since 9/11 has been to kill rather than to recruit [spies]. They just want to get dangerous people off the streets.'[13]

Despite Camp Delta remaining home to the masterminds of 9/11, it will always be a place associated with the power of lies. Although some real intelligence emerged from the horrendous torture sessions endured by the likes of Abu Zubaydah and Khalid Sheikh Mohamed, truth was not ultimately what mattered to the authorities running the camps, nor to their political protectors in Washington. It was the mystery of secret intelligence that allowed it not to matter. The importance of Abu Zubaydah as a source of intelligence was stressed several times by President Bush as justification for his torture at the hands of the CIA; but major doubts as to his real intelligence value are widespread, the US Government case against him appearing increasingly weak, the implication being that he was not as important a figure in al-Qaeda as the White House sought to portray him in order to justify his torture.

But Zubaydah, like the other detainees, could not disprove what they had not been told was the evidence against him – the Afghan farmer whose hearing I had witnessed was not allowed to know what secret intelligence had been used to make the case against him. Meanwhile, those being held there who really did have secrets to tell, had them beaten out of them in a manner which – as the Dublin police had written eighty years beforehand – was unlikely to be wholly reliable; when Khaled Sheikh Mohamed – the 'mastermind' of 9/11 – claimed full responsibility for planning this and numerous other attacks[14] since 1993, he told a representative of the International Committee of the Red Cross who visited him at Guantanamo Bay that he had provided information simply in the hope that it would end the torture.[15]

The detainees could of course be questioned interminably: if what they said under threat of violence proved to be wrong their interrogators could go back to them with more questions until perhaps the 'correct' answer was given. As a senior intelligence officer whose views I have considerable faith in told me at the time, 'I can't think of a detainee that hasn't provided something. Everybody has provided something. Khaled Sheikh Mohamed is saying quite a lot – for them, cooperation offers the only way of improving their situation.'[16] Meanwhile, 'walk-in' agents such Jamal al-Fadl were being used to provide insights into the identities of those being held,[17] the illegal incarceration of the detainees thereby leading to intelligence being gathered – by both brutal and less brutal methods – that has contributed to what the CIA, SIS, MI5, France's Direction Générale de la Sécurité Extérieure (DGSE) and other allied intelligence agencies in Italy, Germany and Australia know about al-Qaeda.

But as the tribunal process progressed at Camp Delta, the 'power' of intelligence took over from the 'weapon' of intelligence in the minds of the CIA's political masters in Washington. The result was the greatest abuse to date of the power of 'the secret state': the invasion of Iraq.

10

KNOW YOUR ENEMY

By the time a cruise missile strike on a Baghdad residence in which Saddam Hussein was thought to be present marked the launch of the invasion on the evening of 20 March 2003, the adaptation of intelligence-gathering methods which had been precipitated two years earlier by the confrontation with al-Qaeda had become a wholesale transformation – not just of methods, but of purpose.

'This is the pre-emptive war. We had good information about the Iraqi weapons programme. It's been difficult to come by, in conjunction with close allies, and now there is a huge weight of responsibility that is foisted on us,'[1] a senior intelligence officer told me as the Baghdad building burned. A major part of that responsibility emerged from the unprecedented pressure to reconcile political demands with the secrets that lay at the heart of what the CIA and SIS had gathered, in addition to what had been learned from Italy's SISMi military intelligence service,[2] and the DGSE in France, both of which had passed intelligence on Iraq's weapons-related and other activities to the British and Americans prior to the outbreak of war.

Thus began a process of turning glaring uncertainties into magisterial truths.

The 'good information' – the secret intelligence – used to justify the invasion to the public in Britain and the United States, was never regarded within the intelligence communities as resembling – in much more than a general sense – how it was portrayed by the political leaderships. The reasons for this were multifold. Central to the differences was that the process of simplifying intelligence for public consumption and political 'soundbites' meant that very different, often contradictory and certainly not mutually supportive issues were forced together as one. That Saddam Hussein was a tyrant about whom there was much justified suspicion, was accepted within the intelligence services; that the Iraqi regime had imported equipment during the 1980s and 1990s that could be used in the development of unconventional weapons programmes was not an assumption confined to the intelligence agencies, and was widely documented;[3] that al-Qaeda had held exploratory discussions with Iraqi officials was substantiated; that there was – and remains – a danger of terrorists acquiring weapons of mass destruction (WMD) was seen within the intelligence services as a very real possibility.

But it was not only the later revelation of the flaws in intelligence regarding the WMD arsenal which marked Iraq out as a challenge to the world's spies. While post-invasion inquiries – which have since led to changes in the relationship between intelligence gatherers and intelligence assessors in the services of both the United Kingdom and the United States – may prevent a repeat of Iraq, at least with regard to the public use of intelligence, the challenge thrown up by Saddam Hussein's regime was far less exceptional than sometimes thought.

Iraq was a very difficult intelligence target; this was in itself nothing new – learning about the Soviet Union's nuclear arsenal had been no less challenging. What was new was the direct linkage between intelligence and action: without the use of intelligence – in whatever manicured form the US and UK Governments decided to present it – there would have been and could have been no invasion, because on its own the political case for it was wholly inadequate; a 'threat' had to be identified. But as has been evident throughout history, while intelligence may provide clues as to what might be going on, it is of limited value unless the *intentions* of the target are understood. It is the combined understanding of intent *and* capability that permits intelligence to feed into policy; while many years before 9/11 al-Qaeda's general *intentions* had been sensed, its *capability* was misjudged; in the case of Iraq, the strategy of the UK and US Governments – intended as it was from the outset to *justify* the invasion – was to focus on the military capability the regime was supposed to possess, and to highlight the alleged existence of this arsenal as proof of the *intent* to use it.

Thus, not only was it necessary to *create* the tangible threat – in the form of the military hardware which did not exist – but also to give the impression that there was certainty on the part of the agencies that Saddam had the *intention* of carrying out that threat.

At the core of the intelligence challenge regarding Iraq was the fact that there wasn't – it transpired in the post-war interrogations of numerous Ba'ath Party officials – a regime: there was, I was later told, 'a man who never spoke to anybody'. To add to the government pressure on the intelligence agencies to provide insights where there were few and certainty where there was none, prior to 9/11 a combination of the challenge it involved and other priorities, meant Iraq had not been a central focus for them. Detailed understanding of the regime was limited, and was heavily influenced – particularly in Washington – by the 'toxic' attitudes of Iraqi dissidents, led by the exiled Iraqi National Congress. What was missing from the intelligence picture was the 'intent intelligence', as one insider explained; the personalities within the regime remained a mystery, and what they might do when under pressure was a part of that mystery.

But where the needs of the political leaderships and the practices of the intelligence communities in Washington and London were fundamentally at odds was over the efforts of the politicians to connect all these very separate elements together. Only when presented as a seamless, overwhelming and potentially apocalyptic threat could all these elements present a credible case for an invasion. But there was no such unifying 'intelligence'. Moreover, the demand that connections be made, assessments drawn up and conclusions reached, forced intelligence officers on both sides of the Atlantic to play roles which were more akin to World War II misinformation peddling than to post-Cold War management of new threats.

Among the many questions raised by the invasion of Iraq was that of whether intelligence is so powerful that it can *create* truths; can secret intelligence *make* history by manipulating knowledge, or is it just a means of playing for time before the truth inevitably emerges?

As they sought to meet the requirements of their political masters, the US and UK agencies saw their material turned from vague hints into cast-iron truths; they saw their circumspection transformed into certainties, and saw the end of the anonymity which is central to their ability to operate, transform them from intelligence gatherers into political pawns.

It was a change they did not like.

Their resistance to this shifting role became evident in private conversations I held throughout the months of war; it was followed by a steady flow of resignations when the war was over, the sentiment underpinning the anger and discontent being made clear to me many months before the March 2003 invasion by a senior intelligence officer, who told me,

> There is a mistake being made in trying to tie Iraq into the War on Terror. We undermine the strong case there is for dealing with Iraq. We also create support for Iraq in the [Middle East] region. The information that I have seen suggests that at one point during the period of intense pressure [on the Iraqi regime] in 1998–99 there were some attempts to open channels of communication between al-Qaeda and Iraq. They didn't work. There was at least one meeting – it's 100 per cent true that there were these attempts *by al-Qaeda* to contact Iraq. I think the US is looking at things that are much more recent – but it's a mistake to project back the al-Qaeda of then and of now, [even though] there are a number of good reasons to deal with the Iraqis.[4]

A few days later, similar doubts were expressed by a second intelligence officer when he told me, 'Traditional terrorism has been associated with rogue states. But this has not been so helpful with regard to al-Qaeda. At a substantial level there are no magic bullets.'[5] A short while later a senior CIA official expressed a remarkably similar view as to the linkages between al-Qaeda – and specifically its Afghanistan-based forces and their Taliban allies – and the Iraqi regime, which was at that time being accused by the White House of connections to Islamists in northern Iraq who had allegedly been developing poisons for military use. He told me, 'It wouldn't be right to say that the Afghans are directly linked to north-east Iraq. What's going on in north-east Iraq? Knowledge of the use of poisons is widespread in al-Qaeda – those who are near the inner core of al-Qaeda had training in poisons. But it appears to be theoretical.'[6]

Against this backdrop of uncertainty, the only way perhaps to find something akin to the truth was to go and look for it myself.

Saddam's presence had been neatly erased from the al-Qaim fertiliser factory. While elsewhere in the country in the weeks after the fall of Baghdad I had seen his portraits with their eyes gouged out or horns painted onto his head, the employees of Iraq's largest fertiliser producer instead took a can of red paint and carefully coated the larger than life image which stood at the factory entrance. For al-Qaim's employees, erasing the past was a duty, a necessity and an obsession. But for Sensitive Sight Team Five (SST5) – a group of US and UK soldiers trained in unconventional warfare – the mission was far more humdrum. Its role was to go painstakingly over old ground – in the hunt for the evidence of the WMD which had brought the dictator's downfall.

Tumbleweed blowing in the teeth of a violent sandstorm sped past the concrete bunkers in a fenced-off inner site of the factory, which lies a few miles from the country's border with Syria, and within which Iraqi scientists in the 1980s had extracted uranium oxide – so-called 'yellow cake'. The 'cake' – if produced in quantities Iraq never in fact achieved – could have been used in the development of nuclear fuel and weapons. The bunkers had been ordered closed and encased in concrete by United Nations inspectors after the 1991 Gulf War, and UN inspectors had regularly visited the site up until early March 2003, days before the US-led invasion. But beneath a building part-destroyed by bombing in 1991, 16 blue plastic barrels lay coated in a thin film of dust. A British specialist with the UK's Nuclear, Biological, Chemical Regiment, seconded to the US-led SST5, surveyed the barrels with an 'Exploranium' chemical detector. Its indicator ticked rapidly, and words on a screen described the contents of the barrels as 'industrial uranium 238' – 'yellow cake'.

A few weeks beforehand, when advancing US forces were regularly proclaiming that they had unearthed evidence of Iraq's WMD, this find would perhaps have been called a 'smoking gun' by the excitable invaders. Instead, by mid-May 2003, expectations of such finds were beginning to evaporate, and suspicion was mounting around claims that major WMD finds made at sites identified pre-war would provide justification for the invasion.

'Our best information is going to come from human sources: Iraqis, when they feel comfortable enough, will come forward,'[7] Lt Colonel Keith Harrington, the US special forces officer heading SST5, told me as we wandered around the rusting pipework and vast machine halls at al-Qaim. 'The new approach will be: piece it together from the human intelligence. We probably won't find the big smoking gun.'

The dependence of the Sensitive Sight Teams – of which there were seven until the entire WMD investigation was reformed in July 2003 and brought under the auspices of the Iraq Survey Group (ISG) – on Iraqi officials, factory employees, scientists and others, left them with little likelihood of unearthing much that the UN inspectors, whose own failure had been used as the excuse for going to war, had failed to find.

But even when the ISG – a 1,200-strong team of weapons experts, intelligence officers and military personnel – took over, it soon became evident that something was very wrong.

'Thank you, Mr Chairman,' said David Kay, a former CIA officer appointed by President Bush as head of the ISG to find the WMD.[8]

It was 2 October 2003, and Kay was making a long-awaited appearance before a joint meeting of several US congressional committees. He took the gathering of Congressmen through a carefully worded assessment of why no weapons had been found, but why they should not abandon the idea of finding them: 'It is far too early to reach any definitive conclusions and, in some areas, we may never reach that goal,' he said.

But only three months later, he delivered a bombshell. Addressing the Senate Armed Services Committee on 28 January 2004, he told the US Government what it did not want to hear:

A great deal has been accomplished by the team, and I do think...it important that it goes on and it is allowed to reach its full conclusion. In fact, I really believe it ought to be better resourced and totally focused on WMD; that it is important to do it. But I also believe that it is time to begin the fundamental analysis of how we got here, what led us here and what we need to do in order to ensure that we are equipped with the best possible intelligence as we face these issues in the future. Let me begin by saying, we were almost all wrong, and I certainly include myself here.[9]

His demolition of the reasons the Bush Administration and the Blair Government had given for the invasion of Iraq was not quite as unequivocally devastating as it may have first seemed. He blamed some of the failure to find evidence of the weapons and weapons programmes on the failure of US troops to halt the looting which took place in the immediate aftermath of Saddam Hussein's fall. But his point was clear:

> I had innumerable analysts who came to me in apology that the world that we were finding was not the world that they had thought existed and that they had estimated... [We've] got a much more fundamental problem of understanding what went wrong, and we've got to figure out what was there. And that's what I call fundamental fault analysis.

American assumptions about Saddam's intent drew heavily on the portrayals of the regime provided to the hawks in the Pentagon by Iraqi dissidents. 'Saddam Hussein is not going to easily give up the horrible weapons that he has worked so hard to obtain and paid such a high price to keep,' the Deputy Defense Secretary Paul Wolfowitz had said on 28 October 2002. This view was echoed across the Atlantic as the war approached, when the UK Defence Secretary Geoff Hoon told the House of Commons on 22 January 2003, 'Weapons of mass destruction have been a central pillar of Saddam's dictatorship since the 1980s. They have built up their WMD, and lied and lied again.' Tony Blair developed the theme on 18 March, telling the House of Commons, 'We are now seriously asked to accept that in the last few years, contrary to all history, contrary to all intelligence, he [Saddam Hussein] decided unilaterally to destroy the weapons. Such a claim is palpably absurd.'[10] On the same day, Bush addressed Americans, telling them, 'Intelligence gathered by this and other Governments leaves no doubt that the Iraqi regime continues to possess and conceal some of the most lethal weapons ever devised.'[11] To this General Tommy Franks, at the first US military 'Centcom' press conference after the launch of the war added on 22 March,

> There is no doubt that the regime of Saddam Hussein possesses weapons of mass destruction. And that – and as this operation continues – those weapons will be identified, found, along with the people who have produced them and who guard them. And of course there is no doubt about that. It will come in the future.[12]

To this, Donald Rumsfeld, the Defense Secretary added eight days later, 'We know where they (the weapons) are. They're in the area around Tikrit and Baghdad and east, west, south and north somewhat.'[13]

But the world was not as the Administration of George W. Bush had made Americans believe it was.

Luckily for Americans, however, the mix of political manipulation and sophisticated propagandising that had taken the media, legislature and public for a ride since the nation decided to pull together in the wake of the 9/11 terrorist attacks, was matched after many months by an equally intense response from the few institutions still capable of resurrecting credibility. It wasn't just that Bush, Rumsfeld, Wolfowitz and all the other players in this unsettling drama were proved wrong about WMD; they also proved themselves wholly unreliable in their claims about the character of the Iraqi regime, the personality of Saddam Hussein, and the policy options that were open to them to confront the regime he led. The Bush Administration portrayed Saddam's regime as *intent* on turning its supposed hatred of the United States into support for al-Qaeda, aggression towards Israel, threats to its neighbours and – if possible – to the entire world. In fact, as the official CIA report into Iraq's weapons programmes concluded in October 2004, 'Iran was the pre-eminent motivator of this [Iraqi military] policy. All senior level Iraqi officials considered Iran to be Iraq's principal enemy in the region. The wish to balance Israel and acquire status and influence in the Arab world were also considerations, but secondary.'[14]

Moreover, the author of the report, Charles Duelfer, told me in October 2004 that Saddam had 'an odd view of the US. He seemed to have the view that it was in the interests of the US to deal with Iraq. I think Saddam Hussein's conclusion was that ultimately the US would come to a deal with Baghdad.'[15] Not that the United States would have engaged in such dealmaking, despite the two countries' close relations as enemies of Iran during the 1980s having led to Rumsfeld paying at least one visit to Baghdad, where he was photographed shaking the hand of the then allied dictator.

What is significant from Duelfer's revelations, based on hours of interviews with the captive Saddam himself, as well as with his senior officials, is the extent to which they show how gravely the US had miscalculated – or perhaps deliberately misunderstood – the regime, rather than whether an alternative to invasion had been feasible. War happened because the Bush Administration wanted it to happen, not because no alternatives existed.

The same was not true of the decision to invade Afghanistan in October 2001, to oust the Taliban and decimate al-Qaeda. But Iraq was different. Why? Because in the final analysis it was the United States and Britain that were the aggressors, as Bush made clear: 'The War on Terror will not be won on the defensive. We must take the battle to the enemy, disrupt his plans, and confront the worst threats before they emerge,' he had told a thousand West Point military graduates and their families on 1 June 2002. The implication was that by taking the war to Afghanistan, overthrowing the Taliban regime and sending al-Qaeda scattering, the battle had not been taken to 'the enemy', that 'his plans' had not been disrupted, and that the attack on al-Qaeda had meant that the 'worst threats' had not yet been confronted. Iraq was – somehow – *worse*, and pre-emptive war thus became the publicly stated – as opposed to privately agreed – doctrine of the Administration.

During the long post-mortem period since the overthrow of Saddam Hussein's regime, the extent to which things were known or could at least have been guessed at during the planning stages, provided an adequate guide as to what could have been a well-founded course of action. UK officials briefed Tony Blair in an 'options paper' in early March 2002 which was referred to by Lord Butler in the report of his inquiry into WMD in Iraq, published in July 2004. Butler also cited an assessment of 15 March 2002 by the UK Joint Intelligence Committee (JIC), the Cabinet Office body by which intelligence assessments are prepared for ministers, which made clear:

> Intelligence on Iraq's weapons of mass destruction (WMD) and ballistic missile programmes is sporadic and patchy. Iraq is also well practised in the art of deception, such as concealment and exaggeration. A complete picture of the various programmes is therefore difficult. But it is clear that Iraq continues to pursue a policy of acquiring WMD and their delivery means. Intelligence indicates that planning to reconstitute some of its programmes began in 1995. WMD programmes were then given a further boost in 1998 with the withdrawal of UNSCOM inspectors.

On Iraq's nuclear weapons programme, the JIC noted that 'Iraq is pursuing a nuclear weapons programme. But it will not be able to indigenously produce a nuclear weapon while sanctions remain in place, unless suitable fissile material is purchased from abroad.' Overall, the JIC judged that 'while sanctions remain effective, Iraq cannot indigenously develop and produce nuclear weapons; if sanctions were removed or became ineffective, it would take at least five years to produce a nuclear weapon. This timescale would shorten if fissile material was acquired from abroad.'[16]

That Saddam Hussein was a tyrant and that the regime routinely tyrannised the Iraqi population was well known. But this was not deemed likely to mobilise the American public behind a war to overthrow him, not least because he had been just as tyrannical when he had been supplied with weapons by the West during the eight-year Iran–Iraq war. To have argued for war on the basis of human rights would probably have led to interminable debates about whether Saddam Hussein was worse than other dictators. Paul Wolfowitz, the US Deputy Defense Secretary, had been the driving force of the Bush Administration's policy of 'regime change' in Iraq. Only days after the 9/11 attacks, Wolfowitz was the first to link state sponsorship with the attacks, defining a policy of 'ending states who sponsor terrorism'.[17] Wolfowitz's opportunism shone through vividly in the immediate aftermath of the terrorist attacks, when it became clear that 9/11 was an *opportunity* as well as a *tragedy*. Bob Woodward, in his account of the Administration's response to 11 September – *Bush at War* – relates how 'the terrorist attacks of 11 September gave the U.S. a new window to go after Hussein.'[18] He adds,

> Wolfowitz seized the opportunity. Attacking Afghanistan would be uncertain. He worried about 100,000 American troops bogged down in mountain fighting in Afghanistan six months from then. In contrast, Iraq was a brittle, oppressive regime that might break easily. It was doable. He estimated that there was a 10 to 50 percent chance Saddam was involved in the September 11 terrorist attacks. The U.S. would have to go after Saddam at some time if the war on terrorism was to be taken seriously.[19]

It is reasonable to assume that the well-informed Woodward's characterisation of the thinking in the White House is accurate. The brittle regime in Baghdad would soon be transformed into a threat to the

United States – which it appears not to have been, according to Duelfer – and one that was allied to al-Qaeda – which it is evident it was not.

To replace truths, the power of secrets was used to launch a war.

As the prospect of invasion loomed, evidence to substantiate the claim that al-Qaeda had ties with Baghdad were demanded of the CIA. It largely failed to provide what the political leadership had asked of it. In his 28 January 2003 State of the Union address, Bush repeated the assertion that 'evidence from intelligence sources, secret communications and statements by people now in custody, reveal that Saddam Hussein aids and protects terrorists, including members of al-Qaeda.'[20] According to UK intelligence officials, al-Qaeda had sought to create ties with Baghdad on at least three occasions, and al-Qaeda operatives are reported to have met Iraqi officials in Khartoum, Cairo and Jalalabad, Afghanistan, in 1994, 1997 and 2000; an al-Qaeda delegation also travelled to Baghdad from Tehran in 1999 to try to build ties.

But these efforts had been rebuffed – by Iraq.

It is nevertheless a prominent characteristic of the ways in which the Bush Administration sought to argue the case for war that at key moments it portrayed the Iraqi regime as having taken steps which were in fact initiated by others. It was at these points that the *use* of intelligence became a clear *abuse*: assertions regarding events in which Iraqi officials were involved were – knowingly – manipulated in order to build the case for war.

It was this practice which had led me to the newspaper stall on the Piazza Barberini in Rome on that hot afternoon in June 2004.

Italy had been thrust into the centre of the intelligence 'war' between supporters and opponents of the Iraq invasion, when its foreign intelligence service became embroiled in the debate surrounding allegations made in the 24 September 2002 UK Government dossier[21] in which it was stated that 'there is intelligence that Iraq has sought the supply of significant quantities of uranium from Africa'.[22]

Central to the intelligence war which then embroiled the Italian SISMi, SIS, France's DGSE and the CIA, was the risk created by the trade in secrets. This trade was real, and centred most prominently on a former officer of the Carabinieri, Italy's national police force – a man called Rocco Martino; it began when thieves stole a steel watch and two bottles of perfume from Niger's Embassy on Via Antonio Baiamonti in Rome at the end of December 2000.

The robbery left many questions and no clear answers as to what the real intentions of the robbers had been, though it was decided later that they had in fact planned to steal embassy notepaper and official stamps which would allow the forging of documents seeming to come from the Niger Government. The documents were then thought intended to be used for one thing: the illicit sale of Niger's uranium deposits.

It was as if I was in sight there on the Piazza – perhaps from a window high up in the shadows – of the man with the precise English who called my cellphone, who instructed me to take one of the streets leading off the Piazza, follow it until I reached a particular building on the right, take the lift to a specific floor, and then ring the bell of the door with a particular number.

A woman in her late thirties, her long blonde hair perfectly coiffed, opened the door; I did not hear her name. She quickly disappeared into a room adjoining one in which three men were sitting in armchairs, a net curtain draped across an open balcony door occasionally billowing in the currents of warm air. A bespectacled man in his thirties introduced himself and the others. The woman brought in some cold drinks. We sat.

All those in the room were Italian intelligence officers, whose first names were all I was given. They had agreed to meet me only after lengthy discussions with an intermediary. These officers didn't meet with foreign journalists, and were slightly nervous about breaking the habit. They observed me intently, aware that the issues we were about to discuss necessitated a new approach.

And this is what I was told.

For a year prior to the break-in, the Niger Embassy had been under surveillance by the SISMi. In fact the building had been bugged after it had been learned that officials may have hosted meetings involving would-be customers for illicit uranium sales. Five countries had been identified as potential customers: North Korea, China, Libya, Iran – and Iraq. The SISMi gathered intelligence on the negotiations, including evidence that Libya was investing in Niger's uranium industry. What also emerged was that the negotiation of sales to Iraq turned on its head the claim by the UK – and later by President Bush – that Iraq 'sought the supply' of uranium. In fact it was the other way round – individuals in Niger had sought customers.

When the evidence gathered by the SISMi between 1999 and 2001 was thrown into the diplomatic furore that preceded the invasion of Iraq, the intelligence gathered in Rome took on major new significance. The Italians had passed the 'raw' intelligence – that is, the unassessed information – to the United States in early September 2001 and to the United Kingdom in March 2002. Five months later, the United States sent the former ambassador Joseph Wilson to Niger to assess the credibility of separate US intelligence which suggested that *Iraq had approached Niger*. Despite subsequently accusing the Bush Administration of 'twisting' intelligence,[23] Wilson wrote in his account of the visit that Mohamed Sayeed al-Sahaf, later Iraq's Information Minister, was identified to him by a Niger official as having sought to discuss trade with Niger. As Niger's other main export is goats, it was assumed that it was in uranium that al-Sahaf had been interested.

Despite having been given the raw intelligence material gathered by the Italians between 1999 and 2001, the only evidence of Iraq's alleged attempts to buy uranium that the United States took into serious consideration was handed to its embassy in Rome in October 2002. That evidence consisted of correspondence apparently sent by Niger officials to their Iraqi interlocutors; when the United States later passed the documents to the International Atomic Energy Agency for verification, they were found to be forgeries. Embarrassed by this revelation, US officials subsequently distanced themselves entirely from the notion that Iraq had been seeking these clandestine deals. But because the letters had emerged in Rome it was assumed they were a key part of the Italian authorities' evidence of illicit uranium sales – which they were not, because they were in fact part of a scam.

The fake documents had been handed to an Italian journalist by the ex-Carabinieri officer Rocco Martino, and were in turn handed by the journalist to an official at the US Embassy in Rome for an opinion as to their authenticity. But a senior officer in another European intelligence service had told me – before I arrived for the July 2004 meeting in Rome – that Martino had first tried to sell the documents to both the

British and French intelligence services, before he had turned up with them in Rome.

Two salient issues emerged from the plethora of claims and counter-claims regarding the Niger uranium issue. First was that Martino emerged as the intelligence 'salesman' *par excellence*, who said of himself – having failed to return my own telephone calls to him – when he later emerged from obscurity and gave an interview to the Italian newspaper *Il Giornale* on 21 September 2004:

> I have been engaged in intelligence for many years, offering my cooperation to various intelligence services, including the French... The hoax began one day when a Nigerien Embassy source who had proven to be reliable on previous occasions and who had contacts also with the collaborator of a SISMi aide, passed on to me a whole lot of information. It is true that that information included some references to a uranium traffic between Niger and Iraq. What did I do at that juncture? I passed it on to the French secret service, with which I am in touch and by which I was remunerated.[24]

The second issue was the rapid immersion of the evidence the SISMi had gathered from its eavesdropping on the Niger Embassy in Rome – the source of its original suspicions about the illicit uranium trade, dating from 1999 – into the welter of other 'evidence', of which the fake documents became the most notorious. As Martino later told *Il Giornale*, 'I am the victim, the tool used by someone for games much bigger than me,' adding that, even though his source within the Niger Embassy was – as far as he knew – also providing information to the SISMi, on this occasion the SISMi 'has nothing to do with it... The truth is that I have been duped, manipulated, used. I would like to figure out why they chose me'.

The wish of the SISMi to weed out the fakes and forgeries, and to let it be known that the separate intelligence – which it said demonstrated that there had indeed been efforts by Nigerien officials to engage Iraq in illicit uranium sales – lay behind the Italian intelligence officers' readiness to meet with me that day in Rome. For my part, all I wanted was the truth, however complex it might be.

The officers told me that two different batches of documents relating to this trade had emerged, which then started to do the rounds of the UK, French, Italian and finally US intelligence agencies. The first were those which included evidence that Martino was right: his trade in secrets was something 'much bigger' than him. He became the servant of many masters, the 'bigger' conflict in which he had been caught being one between two intelligence services – the Italian SISMi, whose Government under Silvio Berlusconi supported the invasion of Iraq, and the French DGSE, whose Government under Jacques Chirac opposed it. 'The most interesting thing is that the French asked Rocco for more [documents],' I was told when I went back to Rome on 30 July for a second meeting in that apartment along the road leading up the Quirinal Hill, where a different woman – dark hair, spectacles – opened the door and offered round a large platter of elaborate sandwiches.

French interest initially stemmed from concern about the security of Niger's uranium – which is in the hands of French companies, which supply France's nuclear power stations – but which then evolved, as the invasion of Iraq drew closer. 'Rocco is a nuisance,' I was told, as we ate the sandwiches.

> He makes his life based on the information that he has. He tries to fulfil demand with the supply. He is present in all the international contexts that may have information – including the SISMi. He comes to us and tries to offer things. When [information traders] understand that they are unable to make a contract, they go somewhere else. And then maybe they come back when the personalities have changed. But sometimes Martino does get good information. This is why the French kept him.[25]

Specifically concerning the market in documents concerning Niger's uranium supplies, one of those present went on to explain that Martino was under surveillance by the SISMi when he met on a monthly basis with the French DGSE at a hotel restaurant in Brussels, the Italians' conviction growing throughout 2003–4 that he intended to say that he believed the SISMi had been responsible for forging the documents which had fallen into his hands: 'He wants to hide the fact that he got them from the forger. Part of the story is about how vulnerable intelligence agencies are to tricksters.'

But the agencies are also part of a trade in secrets, which – the Italian officer explained – can take on a life of its own in ways which can change the course of history:

The French started posing questions about Niger [in 1999]. This is what created the demand [for intelligence, from the likes of Martino]. The demand already existed, but the French pointed the demand towards Martino, and found the supply that passed through his hands. This doesn't mean that Martino created the documents. He just created the market for them.[26]

Rarely have the consequences of this long-established practice of trading created such mayhem. Perhaps similar situations have occurred in the past, but have remained undisclosed; the publicity surrounding the Iraq War intelligence was unprecedented, the discomfort it caused in part rooted in the possibility that poor intelligence was not as uncommon as it might have seemed. Public debate about the quality of intelligence was justified because intelligence was the centrepiece of US and UK Government claims; how the intelligence agencies acquired their intelligence was therefore equally relevant to the debate. But the reality at the heart of this 'craft of cheat and imposter' was always going to be a challenge for all of us on the outside to understand; how could agencies associate with people such as Martino, the traders at the heart of the spying game? The answer is simple: the agencies generally have little choice, obliged as they are to trade and deal with whoever may be able to provide them with the intelligence which may cast light on the issues under scrutiny.

The challenge of gathering accurate intelligence about a regime as isolated and as inward-looking as that led by Saddam Hussein was enormous. Establishing with any precision how much of the equipment acquired during the 1980s with the intention of developing WMD was still in existence would – as the SST5 head Colonel Harrington told me – not be possible without speaking to Iraqis; that in turn was only possible if the country were fully opened to inspection. Saddam Hussein had failed to convince the United Nations that he had nothing to hide, so the assumption was that he was hiding something. But it could only be regarded as an assumption. To give that assumption any credibility required either proof that military hardware was indeed being concealed, or proof that Saddam retained the *intention* of developing WMD. Short of invading the country, concealment was hard to prove; that left the goal of proving the regime's *intent*, and ultimately it was the claims about this *intent* which underpinned the justification for war.

It is a rather overlooked aspect of the intelligence failure which Iraq became that what was completely missing from the intelligence picture was any real idea of what Saddam Hussein's intentions were. Nobody had a clue what was going on inside his mind; nobody really understood the man; certainly nobody understood how he regarded himself, his destiny and his ambitions for Iraq.

Meanwhile, as the political and military juggernauts gathered pace in the winter of 2002–3, exasperation within the intelligence agencies grew. Long-established inter-agency conventions – which had served well during the Cold War, in the Anglo–French cooperation against the PIRA, as well as in the wake of 9/11 – came under threat. The political fault lines between the 'pro' and 'anti' war camps deepened, the role of intelligence became the target of intense media speculation, and the London and Washington political leaderships used secrets as a weapon in debate for the first time, a senior French officer telling me in January 2003,

> The intelligence services are increasingly exasperated by the media drawing links between strands of investigations that in reality have no connection. The sharing of information has been transformed, but it is still not organised as well as it needs to be. Different agencies are still concerned to guard their own sources, and that affects the information that is shared, as the loss of sources outside the West is the worst thing that could happen. What really has to be understood is that really nobody understands what is happening – none of the security services or intelligence agencies. We can all agree that there's no support for Saddam anywhere. But the response to a war in Iraq will be driven by the strength of feeling against the Americans and American policy. This is what makes the situation so dangerous.[27]

As the dangers grew, so did the conflicts between – and within – the intelligence communities. In this the agencies in Washington were not alone.

In London an SIS officer was invited to the headquarters of MI5 at Thames House to explain to a group of senior MI5 officers how confident SIS was about the intelligence it had gathered on Iraq's WMD, and specifically whether it had confidence in its sources. Judgement was a core concern, MI5 having established precedents in its history of 'speaking truth to power', perhaps most memorably in 1936 when its first Director General, the long-serving Vernon Kell, submitted a memorandum concerning the threat from the 'totalitarian governments of Germany and Italy' which illustrated MI5's prescient and accurate reading of Hitler's *Mein Kampf* at a time when the Governments of Stanley Baldwin and subsequently Neville Chamberlain were advocating appeasement; a further MI5 report, in 1938, pointedly included excerpts from Hitler's own notes in which he described Chamberlain as an 'arsehole' – the Security Service's aim being to ensure that the threat from the Führer was taken seriously by the Government.[28]

Lying behind the MI5 invitation to SIS seventy years later, was growing concern within the UK's broader intelligence community that if the intelligence supporting the Government's argument that the ultimatum delivered to Saddam Hussein's regime was not based on firm ground, all the intelligence agencies would be tarnished with the same brush. As one MI5 officer who attended the meeting told me shortly afterwards, 'We didn't want to find that people thought all intelligence was crap, if we were all to be seen in the same way.'

For MI5 the issue was of crucial importance, as it sought to grapple with a domestic threat from individuals inspired by al-Qaeda, whose activities, capabilities and intentions were at that time proving extremely difficult to discern, infiltrate and thwart. MI5 needed public opinion on its side, most particularly among Britain's Muslim population, from within which it was hoped intelligence leads regarding the 'home-grown' terrorist threat might emerge; the last thing it needed was for its sister agency at Vauxhall Cross to be seen to be at the heart of an intelligence failure which would lead to the invasion of a Muslim country.

But the Thames House staff were to be disappointed.

The visiting SIS officer was asked about the intelligence from which the assessments that had formed the basis of the Government's key dossier on Iraq's WMD had been drawn; he was then asked for more detail about the sources SIS had used to provide the intelligence which – in a sanitised form – had been placed in the public domain by the Blair Government. At this point the temperature at the meeting rose, when the SIS officer told these 'fellow members' of the UK's intelligence 'community' that he was sorry, 'but I can't tell you who our sources are.'

His refusal to share the identities – or, when asked to do so, even to share a sense of how well-placed the sources were and therefore what degree of confidence one could have in them – left the MI5 gathering wholly dissatisfied and increasingly edgy about what lay in store once the US ultimatum to Saddam Hussein had expired, the tanks had rolled across the Kuwait–Iraq border, and the country lay open for the relatively unhindered inspection of sites allegedly connected to WMD development.

But just as MI5 was looking askance at SIS over the Iraq intelligence – while nevertheless maintaining without any interruption the two services' ever-closer cooperation in the counter-terrorism effort against al-Qaeda and its affiliates – the emergence of doubts from within the MoD's Defence Intelligence Staff (DIS) caused further ructions. Some within the DIS – whose primary role is to provide senior military officers with intelligence relevant to battlefield situations – had let it be known that it saw flaws in the UK Government's intelligence-based dossier which had been published on 24 September 2002. These differences intensified with the publication by 10 Downing Street in January 2003 of a second report[29] – entitled *Iraq – Its Infrastructure of Concealment, Deception and Intimidation* – which came to be referred to as the 'dodgy dossier' following the revelation that it was in part based on open-source material culled without attribution from research by a California-based academic.

Criticism emanating from within the DIS was met with a response from elsewhere in the intelligence community: 'The DIS assessment is wrong, and these are not the views of the intelligence community,'[30] I was told. This was soon followed up by more detailed explanations from other quarters, another senior official telling me,

> The Joint Intelligence Committee does assessments: these are the ones that matter. The DIS is not an intelligence-producing agency. They get themselves into trouble when they go beyond that. The JIC does the assessments; the DIS doesn't have its own sources, and this is the political use of intelligence. The [DIS] assessment is based on misunderstanding of the situation in Iraq. If it had gone through the JIC it would have been ripped apart.'[31]

This view was followed by one from another official:

The DIS' role is to inform the management of the MoD. They produce assessments and analysis. They do it from a number of sources. But they don't run intelligence assets (that is, agents). The MoD officers abroad do get some intelligence – it's information. There are military sources of intelligence. But the DIS isn't a[n intelligence] collection agency. There are issues with the Defence Intelligence Staff – it is a bit spare, and they would like to do more. That's what this is.[32]

But this friction – which had led to the effort to portray the DIS as outside the intelligence community – between different parts of the Whitehall machinery, whose scepticism of each other was beginning to mirror that which had stymied the CIA and the FBI in the years prior to 9/11, was then calmed by a fresh attempt from within SIS to demystify intelligence and the role of the hitherto wholly mysterious Secret Intelligence Service. The method was straightforward, and simply involved providing explanation as to which parts of the 'dodgy dossier' were based on publicly available material, why using such material was not a reason to doubt the credibility of the dossier, and in general terms to give the public insights into the breadth of material that was drawn together when the 'secret' world of spies was doing its normal work. Thus, I was told, the first and third parts of the dossier were 'drawn from intelligence material',[33] while the second part – which focused on the structure of the Iraqi regime – was, as I was told by one official,

> pulled together from overt sources. For source protection we didn't put in everything we know. The guy in California was relying on Iraqi documents. For some reason people want to play this up, to rubbish the whole piece. There's a feeding frenzy. People in the intelligence world are frustrated, because there isn't maturity as to what intelligence is likely or not likely to be. We don't have that American system, where you have that omniscience when it comes to intelligence. The difficulty is to tell people things without killing your sources. It was an internal paper that was made public. But it had no pretence to being a 'dossier'. Nor was it meant to eventually be made public. The crucial point is that some of it came from overt sources, and we believe them to be largely accurate.[34]

Then, on 20 March 2003, Iraq was invaded.

11

'HAIL THE CHIEF'

The advance of the invading army was assisted by the presence of deep cover agents inside Iraq who were working with both the US and the UK intelligence services. The focus on the military campaign provided some relief for the intelligence community, diverting attention – at least temporarily – away from the claims and counter-claims regarding the intelligence that had been used to justify the invasion, one official telling me on 19 March, 'This is a military operation; covert activity to unseat Saddam Hussein is unlikely. In military operations what you do are things to control ground and preserve life. Getting a grip on WMD is important, but the priority is getting control of Iraq.'[1]

A crucial point came when British troops arrived on the outskirts of the southern city of Basra, a few days after crossing the border from Kuwait. It was while the forces were watching events from the outskirts that Iraqis spying for Britain from within the city provided intelligence that can be regarded as having determined the course of the military campaign in its early stages. It was also at this point that the intelligence community's ability to function as a counterweight to ill-informed speculation appeared to emerge.

One aspect of the media speculation at the time was focused on whether – as had been the case when the US-led coalition had forced Iraqi troops out of Kuwait in 1991 – the Shia population of southern Iraq would derive inspiration from the invasion and rise up against Saddam

Hussein's regime. In newsrooms across the West – including the one in which I was working, at the *Financial Times* – the assumption that this would indeed happen was widely discussed as being 'just a matter of time'. The newsroom chatter – mostly opinion dressed up as fact – became increasingly passionate when British journalists 'embedded' with UK forces on the outskirts of Basra were told on 25 March by the military personnel under whose charge they were, that there were signs of violence within the city. The long-predicted 'uprising' must therefore have begun, the media assumed, seemingly encouraged to do so by the Army, whose deputy commander, Major General Peter Wall, told the media that 'we do not have an absolutely clear indication of the scale and scope of this uprising or exactly what has engendered it...But the General on the ground is going to exploit the potential,'[2] before going on to caution that whatever was taking place 'was only in its infancy'.

The first report to grab the attention of the *Financial Times*'s news editor was an ITN bulletin, broadcast early evening over the news desk, which sent a flurry of excitement among the editorial decision-makers about the 'uprising' it was assumed was taking place. General Wall's choice of words had – unsurprisingly – given this assumption added weight. A judgement could be made on the basis of what a man in uniform had said, what a television channel had broadcast, and what was assumed was going to erupt from within the oppressed Iraqi population that was awaiting liberation by the forces of good.

But in the city the real story was a different one, ignorance of the Iraqi population's *intent* becoming as evident as that regarding Saddam Hussein's.

The challenge SIS had faced in recruiting agents inside Iraq who had a detailed inside knowledge of the regime's weapons programmes was far greater than the challenge of recruiting 'eyes and ears' on the ground who were able to provide intelligence on more visible issues. Spies had provided on-the-ground intelligence from Basra for years prior to the 2003 campaign, and this capacity had been built up in the months prior to the 20 March invasion, in order to learn as far in advance as possible – through visible signs as much as from insider intelligence – about regime and popular responses to the military advance. The intelligence provided on the evening of 25 March 2003 by one such agent on the ground in Basra was of a kind that starkly demonstrated the difference between 'intelligence' and the 'indications' conveyed by television.

Liaising with two UK special forces officers who had been deployed to the city by SIS, and who had been undercover in Basra for several days prior to the invasion, one such agent – an Iraqi – knew what was really taking place when the violence seen from the outskirts erupted. One thing was clear: there was no uprising to which the British forces waiting outside the city could attach their military campaign; there was no opportunity to 'exploit the potential' – because there was no potential. Having seen themselves as betrayed in 1991, when the US-led coalition fell back from Iraq after the expulsion of Saddam's forces from Kuwait, the Shia of Basra were in no mood to revolt, as a senior intelligence officer made clear to me at the time, when he said bluntly, 'We are not expecting the Iraqi population to rise up in support [of the invasion].'[3] Iraq's Shia could not rely upon the United States, Britain or anybody else. The brutality of Saddam's suppression of their revolt in 1991 was extremely fresh in their minds, and even the sight of British tanks on the edge of the city was insufficient to inspire a repeat of what had been attempted a decade earlier.

Even so, Saddam Hussein's ruling Ba'ath Party had problems on its hands in Basra. It was internal tensions within the Party which had erupted into the violence that on that night of 25 March were being wrongly reported as signs of an uprising. The gulf between perceptions and reality was stark. What *seemed* to be the logical consequence of the invasion – that the liberators were unleashing Iraqis' pent-up desire for liberation – was nothing of the sort. But logic was what the media decision-makers wanted to hear.

As the *Financial Times*'s news desk prepared its story, I called the number I had called innumerable times that day, had called many times since 9/11, and would call many times in the weeks and months which followed. Gone were the days when the London-based dissidents, exiled propagandists, Washington think-tanks or regional 'experts' could be treated as speaking with authority about what was taking place in Iraq. That night in Basra only the spies on the ground had an insight into what was really happening. Logic suggested that they would like there to have been a Shia uprising in the city; to have portrayed it as such would have bolstered the propaganda role that spies have played throughout history. So, when the telephone was picked up and I spoke with a familiar voice about what might be going on in that city many thousands of miles away, I was expecting the same line to be taken as that conveyed by the Army – the line the news editor had adopted, which somehow *must* be true because that was what was appearing on the television screen above his desk.

'I will see what I can find out. Call me back in thirty minutes,' my contact at SIS told me.

Darkness had fallen over London; the first edition deadline was approaching; I waited, then called back. 'It isn't a Shia uprising, it's a Ba'ath Party feud,' he said.

The spies in Basra had reported back via the special forces officers in the city, whose radio communications with SIS desk officers posted in the Gulf had allowed the intelligence service to gather very quickly that what the Army could see from the outskirts of Basra was far from being an uprising in support of the invaders. My contact explained that the fighting in the city had erupted when Ali Hassan al-Majid – Saddam's first cousin, former intelligence chief, and the man more widely known as 'Chemical Ali' owing to his role in the use of chemical weapons during the regime's attack on the Kurdish town of Halabja on 16 March 1988 – had ordered the execution of a senior Ba'ath Party official whose support for the regime's strategy in the face of the invasion was in doubt. The killing had split the Party leadership in the city, unleashing feuding which was quashed by militia loyal to the regime. This was the violence that could be seen by the British forces watching from afar.

It was unfortunate for the readers of the *Financial Times* that my intelligence contact's detailed explanation of what was really happening was cut down to only a paragraph buried deep inside a television-led story headlined 'Reports from Basra of Shia uprising against Saddam'.[4] The television reportage that oozed out assuredly from the screen above the news editor's desk apparently could not be defied. The newspaper's story that appeared the following day told of an 'uprising' and a 'revolt'; in doing so, and by using such words, it took readers into a situation that was fictitious, amid claims that were wrong. The intelligence provided by SIS agents via their special forces interlocutors, which was then assessed by agent handlers and desk officers, and then – in that emerging era of relative openness which the Iraq War had forced upon a reluctant intelligence service – shared with me, was not going to impede the decision-makers of the 'quality' media once they had made up their minds.

But in the days which followed, as the occupying forces reached sites in southern and central Iraq at which they expected – and failed – to find the WMD, the agencies' discomfort intensified.

Just as the United States and the United Kingdom never agreed on whether links existed between al-Qaeda and Saddam's regime, so they did not agree on whether a 'red line' existed around Baghdad, which, when crossed by the invading forces, would lead to Saddam Hussein ordering the launch of his arsenal of WMD. This difference between the two allies ought to have been highlighted as demonstrating the most fundamental of all the flaws in the argument in favour of war: while one official in Washington was telling me that he was 'not aware of any information that establishes a "line on a map" [after which WMD would be used by Saddam],'[5] one in London was saying that such a line was indeed 'thought to exist'; then another US official told me,

> We have to assume that the Iraqis have done all sorts of advanced planning. They have had plenty of time to think about these things. There are always levels of desperation – which disturbs me a little bit. It comes down to Saddam's perceptions. So far he has probably got reasons to keep up some hopes, and that's reflected in the fact that he hasn't used WMD so far. It will all turn around really quickly.[6]

But when asked a few days later for his view as to why the 'red line' had been crossed without the nuclear missiles having been unleashed, the official in London revealed how uncertain was the real reading of Saddam's intent, telling me,

> The basis on which they might not be used would [result from] overconfidence on Saddam's part, so that he may string things along and believe that he can stay in power. But then events could overtake him. I think there is still a reasonable basis for that. There are reasons to believe that he has been overconfident. He may think he can string

things along. But he may be wrong – he is a dictator who has restricted sources of information. He is not necessarily getting all the bad news. The whole situation might just take him over.[7]

It was illustrative of how similar Iraq was as an intelligence target to other targets throughout history, that the absence of *intent intelligence* was starkly revealed: when the 'red line' was crossed nothing happened. The failure to know the enemy was being exposed, and the enormous error that the UK and US Governments had made in depending on intelligence as the sole justification for going to war, was revealed. The agencies' role – and the understanding of what intelligence is and therefore what its role can and cannot be – fell under increasingly bright light. The perennial, unchanging needs of the 'craft' were at the heart of the discussions being held behind the walls of their imposing offices. The contrast between what *had* happened in Basra on 25 March and what then did *not* happen as the 'red line' was crossed near Baghdad a short while later, is illustrative of how crucial intelligence can be when its time-tested function is retained, but how distracting it can be when it is not set against a background understanding that – in the absence of hard facts – can assist at the very least in facilitating informed judgement. Thus it was that the 'humint' – human intelligence, as opposed to the 'sigint' gathered electronically – gathered by spies on the ground in Basra was quickly passed to the UK military command on 25 March. Al-Majid was reported to have convened a meeting at the Ba'ath Party headquarters in the city; the SIS agent in the city guided the British special forces officers to the building, which they then highlighted with a laser; the coordinates were transmitted to the UK military headquarters, and within minutes the US Air Force had directed bombers to the site and flattened it.

'Chemical Ali' escaped, evading the onslaught until he was captured and later hanged. But the attack on the Party headquarters nevertheless had a profound effect, destabilising the regime's grip on the city, which was occupied by British forces a short while later. The use of 'humint' in Basra had thus been as effective as the 'red line' around Baghdad had proved non-existent. Intelligence on regime *intent* was as evasive as the crumbling of that regime was evident. Nobody, it seemed, could get inside the head of the leader, and the failure to do so – a failure which, given the character of the regime, is understandable though not excusable in view of the action that was then taken to overthrow it – plagued the entire 'intelligence war' against Saddam Hussein.

But in the end the world's first intelligence-based 'pre-emptive war' was a defeat for all sides.

The defeated regime's palaces were turned to rubble, its pleasure gardens transformed into killing fields, its leaders hanged. And for the people of Iraq, the cruelty of dictatorship was replaced by carnage.

However, it was for the invaders that defeat was perhaps the bitterest of all, because for them there is no chance of a full recovery. However many foreign soldiers died, however much money is spent on reconstruction, whatever signs there are that Iraq has now emerged from the bloody turmoil, the invaders will never be released from the burden of having launched a war on the basis of claims which served only to reveal how deep are the flaws in the political establishments of Britain and the United States. While to this day the media focuses on Iraq's parlous state, the real problems lie in London and Washington, where institutions creaked, civil servants considered treachery in response to what they were being required to do to support the 'war effort', and Whitehall mandarins found themselves at odds with the civilised society of which they thought they were a part – most devastatingly when the government scientist who had done more than most to find the evidence of the dangers posed by Saddam Hussein's regime was found dead in an Oxfordshire woodland.

The suicide of David Kelly on 17 July 2003 exposed just how vulnerable the British Government was to the accusation that its case for war had been based on a fiction. The MoD's exposure of Kelly – by way of its confirmation to journalists who asked, that he was indeed the source of a story broadcast by the BBC which appeared to question the validity of UK Government claims regarding the threat from Iraq's weapons – exposed the depths to which the Government had sunk.

But it was during the subsequent inquiry into Kelly's death that the extent to which the flaws in the Government's argument were fully exposed. In a key email referring to the dossier which was shortly to put forward the Government's case for war, Jonathan Powell – Tony Blair's Chief of Staff – stated,

The dossier is good and convincing for those who are prepared to be convinced.

I have only three points, none of which affect the way the document is drafted or presented.

First the document does nothing to demonstrate a threat, let alone an imminent threat from Saddam. In other words it shows he has the means but does not demonstrate that he has the motive to attack his neighbours, let alone the west. We will need to make it clear in launching the document that we do not claim that we have evidence that he is an imminent threat. The case we are making is that he has continued to develop WMD since 1998, and is in breach of UN resolutions. The international community has to enforce those resolutions if the UN is to be taken seriously. Second, we will be asked about the connections to Al Qaida. The document says nothing about these … [the remainder of this sentence is blacked out].

Third, if I was Saddam I would take a party of western journalists to the Ibn Sina factory or one of the others pictured in the document to demonstrate there is nothing there. How do we close off that avenue to him in advance?[8]

The controversy into which David Kelly was later thrust – cast adrift by the MoD, who saw him as a scapegoat, the sacrifice of which could have helped their case had it not led to his suicide – would be unlikely to have happened had the weeks after the invasion produced the evidence of WMD both the UK and US Governments said they expected to find. But as the hunt for weapons got underway, no dissent was permitted. 'What is being found so far isn't surprising, given the way that their (Iraq's) standing holdings of weaponry were quite limited. We are not surprised that we haven't come across large amounts,'[9] I was told in late-April 2003, as it became clear that the locations identified pre-war as possible weapons sites were not what they had seemed, my interlocutor continuing,

Nor are we surprised that there are all these false alarms. It's taking a while getting organised for the search. Nobody is going to find large sites of the size UNSCOM inspected or of the kind that made up the September 2002 dossier. What you're likely to find is mobile rather than industrial sites. We reckon that we are going to be able to find WMD when Iraqis are able to speak freely with us.

A month later I was given the same message, another UK insider seeking to reassure me,

> It's going to take us a few more weeks for us to get a clear picture of what happened to the [WMD] programme. Essentially, we are going to learn about the programme from the people who were operatives in it. People are afraid to speak. There was a massive programme of deception. If you have nothing to hide then why have such a programme if you have nothing to hide? It will eventually come out. There will be a much better story to tell by next month.[10]

The same official told me a few days later, 'I'm not sure that we knew what we were going to find. We had no way of knowing what we would actually find.'[11] The following day came a further step away from predictions: 'We are quietly confident that in the fullness of time most if not all of the points made in the dossier will be proven to have been based on fact. But we can't do that now.'[12]

Across the Atlantic, attitudes within the intelligence community – even among those who had, privately, during the previous months aired deep criticism of President Bush and in particular the Defense Secretary Donald Rumsfeld – remained similarly intent on peddling vagueness, one senior intelligence insider whose views had proven highly informed during the previous months telling me,

> I don't think there have been particular bombshells that have caused analysts to revise their thinking [regarding the WMD]. The fact that some weeks have gone by hasn't led to analysts saying that they think they were wrong. The suspicion was and is a factor. A typical intelligence assessment of this kind of topic is going to have lines like: we don't know what we don't know. Was that taken too far? It's too early to say.[13]

But by the time the territory of Iraq was largely in the hands of the invaders, and still no weapons had been found, he was less reassured, telling me in early July,

> Whenever our credibility is called into question, of course that's an issue of concern. These are difficult times for that reason. It's not been quite as acute a set of recriminations as in the UK. This year has been pretty difficult. But the great majority of officers in the intelligence community believe that the basic integrity of the intelligence has been maintained.[14]

The crisis facing both SIS and the CIA stemmed in part from the fact that this 'basic integrity' had indeed been maintained; as had been made clear to me on numerous occasions, *intelligence is not truth*; intelligence is an element which forms a part of the whole. The intelligence regarding Iraq's WMD was extremely thin and – as I was later told – 'it wasn't a rich enough picture. There was undoubtedly pressure put on us to find intelligence on WMD. We were relying on two or three sources – two or three who were liars,' the most notorious of which was the informer codenamed 'Curveball'.[15]

By mid-July 2003 the futility of the hunt for WMD – which I had joined in May as part of the team scouring the Iraqi desert under the command of Lt Colonel Harrington – had led to an intensification of the pressure on the intelligence community to seek ways of reminding the public what intelligence is and what it is not. Moreover, it became a priority to ensure that popular views did not start to mistake spies for decision-makers: 'The successful transposition of intelligence into policy depends on the policymakers. The question isn't quite as simple as "have they made their case well enough?", but "have they used the information at their disposal well enough?"'[16] a very senior intelligence officer insisted to me, continuing,

> The material from the [intelligence] agencies was the only basis for them (the Government) to make their case for an armed resolution. They didn't start off by saying, 'We are going to go to war.' They said, 'We are going to put Saddam under pressure.' But if an intelligence source is saying that Saddam has a capability, it's not for us to say whether that is the basis for military action. That's for the Government to decide. We can be criticised if facts are wrong or misleading, but not for the decision to go to war or not. We didn't make a case for war.

It is a view which prevails within the intelligence community, bruised as it remains by the experience of being pressured to serve its political masters in ways which it had neither the resources nor the foundation nor the will to do. In the end, it could not – if indeed it ever really tried to – *create* truths about Saddam Hussein, his regime, its intentions and its capabilities. The truth would always out.

Within the UK intelligence community there is a strongly held view that the fiasco of Iraq was rooted in a misunderstanding of what intelligence is. Intelligence should not be confused with truth, though it may help clarify what the truth is. As had been the case in Ireland throughout the intelligence history of Anglo–Irish relations, as was ultimately ignored by the CIA when it decided that Congo under Patrice Lumumba was facing a 'commie takeover', as dominated the travails of 'Alec Station' in the 1990s when attempts to truly *understand* the intentions of Osama bin Laden proved so elusive, 'truth' was a combination of facts and understanding of intent; it was not just the 'what' but the 'why' which mattered; without knowledge of Saddam Hussein's *intent*, knowledge of how many chemical warfare suits he might have stored away was less than useless; when Oleg Gordievsky told the British and American Governments of Russia's deep and genuine worry that the United States might launch a pre-emptive nuclear strike against the Soviet Union, it transformed UK and US understanding of Moscow's 'intent'. Spies like Gordievsky can change the course of history; major successes in warfare or diplomacy are usually dependent on superior intelligence, as the British learned to their cost in 1921, at the hands of Michael Collins. But intelligence very rarely gives pre-emptive warning of a threat. It is, as one long-time officer told me, 'shafts of light, and about understanding'.

Iraq was a war for which intelligence was not used as intelligence but as justification. The war did not stem naturally from the intelligence that was gathered, because in the end that intelligence was not in the hands of the intelligence agencies – it was not in anybody's hands, because it did not exist. Instead, what was available – the small nuggets, devoid of substantial context or deep understanding of Saddam Hussein's *intent* – was dressed up into a weapon *intended* by the political leaderships in London and Washington to mystify the public – a public that could not disprove what it was being offered, because there was no other intelligence by which it could be disproved. The two Governments created an elaborate ploy, by which they – or at least their two leaders – convinced themselves that they could get away with invading a state and overthrowing its leader. Their ploy left the credibility of intelligence and the intelligence agencies in tatters, at the very time when the need was apparent for these still highly secretive agencies to become more visible in the face of the separate – and far more pressing – terrorist threat; as a very senior British intelligence official said, when I asked him for his assessment of the damage to SIS's reputation caused by the Iraq debacle, 'Only time will tell whether the problem is that the intelligence service is not very good at what it does.'[17]

Across the Atlantic there was a similar sense of anxiety, as a senior American officer told me:

> I think there have been a lot of bruises that have been inflicted that are going to take a while to be healed. There are still questions, which will focus on whether the intelligence community allowed itself to be used. There are a lot of arguments on both sides. But it's not like the 1970s, when the CIA and FBI were dirty words.[18]

And just as US domestic critics of the CIA took some degree of pleasure in seeing the Agency embarrassed, so SIS in London found itself isolated in Whitehall, an officer telling me,

> There are some people within Whitehall who will be very pleased that the position of the intelligence agencies – particularly SIS – has been cut down to size somewhat. As the Foreign Office has lost ground SIS has seen itself thrust into the limelight, particularly because of issues that can't be dealt with by diplomacy, specifically terrorism, Iraq and Afghanistan. SIS will definitely learn from this experience. It will also have learned from the Government putting its information in the public domain – where it doesn't belong and shouldn't belong.[19]

But such lessons for the future aside, what became far more urgent for the discredited intelligence community was the need to have an intelligence 'success' which would help to rescue a tarnished reputation.

12

SHADOW WARS

Mizran Street was athrong with exuberant revellers drifting away from the parade that had transformed into a military camp the waterfront road that led to Green Square (called Martyr's Square since the fall of the Libyan despot Muammar Gadaffi in 2011). Beneath a striped awning which kept the sun off the viewing stand from where famous faces from bygone revolutions were looking out across the harbour and beyond to the sparkling Mediterranean Sea, Gadaffi had been lounging on a gold throne, resplendent in a crisp white uniform that jangled with rows of medals. He had taken the salute from the ranks of fit and fierce commandos, naval officers, women-only army units and fighter pilots, who had earlier marched in perfect lines under the hot sun along the harbour road in celebration of National Day.

It was 1 September 1999, and the Great Socialist People's Libyan Arab Jamahiriya was celebrating its thirtieth birthday.

But it was when a low, powerful hum replaced the sound of marching, and the waterfront road turned from a military camp to something far less carnival-like, that the polite smiles of the Brother Leader's guests appeared to turn from fervour to anxiety. For rumbling down the road was a slow-moving convoy of enormous trucks; more enormous, however, were the missiles carried on their backs.

It was explained to me later that 'of course' they were not functional missiles – just rusting cast-offs which had been freshly sprayed with white paint. A quick look behind the scenes then enabled me to establish that in fact the convoy only appeared so long because after each truck had crawled ceremoniously past the distinguished gathering, it was driven at high speed along a back road in order to rejoin the rear of the convoy, thereby giving the impression that the Jamahiriya did not boast just a few missiles but in fact had an extensive arsenal.

The joke might well have been on the jokers who mocked this show of force; the real concern was expressed to me weeks later in Khartoum, when a member of the Sudanese Government who had been at the parade in Tripoli told me how shocked he had been to see the Libyan missiles: 'After all, missiles like that only have a certain range, which means they could strike at their neighbours – which means us.'[1]

But without knowing precisely why, the Sudanese – and others – had even more reason to worry than they could possibly have known that afternoon.

Since 1988 Libya had been accused by the United States of developing a chemical-weapons capability at a military-industrial base at Rabta, south of Tripoli;[2] a year earlier, Libyan weapons destined for the PIRA had been captured on board the MV *Eksund* in the joint Anglo–French operation referred to earlier, which had involved tracking the arms shipment using a submarine and a reconnaissance aircraft after it left the same port at Tripoli across which Gadaffi's guests were gazing that day in September 1999. I had just wandered past that port when an Italian friend who was well connected in the city stopped me as I crossed Green Square and beckoned me to come and meet a Libyan acquaintance of his.

Despite his smile, the Libyan first eyed me cautiously. Then he shook my Italian friend's hand warmly, and they spoke in English. My friend introduced me. 'Hello,' the Libyan said, 'I am Musa Kusa.'

Libya's then intelligence chief – head of the External Services Organisation – had been expelled from the UK in 1980 for his alleged involvement in action against Libyan dissidents in Britain. Just as with the United States, UK relations with Gadaffi's regime had deteriorated from then on, Kusa's name occasionally emerging as a key figure in what that regime became during the years that followed. Seemingly relaxed on his home turf, there, just off the square, as he leaned against his car, Kusa talked about the parade, the impressive display of military hardware, and the impact of the recent decision by the United Nations to lift the sanctions it had imposed on 31 March 1992. The sanctions had been a response to the country's refusal to meet demands that it hand over two Libyan intelligence officers accused of organising the bombing of PanAm Flight 103 over Lockerbie, Scotland on 21 December 1988. 'I drove through Lockerbie a few hours before the plane came down,' I told Kusa. He looked at me, nodded good-bye, said nothing more, got into his rather battered car, drove down Mirzan Street, and was soon lost in the crowd.

But his presence lingered and would continue to do so, as the regime within which he was a key player sought to emerge from its isolation, from the sanctions which cost the country $5 billion a year in lost revenue,[3] and from its status as an international pariah. Kusa's role would grow as the world coasted towards 9/11, then lurched from one crisis to another in the wake of that tragedy, as the 'issues that can't be dealt with by diplomacy' began to overwhelm the ones that could. As a consequence of this the intelligence services of influential states became not merely the foot-soldiers of foreign policy but the architects of actions that would be at the heart of what that foreign policy might become. The 'shadow wars' fought between the intelligence services of rival states – in which the dead were not victims like those which had littered the battlefields of Angola and elsewhere, but were the secret operations which failed, the careers which did not progress, the small efforts at manipulation which did not succeed – were the test of whether this alternative to diplomacy could be made to work.

It was consequent to its dealings with Gadaffi's Libya that SIS – in close cooperation with the CIA, though the latter remaining occasionally at arms-length – found itself in the mid-2000s very clearly at a crossroads, as it sought to evaluate its methodology in light of the rapidly changing world it was seeking to understand. In one direction lay al-Qaeda, with whom the trade in secrets was dead in the water; in the other direction was Gadaffi. While bin Laden the 'non-state actor' had forced a rewriting of the intelligence rule book, the state actor – the Libyan leader in need of building bridges with the West in order to attract investors – had sought to draw closer to the Western states which had once vilified him.

What is more, the West needed him.

More of a test than any other, the ability of the intelligence services to adapt to the sudden eruption of non-state power – in the form of al-Qaeda and its adherents from Bali to Karachi to London – was what precipitated the massive and ongoing investment in electronic surveillance and other 'sigint'. But with state actors – national leaders like Gadaffi – the long-established means of espionage could be used. With the prison at Guantanamo Bay having created a captive pool of intelligence sources – in itself an acknowledgement that at least with regard to the threat from al-Qaeda the days of trading secrets had largely come to an end, the rules having changed and the Western agencies unable to rewrite them – grappling with the intelligence challenge from the 'non-state' threat had begun. But what of emerging threats from states? Were the traditional ways of the spy wholly defunct? Would the arrest of suspects and their incarceration at Camp Delta fully replace the long-established practice of 'making spies'?

When it became clear to policy and intelligence insiders that President George W. Bush was casting around post-9/11 for eligible targets in the Arab world upon which he could rain bombs to the sound of popular applause from his political heartland, a priority for US allies was to argue that Libya was a potentially significant ally in the global conflict with al-Qaeda. This potential derived both from the Gadaffi regime's avowed secularism, as well as from it having been the state that took the first step against al-Qaeda, by issuing the international arrest warrant for Osama bin Laden and three of his associates on 16 March 1998 in response to the killing of two German citizens in Libya on 10 March 1994.

Individuals associated with al-Qaeda – and specifically its offshoot, the Libyan Islamic Fighting Group (LIFG), which had been of concern to MI5 and SIS due to the presence of Libyans in the UK – meanwhile languished in Libyan prisons, until their release in 2011 as Gadaffi fell and Islamists became key figures in the Transitional National Council which replaced him. In the aftermath of 9/11, however, the incarceration of these prisoners was talked of as demonstrable proof that the Gadaffi regime was on the 'right side' in the 'GWOT', and that it should be spared an invasion; Iraq was – in part – chosen instead.

Spying was at the heart of all that happened next, because Libya under Gadaffi had two things: oil and secrets, and the regime wanted to trade both.

The Gadaffi mystique had thrown a cloak around the regime and the country for much of the previous thirty years. But what Libya needed was investment in its oil industry, whose out-of-date equipment and lagging production levels were causing discontent within the country as well as within the leadership. To address the economic problems the regime started to explore what bargain could be reached if it traded its secrets in return for the political rehabilitation that would lead to hungry investors flocking in to accelerate development of its oil reserves.

The first stop was Paris.

Ever since the French investigative magistrate Jean-Louis Bruguière had identified five Libyans as responsible for organising the bombing on 19 September 1989 of UTA Flight 772 over Niger, the French Government had been as aggressive in its criticism of the Gadaffi regime as the United States and Britain. The regime's realisation that crime does not pay, that the lifting of sanctions was desirable, and that the issues of the Lockerbie and UTA bombings had to be resolved before there was any hope of sanctions being lifted, marked a seachange in Tripoli's thinking. But the regime also foresaw that opening the terrorist files would lead to discussion about its ambitions on the issue of WMD, as was explained to me by a pivotal figure in the negotiations that followed, who was very familiar with Libyan thinking: 'The discussion about sanctions meant it was necessary to solve the problems of Lockerbie and the French plane, and during the process the WMD file was opened. Lockerbie and the French issue were not going to be solved on their own.'[4]

He went on to explain that Gadaffi first approached the French Government in early 2000, to discuss the WMD issue:

It took the French a long time to come back. He [Gadaffi] wanted the French to come back and be the interlocutors, and he offered them the management of the Rabta [military-industrial] factory. But the French never came through. It was then that it was decided that the UK and the Americans were the only ones.

205

The realisation in Tripoli that it was likely to be more productive in the long run to seek a dialogue with the British and Americans came as the potential fallout for Libya of the US-led invasion of Iraq was causing growing alarm within the Libyan leadership. Moreover, the British were strongly of the view that the United States should be discouraged from drawing Libya into the 'axis of evil'. Thus it was that 'the British opened up, and there were immediately meetings between them and Musa Kusa,' the figure familiar with Libyan thinking told me. The first was with British diplomats in Tripoli in March 2003, he explained, continuing,

> They told the British 'There's a file we would like to discuss'. But after there had been a meeting between Musa and a bureaucrat in London we realised that SIS would be more professional in taking the initiative. At the time there was a vibrant discussion with SIS on other issues, specifically [the killing of WPC Yvonne] Fletcher[5] and Lockerbie. The Libyans didn't think that the WMD issue was a priority – but Musa Kusa was convinced [by others] that it was an issue. They had thought that the Lockerbie issue might be enough.

Thus it was that something akin to the long-established trade in secrets was revived. It was not that the Western interlocutors would be offering up any of *their* secrets; instead they would offer the chance of credibility and rehabilitation to the regime, from which investment might then flow. For its part, Libya would share what it knew of the role played by the LIFG within the al-Qaeda network. Meanwhile, the UK would stealthily focus on the issue which was of increasingly major concern: the global procurement network which had permitted the regime in Tripoli to develop its WMD programme. Having been sidestepped by al-Qaeda's refusal to 'trade', and then bloodied by the abuse of intelligence in order to seek ways of justifying the invasion of Iraq, the spies were on familiar ground with Gadaffi: it was back to the Cold War practice of 'give and take', surrounded by the veil of secrecy necessary to help it happen.

The dual US–UK negotiation with Kusa which followed these initial steps was – seen from the Libyan side – marked by the different approaches of the two allies at the meetings, which took place monthly from March 2003, mostly in London. While they saw their SIS interlocutors as 'consistent', my source familiar with the discussions told me, the arms-control and CIA officials who were part of the discussions were, he said, 'not so consistent. The UK were harder than the Americans in some meetings; the CIA would not be so hard. But in the end Libya was very appreciative of the British position: they played it bluntly, but SIS was the best organisation to do this.'

As the covert diplomacy went on, the Libyan leadership was trying to reconcile the need to project itself as no longer a 'rogue' state with the fact that it had long sought unconventional weapons and that it had at one time – at least in theory – seen possession of such weapons as part of a military strategy, as my source explained:

> The Libyan position came to the point where they were asking: 'Why are we developing these? Against whom? We are not going to use them against our neighbours, so the only offensive weapon could be used against Europe. And with the New World Order it would be suicide to even threaten with such a weapon.'

The Libyan decision to make tentative moves towards addressing US accusations regarding its WMD programme was made prior to the 20 March 2003 invasion of Iraq, though the invasion certainly accelerated the pace at which the leadership made efforts to come to the negotiating table, with some of those close to Gadaffi openly discussing – as the war drums sounded in Washington – whether it was to be 'Libya or Iraq that will be bombed first'.

But the shift in outlook made by the Gadaffi regime during the 1990s – as it had limped along under the yoke of sanctions – had long led to those within the inner circle asking themselves another question: 'Do we use the WMD issue as a bargaining position?' Having then shifted their focus from dealing with the diplomats of the UK Foreign Office to the hardball players of SIS, they found themselves steadily reduced in determination and ability to throw the ball back as robustly as it was being thrown at them, as my source told me:

> The British didn't tell the Libyans what they wanted [regarding WMD]. The British view was: 'The Libyans know what they have, and they should come clean on the issues.' The way the British played it was very clever. They asked the Libyans to come clean, as a check to see if they were serious. And the British could check some of the information to see if it was a manoeuvre or a real process.

Meanwhile, the holding of the secret negotiations was causing a rift in Washington, with the Libyans aware that while Secretary of State Colin Powell, CIA Director George Tenet and National Security Advisor Condoleezza Rice were supportive of the discussions, Vice President Dick Cheney and Defense Secretary Donald Rumsfeld 'were against it, and wanted to keep the military option'.[6]

But another issue preoccupied the regime in Tripoli.

The London meetings held between March and December 2003 – which involved two officials each from the United States, Britain and Libya – were kept secret not only because of the sensitivity of the subjects under discussion, but also because of a wish on the Libyan side to minimise the possibility that other Middle East states would seek a role, as my interlocutor explained:

> The Libyans were very cautious concerning other Arab states, because countries like Tunisia and Egypt were acting like pimps. And they were approached by the Qataris. But the Libyans knew they had to do it directly. They didn't allow any of the Arab countries to do it on their behalf. Egypt in particular liked to play the role of being indispensible as an interlocutor to the Americans.

The risk of being seen to 'lose face' by rescinding the weapons programme without earning much in return was a similarly important factor in Libyan thinking, despite the decision having been taken by the leadership that such a WMD programme had no real purpose and that possession of it could – in the opinion of some – prove 'suicidal'. However, as the monthly meetings progressed, the difference between the US and UK approaches became troubling to the regime: 'It was very important for Gadaffi to have a face-saving exercise. He couldn't give up something without having something to show for it. The British were the ones who could understand this – the SIS people,'[7] my source explained, fully aware that when – under cover of darkness, on 4 October 2003 – a ship bound for Tripoli en route from Malaysia was secretly boarded by Italian and UK intelligence officers at the southern Italian port of Taranto, it had been the SIS officers whose 'understanding' was the most potent element in the negotiators' armoury.

The ship – the *BBC China* – had been under surveillance since leaving Malaysia in August 2003, from where it made a stopover in Dubai.

It was there that it was loaded with forty wooden crates containing the equipment which when assembled would provide Libya with the centrifuge capacity to produce the highly enriched uranium it required to achieve its aims – the creation of a nuclear bomb: a bomb that it was perhaps intended would be delivered via one of the missiles I had seen paraded along the Tripoli seafront four years earlier.

The team of UK and Italian intelligence officers that boarded the *BBC China* at Taranto found what they were looking for. The ship had been diverted there by its German owners on the orders of the German intelligence service, who had been approached by the British though not told of the ongoing negotiations with Tripoli. A tip-off from within the network of the Pakistani nuclear scientist A.Q. Khan – which was supplying the Libyans via a Malaysian company called SCOMI, and which had also provided the technology that allowed Iran and North Korea to develop their nuclear programmes[8] – led to the discreet removal from the ship of the containers they were certain contained the evidence that Tripoli's nuclear programme was still underway. A meeting with Musa Kusa was immediately requested, and as one senior figure intimately acquainted with the details of the negotiations told me, 'They couldn't deny what we were saying. They went into the room to negotiate – and then we switched on the lights ... The ship made it impossible for the Libyans to deny what they were doing.'[9]

In light of the general acceptance within the intelligence community in 2003 that the Libyan leadership no longer saw its nuclear ambitions as serving a strategic purpose, its plans for the cargo discovered at Taranto remain something of a mystery. Musa Kusa told the CIA and SIS officers who pressed him for an explanation, that the cargo was just the latest of several, and that the items would have been surrendered as part of any deal.

Believe Kusa or not, the unravelling of both Libya's nuclear programme and subsequently the A.Q. Khan network which sustained it, marked the moment when intelligence was the crucial element it had failed to be in Iraq, a senior official telling me later, 'The [Secret Intelligence] Service has got to move on [from the Iraq debacle]. It has to rebuild its reputation. The Libyan WMD came at just the right moment.'[10]

A major intelligence success was achieved by combining covert diplomacy, high-quality human intelligence from within the A.Q. Khan network, and an understanding of the intentions of and political currents within the Libyan regime. Some leaders wouldn't have responded as Gadaffi did to the moment when SIS and the CIA 'switched on the lights'; but Gadaffi – despite the discovery of the evidence on board the *BBC China*, which suggested that he may have been bluffing – ultimately needed 'rehabilitation' in the eyes of the world, otherwise he risked overseeing Libya's terminal economic decline.

So he traded his secrets in return for a face-saving diplomatic gesture.

For SIS the 'rebuilding' of its reputation after the intelligence catastrophe of Iraq was of importance not because of public perceptions about it – based as they were on what some within the Service regard as the 'media event' of Iraq – but because of much more significant changes in its relationships with the two most important institutions with which it interacts in its daily operations in the counter-terrorist effort: MI5, and the agency that was becoming increasingly vital in gaining the upper hand against al-Qaeda and its affiliates – the Government Communications Headquarters, GCHQ.

The fundamental reworking of these relationships came in the period which would subsequently be seen as the build-up to the '7/7' suicide bombings in London on 7 July 2005. While it would be a misinterpretation to characterise the organisational changes that were well in train prior to 7/7 as any kind of trade-off between SIS – which had been bloodied by the Iraq issue – and MI5, which had privately cast considerable doubts on the credibility of the SIS intelligence on Iraq's WMD, certain views were widely held across the UK intelligence machinery. One was that the SIS Chief during the Iraq War, Sir Richard Dearlove, had been – as one of his former colleagues described it to me – 'seduced' by Downing Street in the run-up to the invasion, and that his seduction had diluted SIS's professional standing.

But the need to rework fundamentally the relationship between the three UK agencies was anyway being recognised, primarily because of changing perceptions of the threats with which they were responsible for dealing.

Dearlove's replacement as Chief on 6 May 2004 by the long-serving SIS officer John Scarlett – a controversial choice, in light of Scarlett's role while Chairman of the Joint Intelligence Committee in building the Blair Government's case for the invasion of Iraq – was generally welcomed, though with some reservations, within the intelligence community. Morale during Scarlett's five-year tenure as Chief – dominated as it was by the London bombings of 7 July 2005, which left 52 people dead – had already been boosted by the success (under Dearlove) in persuading Libya to abandon its WMD programme; it was an intelligence success which it was seen as necessary to trumpet, with details of the crucial 16 December 2003 meeting when the deal was sealed at the Travellers Club on Pall Mall being revealed in an unprecedented manner intended to demonstrate, via the media, that given the time and resources the intelligence community could make a dramatic difference.

With the security stakes so high and intelligence community morale boosted but still at a low ebb following the Iraq fiasco, successes were necessary. What was also necessary was recognition that the countries that had been forced, cajoled or blackmailed into joining President Bush's 'GWOT' had now to break out of the ideological straightjacket and foreign-policy catastrophes the Bush years had foisted upon them.

The splits within the Bush Administration regarding Libya – with the extremist 'neo-con' wing repelled by the idea of dealing with Gadaffi whatever the benefits, and the less extreme wing going along with the CIA view that it was worth a try – demonstrated how 'political' the practice of using the means and methods of the intelligence community remained. In London, the realisation came in 2004 that US and UK security priorities were diverging, and it is this realisation that has steadily re-forged the relationship between SIS, MI5 and GCHQ. For while the US under Bush cast all foreign-policy decisions within the context of the 'GWOT', Britain's intelligence services in the year prior to 7/7 came to the conclusion that they were no longer fighting a 'global' war on terror, but were in fact primarily concerned about stopping bombs from going off in London and other British cities.

The reality of the 'desperate scramble'[11] with which the security establishment characterised Britain's counter-terrorism effort in the months before 7/7 was plain to see as a ball of fire erupted from the World Trade Center, tumultuous cries of 'Allah akhbar' echoed around the main hall of the Quaker Meeting House in London's Euston Road, five hundred people watched an out-of-focus film of the 9/11 terrorist attacks, children played among the seats, adults cheered as the Twin Towers crumbled, and I sat surrounded by a ring of empty chairs, awkwardly wondering why I had been invited to attend a meeting during which I – the sole outsider present – was at points singled out for attack by the succession of firebrand speakers who took to the stage.

The irony of the Quaker Meeting House – a haven for peaceful reflection – having been made available for the purpose of drawing together so many people filled with hatred and anger made that meeting on 8 January 2005 – to which I had been invited by the leader of the since-banned radical group al-Muhajiroun, Omar Bakri Mohammed – all the more significant. Although none of the 7/7 bombers – nor the would-be bombers arrested after the attempted suicide bombing of London on 21 July 2005 – were known to have attended this event, the radicalised environment in which they had moved was vividly on display. Speaker after speaker asserted that a 'covenant of security' which allegedly existed between Muslims and non-Muslims – whereby both sides would leave each other in peace – had been broken as a result of Western aggression in Iraq and elsewhere in the Islamic world, and that therefore Muslims had a right to launch a *defensive* jihad. Omar Bakri – who was later obliged to leave the UK – had told me earlier that week,

> The mosque is no longer a mosque in the UK. Many of the Muslim youths don't go, because they are dominated by communities that have sold out to unbelievers. I cannot be a Muslim and live in the UK. We have been forced to make a stand. We are not going to be integrated. Some Muslims believe they are British citizens. It's really very strange. Either you migrate, or you prepare yourselves.[12]

The radical community – which has gone through many organisational changes since 2005 – remains an alternative to those in control of the mosques, as Abu Yahya Abderahman, a vocal proponent of conflict, made clear at the London meeting, telling the cheering crowd,

We are no longer living with the *kufr* with a covenant of security. That means that we are at war. For years we have been living in peace. They have violated the covenant. If they are going to come together to fight us, we now realise we have to have a global coalition to fight them. We are at war. It's time for brothers, sisters and children to prepare. Prepare as much as you can, whether with sticks or stones or bombs. Prepare as much as you can, to defeat them, to terrorise them. That is what the message of Mohammed was. Just by terrorism alone. Is it not the case that when Sheikh Osama bin Laden speaks, that kings and queens and prime ministers stop to listen? Why? Because he terrifies them. Thus, you have to want to give up your lives for the sake of Allah. He gave us this life, and he wants you to give it back.[13]

The conditions into which the post-9/11 language of extremism has been inserted has provided fertile ground on which such views can flourish. But as the 'GWOT' developed, so too did identification of how distinctly different were the threats in different countries, and therefore how very different were their security and intelligence needs. It became clear that the United States and Britain had both different needs and different aims, those of the CIA – working with the FBI – being to identify people of potential or actual concern and 'take them off the streets', while in the United Kingdom the aim was to stop any of the hundreds of UK-based conspiracies seen as 'domestically generated' evolving from the nascent into the fully formed. MI5, SIS and GCHQ came to see that they had a 'British problem to deal with' which was distinct from the 'GWOT', and which had to take precedence over the threat to America.

This view should not be seen as having *suddenly* become apparent; it evolved over time, though it was clarified publicly with the establishment in March 2007 of the Office for Security and Counter-Terrorism (OSCT), the Home Office department which today coordinates all UK counter-terrorist activity.

In the wake of the 7/7 attacks, an increasingly significant feature of this activity has been focused on developing a highly detailed understanding of the UK's Muslim community, and channelling that understanding directly into the strategic thinking of the intelligence services. Thus it was that the need to 'understand' was being called for by some while being regarded by others as a distraction, a senior counter-terrorism officer telling me in 2006:

It's not our role to consider all the additional consequences of what we do. Our primary aim is to prevent atrocities, save lives, and make the public feel secure. We know that there are vast issues and that we are – in a sense – dealing with the tip of the iceberg when we spy on people, bug telephones, intercept Internet traffic, knock down doors and arrest people. But the counter-terrorism strategy has in essence to be informed primarily by knowledge of specific threats – of which we are currently dealing with around a hundred simultaneously in the UK – while we have to leave to others the task of social engineering and developing foreign policies which can dilute the anger. Bridging the gap between understanding the underlying issues and designing a counter-terrorism strategy in response to that deeper understanding just isn't possible in the current climate, when the threat is real, urgent and highly dangerous. There are too many lives at stake for us to become overly academic.[14]

Despite such views being deeply engrained within the intelligence community, however, initial steps towards 'bridging the gap' between confronting immediate security threats and developing a deeper understanding that could assist in informing the evolution of those threats, became a major stride in 2008. It was then that a study based on 20 'deep dive' reports into radicalism within Britain's Muslim community was launched from within the intelligence community. These reports combined open-source material, interviews and intelligence, and were aimed at providing a detailed, nuanced study that would place *understanding* close to the centre of intelligence gathering and assessment. As with much that has influenced UK intelligence gathering, the value of seeking to understand the conflict in Northern Ireland was influential, an experience which – through its absence – had crippled the CIA in its assessments of al-Qaeda throughout the 1990s, and which by being the *missing* element in the intelligence 'war' with Saddam Hussein's regime had denied the intelligence communities in the United States and Britain any claim to understanding the *intentions* of that regime.

The 2008 study, which today underpins much of the intelligence agencies' understanding of the threat from violent extremism within Britain, found that there was no link between the size of a particular Muslim community and levels of extremism within it; it also found that there was no relationship between deprivation and extremism, and that, while there is a 'pipeline' to violence, it is not operated by identifiable Muslim organisations such as that which I had been among at the Quaker Meeting Hall in January 2005. It went on to find that the patterns of influence within groups of potential extremists were determined by a small number of 'radicalisers', who had proved adept at weaving the local into the global picture, but who to be effective had to be part of global networks in order to be able to despatch would-be participants to places where planning and training could be provided.

Pursuit of these links between the local and the international – which had long been assumed but which have proved very difficult to map – has determined the re-forming of the counter-terrorism effort, which now accounts for around seventy percent of MI5 resources, and which since 2004 has transformed the relationship between MI5 and SIS. Today, the SIS role as the overseas 'arm' of MI5 is more pronounced than ever. Although SIS had always been 'tasked' by MI5 when necessary, a decision was taken that MI5 would lead the counter-terrorism effort and that SIS would become the overseas component of the MI5 strategy, coordinated by the OSCT.

It is a strategy that has brought numerous 'new faces' – those of MI5 officers – into SIS's space-age-cum-Babylonian headquarters on the Thames at Vauxhall Cross, and has seen MI5 consolidate its role at the centre of Britain's global counter-terrorist effort, building on that developed since the creation of the multi-agency Joint Terrorism Analysis Centre (JTAC) formed in 2003 as what quickly became a highly effective 'clearing house' for all intelligence regarding the terrorist threat.

The major domestic counter-terrorist investigations since 9/11 – which had by early 2010 involved the unearthing of thirty plots, the identification of two hundred cells or networks, and surveillance of individuals from within a two-thousand-strong pool of potential or actual recruits to the jihadist cause – exposed the radicalism that has taken root within a section of the British population.

But the same investigations also exposed the extent to which Britain was unprepared for what emerged in the early 2000s. As the report,[15] published in May 2009, of the UK Parliamentary Intelligence and Security Committee into the London bombings of 7 July 2005 stated, 'throughout 2004 and 2005 MI5 were playing catch-up, moving resources from one plot to the next, whilst each time unearthing still more people of interest on the sidelines of each plot that they would need to return to and investigate when they had time.' Senior security officials acknowledge this to have been the case, one telling me, 'Post-9/11 we didn't really know whether there was a threat within this country or not. During 2002–3 it was a question of finding out where the people were who had been in the Afghan camps. And it was only in 2004 we found that we had home-grown groups.'[16]

The process of 'catching up' has led to what is little short of a revolution within Britain's security establishment. Acknowledging that there was little detailed intelligence on the domestic threat until at least three years after 9/11, the security official was clear: 'It was detainee interviews [such as those held at Guantanamo Bay] that were the only game in town, until around 2004. The picture they painted gave us an idea of what we needed to look at. The material was the best stuff we got at that time.'[17]

In light of the paucity of intelligence, part of the challenge for those seeking to improve intelligence gathering was to know what to change – in terms of practices and techniques – and what to retain of the traditional methods that had stood the test of time. A senior security official who has been part of the 'machinery' since the 1980s explained:

> When I was recruited...most of the colleagues were retired colonels coming up on the 8.35 from Tonbridge. I recall one of that generation seeing me and referring to me as 'one of the young intellectuals'. It wasn't hostile – but it was a vignette. There was an old establishment, but not one that was overly grand. They had rather good value sets, but not absolutely reflecting what the UK was like in the 1980s. There was a social conservatism, with an office cocktail party every three months. In that sense there has been a discontinuity [within MI5]: now the average age is much younger. But some of the good things do continue: from an early stage the Service was quite informal – there was a 'first name' culture. This is a rather good thing. It's always been like that.[18]

Broadening the recruitment net – and thereby inevitably increasing the risk of infiltration – and somewhat diluting the high-value mystique by becoming more visible, has been a significant trade-off for the agencies. The public use of SIS intelligence in the Iraq dossiers, the appearance of the MI5 Directors General Eliza Manningham-Buller and subsequently Jonathan Evans at semi-public events, and the appointment of the senior and already well-known diplomat Sir John Sawers as Chief of SIS in 2009, have given spying something of a public face.

But while on the one hand the agencies' greater visibility may have encouraged recruitment from the ethnic and religious groups into which the agencies previously had least access, the concern remains very real that agents – the 'touts' and others – who are the sources of intelligence, may feel less comfortable taking the risks they do if the intelligence officers they are working for are no longer operating as deeply within the shadows as has been the case for centuries. Although there is no proof of it, by becoming more visible the agencies may *seem* to have become less secret, and perhaps less discreet. Operationally this is certainly not the case. However, if spies don't feel confident that their intelligence will be tightly guarded – and may even find its way into a public 'dossier' used to justify a war – they are certainly less likely to share what they know. The risk to them can occasionally become evident in the most unforeseen circumstances, a former SIS officer telling me in one unguarded moment that a well-known journalist who still works for the *Guardian* newspaper had been 'one of my agents', a member of another intelligence agency telling me that a reporter on the *Sunday Times* was 'with SIS', and a former SIS officer now in the private sector causing consternation among several of his former colleagues when it emerged that he had shared with me the highly secret codename of a key player in the intelligence operation that led in 2003 to Libya abandoning its WMD programme.

For the rather more discreet majority within the intelligence community, meanwhile, it irks them that the era of the agencies' greater openness – as well as of the greater need for public confidence in their abilities – coincided so closely with the greatest intelligence fiasco in living memory, that of Iraq. Even though the inadequacies and imperfections of intelligence are widely recognised within the fractured world of espionage, the combination of misjudgement and political meddling that led to inadequate intelligence on Iraq's WMD being used as the Government's core justification for the invasion, served to diminish the validity of intelligence at just the moment when the services had taken their early steps towards seeking to gain the confidence of a public they knew they needed to have on their side in the counter-terrorism effort.

But the real effectiveness of the reformism and 'joining up' of MI5 and SIS has been cemented by the rapidly expanding and all-important role of the third arm of Britain's 'secret state': GCHQ.

While MI5 has deepened its understanding of the complexion of the radicalised world from which the terrorist threat is emerging, and has been able to infiltrate groups plotting attacks in the United Kingdom, and SIS has run agents and developed liaison with foreign intelligence and security services to an extent that is unprecedented, the limitations on the effectiveness of traditional methods of intelligence gathering has been exposed by al-Qaeda and the groups it has inspired. A key aim of the 2008 UK study of radicalisation was to try and identify how, when and why extremist thought turns into extremist action. The study – as well as the accumulated intelligence gathered in the aftermath of 9/11 – helped in the process of deciding how networks form and operate, and how lines of communication and influence function.

But knowing these things was not going to stop bombs going off. To achieve that it was – and remains – necessary to get inside the groups of plotters.

As was clear when al-Qaeda was based in Sudan, counter-intelligence – specifically, preventing infiltration – was a preoccupation of the organisation's leaders. On the local level, infiltrating a group of acquaintances or friends who decide – as the report of the official inquiry into the 7/7 bombings explains[19] – to become a terrorist cell is almost impossible, though it has happened. This realisation has led to a massive expansion in the role of signals intelligence – 'sigint' – captured from telephone intercepts and other electronic communications, by the 5,300[20] staff inside the 'Doughnut' – the imposing building on the edge of Cheltenham which houses GCHQ.

If Britain, the United States and others are to keep ahead of the terrorist threat, it is the signals intelligence – the eavesdropping – which is likely to give them the advantage, owing to their superior capacity over all but other advanced states. Its rapidly expanding use has brought with it a change in spy-craft which is in many ways as dramatic as that which was forced upon the spies with the end of the practice of trading secrets brought about by al-Qaeda's rejection of the old rules of the game. For a major strength of 'sigint' is that it has reduced – almost to zero – the *need* to trade; while listening devices, tracking equipment, satellite imagery and the like will not *replace* human intelligence sources, their expanding use is providing the intelligence agencies with the means to keep a step or more ahead of the terrorists who sidestepped the spies. It has – as the leading expert on GCHQ, Richard Aldrich, has written – transformed the role of the Cheltenham staff from being one primarily focused on intercepting communications abroad to being one whose focus on counter-terrorism has come to 'mean that GCHQ has little choice but to head down the road towards wholesale collection [of intelligence], since many international groups such as terrorists and criminal gangs overlap seamlessly, with dispersed elements within British society'.[21]

Intense political debate about the expansion of eavesdropping capability – particularly programmes such as the planned £12 billion Intercept Modernisation Programme (IMP),[22] which would store all data on telephone and Internet communications (though not the actual content) generated in the UK – placed GCHQ in the limelight at the very time when it was seeking to follow MI5 and SIS and demystify itself somewhat.

So it was that in February 2003 – as a small sign of this demystification – the glass doors of the 'Doughnut' swung aside and 'Britain's most secret intelligence agency'[23] opened up before me.

The building was empty, but the days when even the colours of the carpets in such buildings were rumoured to be state secrets had long gone. A carefully drawn deskplan was shown to me, detailing where on the acres of neutral grey-brown floor the Director would sit when the surrounding shambles of fifty wooden huts and other buildings scattered around Cheltenham was vacated and the new £800 million headquarters started to hum to the sound of spying. But the move to the new building – today surrounded by residential streets named after characters from James Bond movies but which during my visit just before it opened was the 'world's most secure building site', the 10,568-page project agreement including 1,056 pages devoted solely to the security arrangements agreed with the private-sector contractors – was and is intended to be far more than just a change of scenery. Close to the heart of the plan was an attempt to alter staff attitudes, as Ann Black, GCHQ's spokeswoman at that time, explained:

> We were asked by an external adviser: what are you doing to prepare your workforce for the twenty-first century? The traditional attributes of the GCHQ person are that they are introverted and analytical. We wanted a shift. The aim has to be to move away from tribalism. There's now much more dialogue, so that the technical people really understand what is being asked of them.[24]

A part of the process of 'preparing' staff for the new century was to have them analysed using the Myers Briggs Type Indicator (MBTI) – a process which defines sixteen personality types and permits employers to tailor management styles to the character of staff. The results at GCHQ were explained by a senior staff member, who told me,

> From Myers Briggs we have learned that we have a lot of thinkers and sensors but not enough intuitors and feelers. This process made people think about how their way of doing things impacted on other people. It enabled our very analytical staff to see how to operate in a way that was more sensitive to other people.[25]

Equipped with the MBTI conclusions, the 'tribalism' and introversion were then analysed against the background of GCHQ's functions as the gatherer of intercepted intelligence from all over the world, the senior official explaining, 'Civil servants are supposed to be very hung up on organisation, and there were parts of our organisation that hadn't changed in decades. Then suddenly everything changed, and we couldn't respond to the changing demands, with our existing, rigid organisational structure.'

The big change was the end of the Cold War and its replacement by al-Qaeda, as Ann Black said: 'During the Cold War, GCHQ had a monolithic target. And its approach was monolithic. With the end of the Cold War we had to be much more adaptable and flexible.' Flexibility is now central, with GCHQ staff accompanying British forces to battlefronts. SIS and MI5 staff work alongside them at the Cheltenham headquarters to interpret the 'sigint' the GCHQ linguists are there to translate. Meanwhile, the vast computing capacity that is today housed in the seemingly endless ground floor of the building, which on the day of my visit was not even home to a plug in what one staffer there that day described as 'a plug-and-play building', was described simply by one long-serving GCHQ staff member as 'future-proofing our business'.[26]

EPILOGUE

Future-proofing the business of spying is nothing new. The view of the Florentine political theorist Niccolò Machiavelli – that the failure of the 'Prince' to protect the people from internal or external threat can usually be traced back to his failure to 'know his country' – is as relevant today as it was in fifteenth-century Europe.

In the case of the British in the Ireland of 1798, the spy Francis Higgins kept the British not only well informed of the social, political and religious currents about which he – despite his bias – was extremely well informed, but also assisted in orchestrating the surprise that stopped a rebellion. By 1919 the roles had reversed; the British official hidden inside Dublin Castle was no longer somebody who 'knows his country'; the rest is history. For the United States today – its identity built upon the assertion of *global* influence and the exercise of *global* power – the need for knowledge is the same but the scale immeasurably larger, the results always incomplete, as George Tenet, CIA Director between 1997 and 2004 explained when he wrote,

> First and foremost it must be said that intelligence is not the sole answer to any complicated problem. Often, at best, only 60 percent of the facts regarding any national security issue are knowable. Intelligence tries to paint a realistic picture of a given situation based on expert interpretation and analysis of collected information. The results are generally impressionistic – rarely displayed in sharp relief.[1]

Intelligence is gathered in an atmosphere of vagueness, uncertainty and evolution: ideas that *could* become threats, threats that *could* become plots, and ambitions that *could* become actions, mostly fail to materialise – perhaps because they are thwarted, perhaps because the will to see them through is ultimately not there. Prioritising what to spy on, what to try and infiltrate, and what to place under surveillance, then becomes the challenge.

In Britain it was several years after the 'home-grown' terrorist threat was first discerned that MI5 established the regional offices that have brought its intelligence staff into the closest possible contact with the communities out of which the next 'home-grown' threat may emerge; in the United States the turmoil within the intelligence community that erupted after 9/11 has subsided, but the wounds have yet to heal and the bruises yet to fade, as the agencies that let the hijackers slip through continue to wring their hands.

So, with surprise having found its way onto the side of the terrorists, what is left in the arsenal of Machiavelli's 'Prince' or his successors in the twenty-first century? Put differently: once obtained, what should intelligence be used for?

With terrorism continuing to be the single biggest threat commanding the time and resources of the world's major intelligence agencies – despite the death of Osama bin Laden – using intelligence to confront the bombers is the highest priority. But its use and value goes beyond action by special forces in Afghanistan, police officers in London, or Homeland Security officials in Chicago. The unprecedented level of funding, the broadening of recruitment to the services, and the increased pooling of knowledge and skills by separate agencies, as well as extensive liaison between different countries' intelligence services, means that the global intelligence 'community' is awash with more information, insight and knowledge than ever before.

While using these resources in pursuit of security remains the priority, intelligence-based reporting would be of even greater value if extended beyond intelligence and governmental circles, to the academics, social scientists and political analysts whose often unique ground-level knowledge of the very same issues that haunt spies and politicians in possession of secrets would greatly increase understanding if it were informed as much by the 'covert' as the 'overt'. Although the first experience of intelligence being used in public – to justify the invasion of Iraq – was a disaster, the value of better-informed discussion outside the intelligence agencies on issues ranging from radicalism to weapons proliferation cannot be overestimated; facts are hard to come by, and while secret intelligence is really only of value *when* it is and *because* it is secret, great value lies in the interaction between the intelligence community and the world beyond it.

Of course it will always remain the aim of Governments to fund intelligence gathering with a view to arming themselves with the power such intelligence can bring – over both the enemy, and with regard to influence over one's allies. But in the multipolar world of the twenty-first century – one in which variety has left as an almost distant memory the stark 'East–West' Cold War conflict in which many of today's intelligence professionals cut their teeth, and one in which long-stagnant regions such as the Arab world are undergoing dramatic change – the intrinsic power of intelligence is likely to become less evident. The unearthing of 'smoking guns' – so-called 'Adlai Stevenson moments', when decisive, world-changing intelligence emerges – may come to be less advantageous to decision-makers than will be deep knowledge, understanding and accurate assessment.

This need and role has become of ever-growing importance as terrorist groups – al-Qaeda and its descendants – have become more adept at counter-intelligence, that is – the practice of taking pre-emptive steps intended to hamper the spies in their task. The adaptation of the means of gathering secrets has dominated the post-9/11 history of secret intelligence; to reclaim the advantage, the spies' 'blueprint' forged over many years – so much of it rooted in the British experience of spying in Ireland – has not been torn up; but it is a blueprint which now provides less of a reference point than has ever been the case. The Western agencies' steadily developing knowledge of terrorist counter-intelligence measures has informed much of the pace at which this change has taken place, as the practices employed by 'the other side' have emerged; when two suspects who were under surveillance by MI5 in the UK sensed their discussions might be the target of eavesdroppers, they took to talking to each other while lying face-down at the centre of a children's playingfield – a location it would be difficult to bug, but in which they lay face-down in order to limit the risk that their words would be observed from a distance by intelligence officers capable of lip-reading.

Training undertaken during the 1990s at al-Qaeda's camps in Afghanistan clearly armed trainees with many skills; but the articulation of extremist thought which preceded 9/11 – and which was articulated more forcefully, and globally, in its wake – revealed the extent to which intelligence gathered without deep, inside knowledge of its social and political context can limit understanding of what is taking place. It is for this among other reasons that the once near-invisible world of secret intelligence has – rightly – become more visible; without a flow of insights, information and intelligence coming from within communities, the radical thought which can on occasion turn to radical action, would remain substantially undetected by the established means of gathering human intelligence.

But just as the intelligence agencies have been obliged to change – dependent as they have now become on electronic interception and other 'sigint' – so have those informing them. Is it 'spying' if an imam informs the police of the attitudes or actions of a radical group frequenting a particular mosque? Is that imam a tout? Opinions are likely to be divided, though as no trade in secrets is likely to have taken place the answer will probably be no. Even so, what is clear is that not only has the post-9/11 world of spying seen the intelligence agencies significantly transform from old-style spies to electronic eavesdroppers, so the practice of 'making spies' has also seen change. While of course great efforts continue to be made to infiltrate groups which may be planning to carry out terrorist or other actions, a common interest in seeking to thwart indiscriminate terrorist action has – if only slowly – drawn communities closer to the government agencies (often with the police acting as the interface, though not always) which need to know what these communities know. As Machiavelli would likely say, the 'Prince' has become more focused on the need to 'know his country'.

And all this change has come because even though the trade in secrets is still practised, the secrets which could lead to a terrorist plot being unearthed are largely in the hands of people who have no interest in selling what they know. Consequently, the need to 'future-proof' the business of intelligence gathering – as it is described by those at GCHQ – has meant that the changing relationship between spies and communities has been matched by the overhauling of relationships between the intelligence agencies themselves. As trading secrets has become more challenging, eavesdropping has taken the lead; where once – in the Northern Ireland of the 1980s or in the US counter-terrorism effort of the 1990s – inter-agency relationships were often characterised by friction, the jealous guarding of sources and intelligence, and snobbery, now cooperation and the pooling of knowledge are today largely routine. Seemingly gone are the days when – as the senior Army officer who served in Northern Ireland told me – there was 'little or no co-ordination, due mainly to the intense distrust between the various agencies'.

So, what of the 'gentlemen's game' once played by the older generation of today's spies, those most acutely aware of how the rules of spying have been transformed by al-Qaeda?

While some remain within the agencies, the past decade has seen a new, often younger, more multicultural intake into the intelligence services; people with skills in languages which once had less significance are now playing central roles in the gathering of intelligence; others who have emerged from within communities with particular significance for the intelligence picture – both within the West and globally – are joining the agencies' ranks. The size of the agencies has meanwhile grown, seemingly immune from cuts in other areas of government expenditure.

In the meantime, some aspects of the methodology of spying have become evident in the public domain for rather different reasons. When spies want to make some money they leave government service and join the private sector, whether in India or Mexico, in South Africa or Russia. To varying degrees they are able to keep the secrets to which they were privy when in the service of the state – though not always. Today, many of the private security and intelligence companies that have emerged, build their 'brands' – sometimes in part, sometimes wholly – on the previous connections their personnel may have or have had to military, intelligence or security agencies.

It is a powerful card to play, hinting – as it does – that some privileged access may still be available to them, if the client is prepared to pay.

Sometimes these connections do remain, however: it is only a matter of time before it will become apparent that some of the private companies are not averse to dipping in to the fund of knowledge available to colleagues in the intelligence services who are prepared to break the rules by assisting with inquiries from former colleagues now in the private sector. While the secrets remain secret, therefore, the methodology of intelligence gathering has been privatised, the networks from which it is gathered being increasingly aware of their value in the commercial arena, the allure of the higher rewards tempting at least some of those in the agencies to remain in public service just long enough to earn their spurs, but not so long as to deny themselves access to the richer pickings elsewhere.

So it is that while al-Qaeda's arrival precipitated a drying up of the 'trade' in secrets for governments, for the intelligence officers who become company executives the opportunities to find new ways to transact their business have rarely looked more profitable.

NOTES

PROLOGUE

1   This account was related to me by the SIS officer involved.
2   Sir John Sawers, speech to the Society of Editors, 28 October 2010: https://
    www.sis.gov.uk/about-us/the-chief/the-chief%27s-speech-28th-october-
    2010.html.
3   Niccolò di Bernardo dei Machiavelli, *Dell'arte della Guerra* (*The Art of War*)
    (Florence: 1521).
4   Machiavelli, *The Prince* , (Florence, 1513).

CHAPTER 1

1   Peter Clarke, interview with the author, London, 16 February 2009.
2   Christopher Andrew, *Defence of the Realm: The Authorized History of MI5*
    (London: Allen Lane, 2009), p. 842.
3   UK security official, interview with the author, 13 February 2009.
4   Richard English, *Irish Freedom: The History of Nationalism in Ireland* (London:
    Pan Macmillan, 2006), p. 88.
5   English, *Irish Freedom*, p. 91.
6   Thomas Bartlett (ed.), *Revolutionary Dublin 1795–1801: The letters of Francis
    Higgins to Dublin Castle* (Dublin: Four Courts Press, 2004), p. 58.
7   William John Fitzpatrick, *The Sham Squire and the Informers of 1798* (Dublin
    and London: John Camden Hotton, 1866), p. 17.
8   Francis Higgins, letter to Sackville Hamilton, 10 April 1795, in Bartlett
    (ed.), *Revolutionary Dublin 1795–1801*, p. 78.
9   Letter to Sackville Hamilton, 14 April 1795, in Bartlett (ed.), *Revolutionary
    Dublin 1795–1801*, p. 82.

10 Letter to Edward Cooke, 3 May 1797, in Bartlett (ed.), *Revolutionary Dublin 1795–1801*, p. 153.

11 Letter to Edward Cooke, 2 March 1798, in Bartlett (ed.), *Revolutionary Dublin 1795–1801*, p. 225.

12 Letter to Edward Cooke, 18 May 1798, in Bartlett (ed.), *Revolutionary Dublin 1795–1801*, p. 237.

13 Richard Madden, *The United Irishmen: Their lives and times* (London: J. Madden & Co., 1867), pp. 415–42. A digitised version of this work, including the annex detailing these payments, is available at http://books.google.com/books?id=uFUjAAAAMAAJ&printsec=frontcover&source=gbs_book_other_versions#v=onepage&q&f=false.

14 Senior intelligence officer, interview with author, 13 August 2002.

15 Senior security official, interview with author, 17 March 2009.

CHAPTER 2

1 Richard English, *Irish Freedom: The history of nationalism in Ireland* (London: Pan Macmillan, 2006), p. 120.

2 Paul McMahon, *British Spies and Irish Rebels: British intelligence and Ireland, 1916–1945* (Woodbridge: Boydell Press, 2008), p. 7.

3 Ibid., p. 19.

4 Christopher Andrew, *Defence of the Realm: The authorized history of MI5* (London: Allen Lane, 2009), p. 88.

5 Ibid., p. 9.

6 Senior security official, interview with author, 23 April 2009.

7 McMahon, *British Spies and Irish Rebels*, p. 23.

8 Ibid. p. 27.

9 T. Ryle Dwyer, *The Squad and the Intelligence Operations of Michael Collins* (Dublin: Mercier Press, 2005), p. 36.

10 Tadgh Kennedy, BMHS, WS135, in ibid., p. 63.

11 Dwyer, *The Squad and the Intelligence Operations of Michael Collins*, p. 64.

12 Patrick O'Daly, BMHS, WS220, in ibid., p. 53.

13 Dwyer, *The Squad and the Intelligence Operations of Michael Collins*, p. 73.

14 For an ongoing exchange of notes regarding Quinlisk see http://www.rootschat.com/forum/index.php/topic,414992.0.html.

15 Dwyer, *The Squad and the Intelligence Operations of Michael Collins*, p. 76.

16 Ibid.

17 David Neligan, *The Spy in the Castle* (London: Prendeville Publishing, 1999), p. 56.

18 Dwyer, *The Squad and the Intelligence Operations of Michael Collins*, p. 80.

19 Ibid., p. 89.

20 Ibid., p. 90.

21 Dwyer attributes the comment to Walter Long, the Unionist politician, former Chief Secretary for Ireland (March–December 1905), First Lord of the Admiralty (1919–21) and chairman of the Cabinet's Long Committee on Ireland during the Lloyd George Government of 1916–22.

22 Letter of 18 April 1920, in Dwyer, *The Squad and the Intelligence Operations of Michael Collins*, p. 107.

23 Peter Hart (ed.), *British Intelligence in Ireland 1920–1921: The final reports* (Cork: Cork University Press, 2002), p. 7.

24 Dwyer, *The Squad and the Intelligence Operations of Michael Collins*, p. 107.

25 Tim Kennedy, IRA chief intelligence officer for north Kerry, in ibid., p. 126.

26 Neligan, *The Spy In The Castle*, p. 56.

27 Ibid., p. 59.

28 Ibid., p. 64.

29 Ibid., p. 83.

30 English, *Irish Freedom*, p. 288.

31 Hart (ed.), *British Intelligence in Ireland, 1920–1921*, p. 14.

32 *A Record of the Rebellion in Ireland in 1920–21, and the Part Played by the Army in Dealing with It (Intelligence)*, Imperial War Museum, Sir Hugh Jeudwine Papers, 72/82/2, reprinted in ibid.

33 Hart (ed.), *British Intelligence in Ireland, 1920–1921*, p. 55.

34 Ibid., p. 21.

35 Ibid., p. 52.

36 Ibid., p. 47.

37 Ibid., p. 56.

38 MacMahon, *British Spies and Irish Rebels*, p. 31.

39 *A Record of the Rebellion in Ireland in 1920–21*, p. 28.

40 Ibid., p. 38.

41 Ibid., p. 45.

42 Neligan, *The Spy In The Castle*, pp. 123–25.

43 Senior intelligence officer, interview with the author, 19 September 2002.

44 For a detailed account of how bin Laden was eventually found and killed see Peter Bergen, *Manhunt: From 9/11 to Abbottabad – The Ten-Year Search for Osama Bin Laden* (London: Bodley Head, 2012).

CHAPTER 3

1 Stella Rimington, *Open Secret: The autobiography of the former Director-General of MI5* (London: Arrow Books, 2002), p. 104.

2 Ibid., pp. 105–6.

3 The Provisional Irish Republican Army or 'PIRA' emerged following a meeting of the IRA on 24 August 1969, when the organisation's Belfast-based leadership was criticised for failing to defend Catholics in Northern Ireland. The resulting split in the organisation led to the creation of the PIRA's Provisional Army Council on 28 December and its declaration of intent to bring about a united Ireland.

4 Rimington, *Open Secret*, pp. 104–5.

5 Former senior official with early experience of Northern Ireland, interview with author, 9 September 2010.

6 Former senior British official, interview with author, 8 August 2010.

7 Ibid.

8 Former member of Whitelaw's staff, interview with author, 29 October 2010.

9 This support on one occasion led to 'a benevolent charity' paying for a group of loyalist paramilitary leaders to attend a specially designed weekend seminar in community politics given by the politics faculty of Edinburgh University.

10 Former member of Whitelaw's staff, interview with author, 29 October 2010.

11 Former senior UK official, interview with author, 7 July 2010.

12 Ibid.

13 Ibid.

14 Former official involved with the negotiation process, interview with author, 31 October 2010.

15 Ibid.

16 Former senior intelligence official, interview with author.

17 Former senior Army officer who did three tours of duty in Northern Ireland between 1977–91, interview with author.

18 For a detailed assessment of the role of the RUC Special Branch see Peter Taylor, *Brits: The war against the IRA* (London: Bloomsbury, 2001).

19 See ibid., pp. 138–48.

20 Martin Ingram and Greg Harkin, *Stakeknife: Britain's secret agents in Ireland* (Dublin: O'Brien Press, 2004), p. 31.

21 Ibid., p. 32.

22 Former senior UK Army intelligence officer with experience of Northern Ireland, interview with the author.

23 Former senior British Army officer with experience of Northern Ireland, interview wit author.

CHAPTER 4

1 Sean O'Callaghan, *The Informer* (London: Corgi Books, 1999), p. 120.

2 Ibid., p. 123.

3 Ibid., p. 41.

4 Stella Rimington, *Open Secret: The autobiography of the former Director-General of MI5* (London: Arrow Books, 2002), pp. 91–92.

5 Ibid.

6 For a detailed account of what lay behind the PIRA's plans for these cargoes see Ed Moloney, *A Secret History of the IRA* (2nd edition) (London: Penguin, 2007), pp. 3–34.

7 O'Callaghan, *The Informer*, p. 304.

8 Senior British Army officer, interview with author.

9 The account of the intelligence operation as related in Christopher Andrews's *Defence of the Realm: The authorized history of MI5* (London: Allen Lane, 2009) sums up what was called Operation Flavius in this way: 'The fact that McCann, Farrell and Savage were shot rather than arrested derived from the incompleteness of the intelligence available at the time (a common characteristic of even the best intelligence). There was very good intelligence on the identity of the ASU members, their previous movements and their target. The fact that they were unarmed, however, was not discovered until after they had been shot' (pp. 743–44).

10 Annika Savill and David McKittrick, 'Iran plot to aid IRA exposed: Secret service uncovers scheme involving guns, drugs and money as Ulster violence claims more victims', *Independent* (London), 29 April 1994.

11 Safa Haeri, 'Iran tried to hire IRA hit-men: Provos turned down offer of guns, missiles and cash to murder three dissidents in Europe', *Independent* (London), 3 May 1994.

12 Former official involved in the Northern Ireland peace process, interview with author, 29 October 2010.

13 Ibid.

14 Former senior British official, interview with author.

15 Ibid.

16 Peter Taylor, *Brits: The war against the IRA* (London: Bloomsbury, 2001), p.323.

17 Jonathan Powell, interview with the author, 7 July 2010.

18 Ibid.

19 The phrase is that of Michael Smith in his account of modern espionage, *The Spying Game* (London: Politico's, 2003).

CHAPTER 5

1 John Stockwell, *In Search of Enemies: A CIA story* (New Jersey: Replica Books, 1997; originally published New York: W.W. Norton, 1978), Ch. 3.

2 Former senior SIS officer, interview with author, 8 October 2009.

3 Confusingly, Penkovsky is also portrayed by the former MI5 officer Peter Wright as having been a KGB plant, whose revelations to SIS – which were shared with the CIA – were intended by Moscow to give the impression that Russian missile technology was not as far developed as in reality it was. Wright's explanation for the KGB having placed Penkovsky – who, Wright asserts, operated with a degree of openness as an SIS spy in Moscow which all but proved that the KGB had given him this role of double agent – in the way of SIS was that Moscow wanted to deflect attention from its true missile capability; by preparing to station intermediate-range ballistic missiles (IRBMs) on Cuba, the Soviet leadership would be giving the impression that it did not have intercontinental ballistic missiles (ICBMs), which could reach the United States from Soviet territory, and was thus dependent on IRBMs. Penkovsky's leak of intelligence warning of the plan to station the IRBMs on Cuba was, Wright argues, successful in giving the US the impression that the Soviet Union could not strike the US mainland unless it had missiles close by; by then agreeing to withdraw the weapons, Wright

argues, Moscow also achieved its second aim, which was a guarantee – unwritten – that the United States would not seek to overthrow the Castro regime in Cuba. See Peter Wright, *Spy Catcher: The candid autobiography of a senior intelligence officer* (Richmond, Australia: William Heinemann, 1987), pp. 207–12.

4 Sir John Scarlett, http://news.bbc.co.uk/1/hi/world/europe/8184338.stm.

5 Some details of the section of this chapter referring to the situation in Angola in 1989–93 first appeared in Mark Huband, *The Skull Beneath The Skin: Africa after the Cold War* (Boulder, CO: Westview Press, 2001), pp. 31–57.

6 Senior UK intelligence officer, interview with author, 18 April 2003.

7 http://www.foia.cia.gov: 'UNTITLED (BELIEVE CONGO EXPERIENCING CLASSIC COMMUNIST EFFORT TAKE OVER GOVER'), 18 August 1960.

8 http://www.foia.cia.gov: 'CABLE TO LEOPOLDVILLE RE CONGO COVERT ACTION AGAINST UNIDENTIFIED HIGH OFFICIAL', 27 August 1960.

9 United States Senate Select Committee to Study Governmental Operations with Respect to Intelligence Activities, 94th Congress 1st session, Senate Report No. 94-465, 'Alleged Assassination Plots Involving Foreign Leaders', 20 November (legislative day, 18 November) 1975.

10 Ibid.

11 Ibid.

12 Madeleine G. Kalb, *The Congo Cables: The Cold War in Africa from Eisenhower to Kennedy* (New York: Macmillan, 1982).

13 Ibid., p. 7.

14 Larry Devlin, *Chief of Station, Congo: Fighting the Cold War in a hot zone*, (New York: Public Affairs, 2007), p. 28.

15 The Mitrokhin Archive was published in two volumes: *The KGB and the West* (London: Allen Lane, 1999) and *The KGB and the World* (London: Allen Lane, 2005), both written by Christopher Andrew and Vasili Mitrokhin.

16 Oleg Kalugin, *Spymaster: My thirty-two years in intelligence and espionage against the West* (New York: Basic Books, 2009), p. 92.

17 Christopher Andrew and Oleg Gordievsky, *KGB: The Inside Story* (London: Harper Perennial, 1991). This account of Gordievsky's role as a KGB officer, 1962–85 – including as its head in London in 1982–85, and as a spy for SIS, 1974–85 – reveals how deep Soviet disillusionment with Sub-Saharan Africa's revolutionary movements became.

18 Ibid., p. 25.

19 William Burden, US Ambassador in Brussels, in a cable to the US State Department, 19 July 1960, cited in Kalb, *The Congo Cables*, p. 27.

20 Crawford Young and Michael Turner, *The Rise and Decline of the Zairean State* (Madison, WI and London: University of Wisconsin Press, 1985), p. 364.

21 William Colby, former CIA director, quoted in Michael G. Schatzberg, *Mobutu or Chaos: The United States and Zaire 1960–1990* (Lanham, MD: University Press of America, 1991), p. 3.

22 Stephen Weissman, 'The CIA and US policy in Zaire and Angola', in Rene Lemarchand (ed.), *American Policy in Southern Africa* (Lanham, MD and London: University Press of America, 1981), pp. 444–45.

23 Ibid., pp. 16-17.

24 See Stockwell, *In Search of Enemies*, pp. 54-55.

25 Details of this first consignment are drawn from ibid., p. 55.

26 Fernando Andresen Guimaraes, *The Origins of the Angolan Civil War: Foreign intervention and domestic political conflict* (New York: St Martin's Press, 1998), p. 54.

27 Guimaraes, *The Origins of the Angolan Civil War*, p. 163.

28 Ibid.

29 João Cabrita, *Mozambique: The tortuous road to Democracy* (London: Palgrave, 2000), p. 45.

30 Christopher Andrew and Vasili Mitrokhin, *The Mitrokhin Archive*, vol. II: *The KGB and the World* (London: Penguin, 2006), p. 432.

31 Ibid., pp. 434–35.

32 Ibid., p. 443.

33 Oleg Nazhestkin, in ibid., pp. 444–45.

34 Ibid., p. 447.

35 Ibid., p. 451.

36 Ibid., p. 454.

37 Ibid., p. 456.

38 Ibid., p. 466.

39 Nelson Mandela, *Long Walk to Freedom* (London: Little, Brown, 1994) p. 115.

40 Katia Airola, interview with author, Luanda, 26 August 1993.

41 The Tunney Amendment to the 1975 Defense Appropriations Bill in the Senate terminated financial assistance to US operations in Angola. The Clark Amendment to the 1975 Security Assistance Bill specifically called for a complete termination of funds to Angola.

42 *Africa Report* 19 (May–June 1976).

43 Gerald Bender, 'American Policy toward Angola: A history of linkage', in Gerald J. Bender, James S.Coleman and Richard L. Sklar (eds), *African Crisis Areas and US Foreign Policy* (Berkeley, CA, Los Angeles and London: University of California Press, 1985), p. 114.

44 Republican Senator Bill Symms to Congress, 11 June 1985.

45 George Wright, *The Destruction of a Nation: United States' policy towards Angola since 1945* (London and Chicago: Pluto Press, 1997), pp. 128–29.

46 David E. Kyvig, *Reagan and the World* (New York, Westport, CT and London: Praeger, 1990), p. 129.

47 William Minter, *Apartheid's Contras: An Inquiry into the Roots of War in Angola and Mozambique* (London and New Jersey: Zed Books; Johannesburg: Witwatersrand University Press, 1994), p. 161.

48 Chester Crocker, interview with author, Georgetown, 4 February 1993.

49 Jonas Savimbi, interview with author, Abidjan, 15 December 1990.

50 Maria N'guare, interview with author, Vindongo, southern Angola, 29 August 1993.

51 Minter, *Apartheid's Contras*, p. 161.

52 Former senior CIA officer, interview with author, 4 March 2003.

53 This practice was ended when the law was changed in November 2001.

54 Former CIA Director James Woolsey, interview with author, 11 February 2003.

CHAPTER 6

1 Karim Omar, whose birth name is Mustafa bin Abd al-Qadir Setmariam Nasar and who later adopted the name Abu Mus'ab al-Suri, interviews with author, London, 15–16 January 1997.

2 For a full account of Somalia's crisis at this time see Mark Huband, *Warriors of the Prophet: The struggle for Islam* (Boulder, CO: Westview Press, 1998), Ch. 2.

3 Abdelkadir Hachani, interview with author, Algiers, 19 September 1999; see also Huband, *Warriors of the Prophet*, Ch. 3.

4 Amid Khan Motaqi, interview with author, Kabul, 4 December 1996.

5 *The 9/11 Commission Report: Final Report of the National Commission on Terrorist Attacks Upon the United States* (New York and London: W.W. Norton, 2004), p. 62.

6   For the definitive account of Karim Omar's life and work see Brynjar Lia, *Architect of Global Jihad: The life of Al-Qaida Strategist Abu Mus'ab al-Suri* (London: Hurst & Co., 2007).

7   For a detailed account of Algeria during the mid-1990s see Huband, *Warriors of the Prophet*, Ch. 3, and Huband, *Brutal Truths, Fragile Myths: Power politics and Western adventurism in the Arab world* (Boulder, CO: Westview Press, 2004), pp. 42–49.

8   Richard A. Clarke, *Against All Enemies: Inside America's war on terror* (New York: Free Press, 2004), p. 96.

9   Milton Bearden, interview with author, 8 October 1999.

10   See Huband, *Warriors of the Prophet*.

11   Former senior CIA officer, interview with author, 16 March 1999.

12   Billy Waugh, with Tim Keown, *Hunting the Jackal: A special forces and CIA soldier's fifty years on the frontlines of the war against terrorism* (New York: Avon Books, 2004), p. 193.

13   Ibid., p. 200.

14   Ibid., p. 203.

15   See Huband, *Warriors of the Prophet*, p. 2

16   For a full account of the activities of Ali Mohamed see Peter Lance, *Triple Cross: How bin Laden's master spy penetrated the CIA, the Green Berets, and the FBI – and why Patrick Fitzgerald failed to stop him* (New York: William Morrow, 2005).

17   Testimony of FBI agent Jack Cloonan, in Lance, *Triple Cross*, pp. 104–5.

18   Nabil Sharef, *The Wall Street Journal*, 26 November 2001.

19   Lance, *Triple Cross*, pp. 130–31.

20   Ibid.

21   *New York Times*, 1 December 1998.

22   For a firsthand account of the battle of 3 October 1993 see Mark Huband, *The Skull Beneath The Skin: Africa after the Cold War* (Boulder, CO: Westview Press, 2001), pp. 303–6.

23   Lance, *Triple Cross*.

24   Ibid., pp. 274–76.

25   Ibid.

CHAPTER 7

1 'Anonymous' (Michael Scheuer), *Imperial Hubris: Why the West is losing the War on Terror* (New York: Brassey's, 2004), p.191.

2 Ibid., p.192.

3 http://www.intelligence.senate.gov/iraqreport2.pdf.

4 http://www.intelligence.senate.gov/iraqreport2.pdf, p.318.

5 http://www.intelligence.senate.gov/iraqreport2.pdf, p.309.

6 Reported on *The Spy Factory*, PBS, 3 February 2009.

7 See 'The Path to 9/11: Lost Warnings and Fatal Errors', *Vanity Fair*, November 2004, available at http://www.vanityfair.com/politics/features/2004/11/path-to-9-11-200411.

8 Philip Shenon, *The Commission: The uncensored history of the 9/11 investigation* (New York: Twelve, 2008), p.192.

9 Michael Scheuer, *Marching Toward Hell: America and Islam after Iraq* (New York: Free Press, 2008), p.284.

10 See 'The Path to 9/11'.

11 Michael Scheuer, interview with author, 10 December 2004.

12 Ibid.

13 As explained by Sandy Berger, US Deputy National Security Advisor, in *The Washington Post*, 3 October 2001.

14 The chronology of Mansoor Ijaz's involvement in these issues has been provided by Ijaz to the author.

15 As reported to the author by Ijaz, New York, 2 March 2003.

16 Lt General Gutbi Al-Mahdi, Director General, External Security Bureau, letter to David Williams, Middle East and North Africa Dept, FBI, 2 May 1998. Copy in author's collection.

17 David Williams, letter to Lt General Gutbi Al-Mahdi, 24 June 1998. Copy in author's collection.

18 Yahia Babiker, Deputy Secretary General, Sudan External Security Bureau, interview with author, Khartoum, 17 October 1999.

19 Senior US official, telephone interview with author, 8 October 1999.

20 Yahia Babiker, interview with author.

21 Ibid.

22 Information provided to the author by a Sudanese intelligence official.

23 See Richard A. Clarke, *Against All Enemies: Inside America's war on terror* (New York: Free Press, 2004), p.146–47.

24 Senior US State Department official, interview with author, 4 October 1999.

25 Clarke, *Against All Enemies*, p. 146.

26 Yahia Babiker, interview with author.

27 Gutbi Al-Mahdi, interview with author, Khartoum, 7 November 2001.

28 For a detailed account of these developments see Mark Huband, *Brutal Truths, Fragile Myths: Power politics and Western adventurism in the Arab world* (Boulder, CO: Westview Press, 2004), pp. 56–60.

29 Yahia Babiker, interview with author.

30 United States vs Usama bin Laden, No. S(7) 98 Cr. 1023 (S.D. N.Y.), 6 February 2001 (transcript pp. 218–19, 233); 13 February 2001 (transcript pp. 514–16); 20 February 2001 (transcript p. 890). The transcript of Jamal al-Fadl's testimony is available at http://en.wikisource.org/wiki/United_States_of_America_v._Usama_bin_Laden/Day_2_6_February_2001.

31 Ibid., pp. 235–36

CHAPTER 8

1 For a detailed account of these ambitions see Mark Huband, *The Skull Beneath The Skin: Africa after the Cold War* (Boulder, CO: Westview Press, 2001), Ch. 11.

2 For a detailed account of the Taliban's consolidation of power in Afghanistan see Mark Huband, *Warriors of the Prophet: The struggle for Islam* (Boulder, CO: Westview Press, 1998), pp. 14–22.

3 United States vs Usama bin Laden, No. S(7) 98 Cr. 1023 (S.D. N.Y.), 6 February 2001 (transcript pp. 218–19, 233); 13 February 2001 (transcript pp. 514–16); 20 February 2001 (transcript p. 890).

4 Ibid., p. 192.

5 Ibid., pp. 196–97.

6 Ibid., pp. 203–13.

7 Ibid., p. 266.

8 Ibid., p. 267.

9 Ibid., pp. 268–69.

10 Peter Lance, *Triple Cross: How bin Laden's master spy penetrated the CIA, the Green Berets, and the FBI – and why Patrick Fitzgerald failed to stop him* (New York: William Morrow, 2005), p. xxi.

11 John Miller and Michael Stone, with Chris Mitchell, *The Cell: Inside the 9/11 plot and why the FBI and CIA failed to stop it* (New York: Hyperion, 2003), p. 165.

12 For a detailed profile of al-Fadl see http://www.newyorker.com/archive/2006/09/11/060911fa_fact.

13 Al-Fadl testimony, ibid.

14 See Mark Huband, *Brutal Truths, Fragile Myths: Power politics and Western adventurism in the Arab world* (Boulder, CO: Westview Press, 2004), pp. 96–97.

15 Senior intelligence officer, interview with author, 19 September 2002.

16 Senior European intelligence officer, interview with author, 9 October 2002.

17 Ibid., 11 October 2002.

18 Senior UK official in discussion with author, 11 October 2002.

19 Senior intelligence officer, interview with author, 31 October 2002.

20 Senior CIA officer, interview with author, 29 October 2002.

21 Ibid.

22 Senior Middle Eastern intelligence officer, interview with author, 5 November 2002.

23 Senior European intelligence officer, interview with author, 8 November 2002.

24 For a detailed account of Khaled Shiekh Mohamed's life and role see Huband, *Brutal Truths, Fragile Myths*, pp. 86–98.

25 For accounts of the treatment of Abu Zubaydah, Khaled Shiekh Mohamed and Abdelrahim Hussein Abdul Nashiri, and eleven other 'high-value' detainees, see http://www.nybooks.com/media/doc/2010/04/22/icrc-report.pdf.

CHAPTER 9

1 Some elements of my December 2004 visit to Guantanamo Bay – the first of two visits – appeared in Mark Huband, 'Dock of the Bay', *Financial Times* magazine, 11 December 2004.

2 Senior intelligence officer, interview with author, 5 December 2003.

3 Senior CIA official, interview with author, 13 November 2002.

4 http://www.nytimes.com/2006/09/06/washington/06bush_transcript.html?_r=1&pagewanted=all.

5 http://www.newyorker.com/archive/2006/09/11/060911fa_fact.

6 Senior French officer, interview with author, 3 October 2002.

7 Senior UK official, interview with author, 11 October 2002.

8 Major General Martin Lucenti, interview with author, Camp Delta, Guantanamo Bay, 28 September 2004.

9 Brig. General Jay Hood, interview with author, Camp Delta, Guantanamo Bay, 30 September 2004.

10 Murat Kurnaz, *Five Years of My Life: An innocent man in Guantanamo* (London: Palgrave Macmillan, 2008).

11 Sgt Major Berger, interview by author, Camp Five, Guantanamo Bay, 19 January 2005.

12 Steve Rodriguez, Director of Intelligence-gathering Operations, Camp Delta, Guantanamo Bay, 19 January 2005.

13 Senior European intelligence officer, interview with author, 12 September 2010.

14 http://news.bbc.co.uk/1/shared/bsp/hi/pdfs/15_03_07_mohammed_transcript.pdf.

15 See http://www.nybooks.com/media/doc/2010/04/22/icrc-report.pdf.

16 Senior UK intelligence official, interview with author, 4 September 2003.

17 See http://www.newyorker.com/archive/2006/09/11/060911fa_fact.

CHAPTER 10

1 Senior intelligence official, interview with author, 18 April 2003.

2 Following a restructuring of Italy's intelligence agencies, the SISMi was replaced by the Agenzia Informazioni e Sicurezza Esterna (AISE) on 1 August 2007.

3 Several detailed studies based on research during the years prior to the invasion of March 2003 pointed to Iraq's acquisition of equipment which had not been accounted for during UN inspections – but which may have been unearthed had the inspections been permitted to continue; among these reports were the UN inspectors' Working Document of 6 March 2003, the CIA assessment of October 2002, the UK Government's assessment of 24 September 2002 and the assessment of the UK's Joint Intelligence Committee derived from material gathered in 1999–2000 and the International Institute of Strategic Studies assessment of 9 September 2002.

4 Senior intelligence officer, interview with author, 9 October 2002.

5 Senior intelligence officer, interview with author, 11 October 2002.

6 Senior CIA officer, interview with author, 31 October 2002.

7 Lt Colonel Keith Harrington, US Army, interview with author, al-Qaim, Iraq, 15 May 2003.

8 Statement by David Kay on the Interim Progress Report on the activities of the Iraq Survey Group (ISG) before the House Permanent Select Committee on Intelligence, the House Committee on Appropriations, Subcommittee on Defense and the Senate Select Committee on Intelligence, Washington DC, 2 October 2003.

9 Available at http://www.cnn.com/2004/US/01/28/kay.transcript.

10 http://www.number-10.gov.uk/output/Page3294.asp.

11 http://www.whitehouse.gov/news/releases/2003/03/iraq/20030317-7.html.

12 http://www.centcom.mil/CENTCOMNews/Transcripts/20030322.htm.

13 Donald Rumsfeld, interview with ABC television, 30 March 2003.

14 Comprehensive Report of the Special Advisor to the DCI on Iraq's WMD, 30 September 2004, p.1, http://www.cia.gov/cia/reports/iraq_wmd_2004/Comp_Report_Key_Findings.pdf.

15 Charles Duelfer, interview with the author, Washington, DC, 5 October 2004.

16 Lord Butler, Review of Intelligence on Weapons of Mass Destruction, pp.67–68, http://www.official-documents.co.uk/document/deps/hc/hc898/898.pdf.

17 *Washington Post*, 16 September 2001.

18 Bob Woodward, *Bush at War* (New York: Simon & Schuster, 2002), p.83.

19 Ibid.

20 President George W. Bush, State of the Union address, 28 January 2003.

21 http://webarchive.nationalarchives.gov.uk/+/http://www.number10.gov.uk/Page271.

22 Ibid., paragraph 21.

23 *New York Times*, 6 July 2003.

24 'Italian Ex-Spy Discusses Own Role in Iraq-Niger Uranium Traffic Hoax', *Il Giornale*, 21 September 2004, p.4.

25 SISMi officer, interview with author, Rome, 30 July 2004.

26 SISMi officer, interview with author, Rome, 1 August 2004.

27 Senior French intelligence officer, interview with author, 15 January 2003.

28 Christopher Andrew, *Defence of the Realm: The Authorized History of MI5* (London: Allen Lane, 2009), pp. 198–208.

29 http://tna.europarchive.org/20061101035706/http://www.number-10.gov.uk/output/page1470.asp.

30 Senior intelligence official, interview with author, 5 February 2003.

31 Senior intelligence official, interview with author, 7 February 2003.

32 Senior intelligence official, interview with author, 8 February 2003.

33 Senior intelligence official, interview with author, 7 February 2003.

34 Ibid.

CHAPTER 11

1 Senior intelligence official, interview with author, 19 March 2003.

2 *Financial Times*, 26 March 2003.

3 Senior intelligence official, interview with author, 3 April 2003.

4 *Financial Times*, 26 March 2003.

5 Senior US defence official, interview with author, 31 March 2003.

6 Senior US official, interview with author, 31 March 2003.

7 Ibid., interview with author, 4 April 2003.

8 Email from Jonathan Powell to Alastair Campbell; David Manning, 17 September 2002, ref: CAB/11/0069.

9 Senior UK defence official, interview with author, 22 April 2003.

10 Senior UK official, interview with author, 22 May 2003.

11 Ibid., 28 May 2003.

12 Ibid., 29 May 2003.

13 Senior US intelligence official, interview with author, 29 May 2003.

14 Senior US intelligence official, interview with author, 9 July 2003.

15 For a full and excellent account of just how deceitful was the agent named 'Curveball' see Bob Drogin, *Curveball* (London: Ebury Press, 2008).

16 Senior intelligence officer, interview with author, 11 July 2003.

17 Senior intelligence official, interview with author, 13 July 2004.

18 Senior US intelligence official, interview with author, 7 April 2005.

19 Senior UK official, interview with author, 13 December 2004.

CHAPTER 12

1   Senior Sudanese official, interview with author, 7 December 1999.

2   For an assessment of Libya's activities at Rabta see http://www. globalsecurity.org/wmd/world/libya/rabta.htm.

3   This figure was provided by an advisor to the Libyan Government.

4   Source familiar with Libyan thinking, interview with author, 12 January 2004.

5   WPC Yvonne Fletcher was policing an anti-Gadaffi demonstration when she was shot dead outside the Libyan Peoples' Bureau in St James's Square, London, on 17 April 1984, it is widely assumed by a gunman shooting from inside the Libyan diplomatic office. Following the fall of Gadaffi in 2011, two men – Abdulmagid Salah Ameri and Abdulqadir al-Baghdadi – were identified as possible suspects in the killing; al-Baghdadi was later killed in Libya.

6   Source familiar with Libyan thinking.

7   Ibid.

8   For a detailed account of the activities of A.Q. Khan see Gordon Corera, *Shopping for Bombs: Nuclear proliferation, global insecurity and the rise and fall of the A.Q. Khan network* (London: Hurst & Co., 2006).

9   Senior intelligence official, interview with author, 20 January 2004.

10 Senior intelligence official, interview with author, 13 December 2004.

11 See Ch. 1, n. 3.

12 Omar Bakri Muhammad, interview with author, 5 January 2005.

13 Abu Yahya Abderahman, London, 8 January 2005.

14 Senior UK security official, interview with author, 3 June 2006.

15 http://www.cabinetoffice.gov.uk/media/cabinetoffice/corp/assets/ publications/reports/intelligence/isc_7july_report.pdf.

16 Senior security official, interview with author, 9 March 2009.

17 Ibid.

18 Senior security official, interview with author, 13 February 2009.

19 http://www.homeoffice.gov.uk/documents/7-july-report. pdf?view=Binary.

20 This figures is that used by Richard J. Aldrich in *GCHQ: The uncensored story of Britain's most secret intelligence agency* (London: Harper Press, 2010), p. 526.

21 Ibid., p. 540.

22 For the response of several government agencies to the IMP see http:// cryptome.org/ncis-carnivore.htm.

23 The description is Aldrich's.
24 Ann Black, GCHQ spokeswoman, interview with author, Cheltenham, 13 February 2003.
25 Senior GCHQ staff member, interview with author, Cheltenham, 13 February 2003.
26 Ibid.

EPILOGUE

1 George Tenet, *At the Center of the Storm: My years at the CIA* (New York: Harper Luxe, 2007), p. 741.

BIBLIOGRAPHY

Andrew, Christopher, *Defence of the Realm: The authorized history of MI5* (London: Allen Lane, 2009)

Andrew, Christopher, and Vasili Mitrokhin, *The Mitrokhin Archive*: vol. I: *The KGB and the West* (London: Allen Lane, 1999); vol. II: *The KGB and the World* (London: Allen Lane, 2005)

Andrew, Christopher and Oleg Gordievsky, *KGB: The Inside Story* (London: Harper Perennial, 1991)

Aldrich, Richard J., *GCHQ: The uncensored story of Britain's most secret intelligence agency* (London: Harper Press, 2010)

'Anonymous' (Michael Scheuer), *Imperial Hubris: Why the West is losing the War On Terror* (New York: Brassey's, 2004)

Bartlett, Thomas (ed.), *Revolutionary Dublin 1795–1801: The letters of Francis Higgins to Dublin Castle* (Dublin: Four Courts Press, 2004)

Bender, Gerald, 'American Policy toward Angola: A history of linkage,' in Gerald J. Bender, James S. Coleman and Richard L. Sklar (eds), *African Crisis Areas and US Foreign Policy* (Berkeley, CA, Los Angeles and London: University of California Press, 1985)

Bergen, Peter, *Manhunt: From 9/11 to Abbottabad: The ten-year search for Osama bin Laden* (London: The Bodley Head, 2012)

Cabrita, João, *Mozambique: The tortuous road to democracy* (London: Palgrave, 2000)

Clarke, Richard A., *Against All Enemies: Inside America's War on Terror* (New York: Free Press, 2004)

Corera, Gordon, *Shopping for Bombs: Nuclear proliferation, global insecurity and the rise and fall of the A.Q. Khan Network* (London: Hurst & Co., 2006)

Devlin, Larry, *Chief of Station, Congo: Fighting the Cold War in a Hot Zone* (New York: Public Affairs, 2007)

Drogin, Bob, *Curveball* (London: Ebury Press, 2008)

Dwyer, T. Ryle, *The Squad and the Intelligence Operations of Michael Collins* (Dublin: Mercier Press, 2005)

English, Richard, *Irish Freedom: The history of nationalism in Ireland* (London: Pan Macmillan, 2006)

Fitzpatrick, William John, *The Sham Squire and the Informers of 1798* (Dublin and London: John Camden Hotton, 1866)

Guimaraes, Fernando Andresen, *The Origins of the Angolan Civil War: Foreign intervention and domestic political conflict* (New York: St Martin's Press, 1998)

Hart, Peter (ed.): *British Intelligence in Ireland 1920–1921: The final reports* (Cork: Cork University Press, 2002)

Huband, Mark, *Warriors of the Prophet: The struggle for Islam* (Boulder, CO: Westview Press, 1998)

Huband, Mark, *The Skull Beneath the Skin: Africa after the Cold War* (Boulder CO: Westview Press, 2001)

Huband, Mark, *Brutal Truths, Fragile Myths: Power politics and Western adventurism in the Arab world* (Boulder, CO: Westview Press, 2004)

Ingram, Martin and Greg Harkin, *Stakeknife: Britain's Secret Agents in Ireland* (Dublin: O'Brien Press, 2004)

Kalb, Madeleine G., *The Congo Cables: The Cold War in Africa from Eisenhower to Kennedy* (New York: Macmillan, 1982)

Kalugin, Oleg, *Spymaster: My thirty-two years in intelligence and espionage against the West* (New York: Basic Books, 2009)

Kurnaz, Murat, *Five Years of My Life: An innocent man in Guantanamo* (London: Palgrave Macmillan, 2008)

Kyvig, David E., *Reagan and the World* (New York, Westport, CT and London: Praeger, 1990)

Lance, Peter, *Triple Cross: How bin Laden's master spy penetrated the CIA, the Green Berets, and the FBI – and why Patrick Fitzgerald failed to stop him* (New York: William Morrow, 2005)

Lia, Brynjar, *Architect of Global Jihad: The life of Al-Qaida strategist Abu Mus'ab al-Suri* (London: Hurst & Co., 2007)

Machiavelli, Niccolò di Bernardo dei, *Dell'arte della Guerra* (*The Art of War*) (Florence: 1521)

Madden, Richard, *The United Irishmen: Their lives and times* (London: J. Madden & Co., 1867)

BIBLIOGRAPHY

Mandela, Nelson, *Long Walk to Freedom* (London: Little, Brown, 1994)

McMahon, Paul, *British Spies and Irish Rebels: British intelligence and Ireland, 1916–1945* (Woodbridge: Boydell Press, 2008)

Moloney, Ed, *A Secret History of the IRA* (2nd edn) (London: Penguin, 2007)

Miller, John, and Michael Stone, with Chris Mitchell, *The Cell: Inside the 9/11 plot and why the FBI and CIA failed to stop it* (New York: Hyperion, 2003)

Minter, William, *Apartheid's Contras: An inquiry into the roots of war in Angola and Mozambique* (London and New Jersey: Zed Books; Johannesburg: Witwatersrand University Press, 1994)

Neligan, David, *The Spy in the Castle* (London: Prendeville Publishing, 1999)

O'Callaghan, Sean, *The Informer* (London: Corgi, 1999)

Rimington, Stella, *Open Secret: The autobiography of the former Director-General of MI5* (London: Arrow Books, 2002)

Scheuer, Michael, *Marching Toward Hell: America and Islam after Iraq* (New York: Free Press, 2008)

Shenon, Philip, *The Commission: The uncensored history of the 9/11 investigation* (New York: Twelve, 2008)

Smith, Michael, *The Spying Game* (London: Politico's Publishing, 2003)

Stockwell, John, *In Search of Enemies: A CIA story* (New Jersey: Replica Books, 1997; originally published New York: W.W. Norton and Company, 1978)

Taylor, Peter, *Brits: The war against the IRA* (London: Bloomsbury, 2001)

Tenet, George, *At the Center of the Storm: My years at the CIA* (New York: Harper Luxe, 2007)

Waugh, Billy, with Tim Keown, *Hunting the Jackal: A special forces and CIA soldier's fifty years on the frontlines of the war against terrorism* (New York: Avon Books, 2004)

Weissman, Stephen, 'The CIA and US policy in Zaire and Angola', in René Lemarchand (ed.), *American Policy in Southern Africa* (Lanham, MD and London: University Press of America, 1981)

Woodward, Bob, *Bush at War* (New York: Simon & Schuster, 2002)

Wright, George, *The Destruction of a Nation: United States' policy towards Angola since 1945* (London and Chicago: Pluto Press, 1997)

Wright, Peter, *Spy Catcher: The candid autobiography of a senior intelligence officer* (Richmond, Australia: William Heinemann, 1987)

Young, Crawford, and Michael Turner, *The Rise and Decline of the Zairean State* (Madison, WI and London: University of Wisconsin Press, 1985)

INDEX

251